PUZZLES
OLD & NEW

Jerry Slocum–Jack Botermans

PUZZLES
OLD & NEW

HOW TO MAKE AND SOLVE THEM

Text: Carla van Splunteren–Tony Burrett

In association with the Craft & Folk Art Museum, Los Angeles

Distributed by University of Washington Press, Seattle.

For Margot

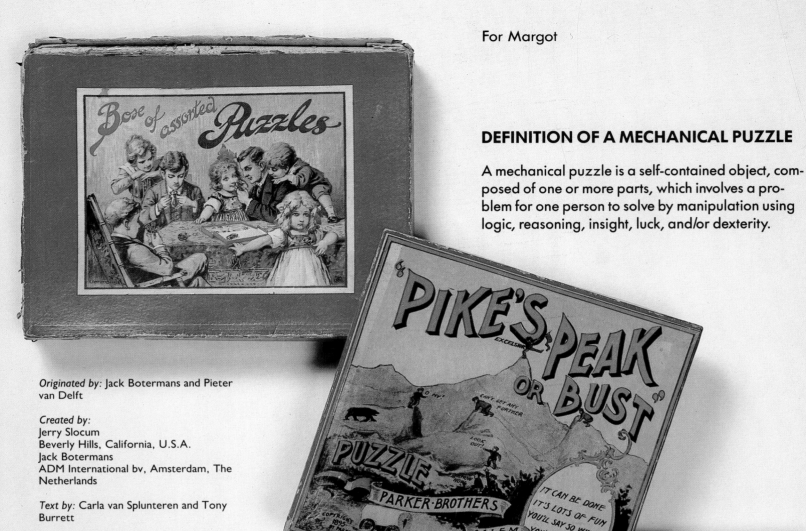

DEFINITION OF A MECHANICAL PUZZLE

A mechanical puzzle is a self-contained object, composed of one or more parts, which involves a problem for one person to solve by manipulation using logic, reasoning, insight, luck, and/or dexterity.

Originated by: Jack Botermans and Pieter van Delft

Created by:
Jerry Slocum
Beverly Hills, California, U.S.A.
Jack Botermans
ADM International bv, Amsterdam, The Netherlands

Text by: Carla van Splunteren and Tony Burrett

Photography: John Koopman, Susan Einstein, David van Dijk, Pieter van Delft, Jack Botermans and Jerry Slocum.
Illustrations: Anne-Claire Alta and Utte Middelhoek
Design: Jack Botermans, ADM International bv

© 1986 Plenary Publications International (Europe) bv, De Meern, The Netherlands and
ADM International bv, Amsterdam, The Netherlands
© 1986 Bibliography Jerry Slocum

Puzzles on pages 8, 9, 12, 38, 49, 51-54, 58, 65, 66, 70, 72-74, 77, 80, 84, 85, 87, 92-95, 100, 106-110, 114, 121-125, 128, 131, 136, 137, 140, the frontispiece and cover are from the collection of Mr James Dalgety and published with his kind permission

First paperback edition © 1987

ISBN 0-295-96579-7

PUZZLE CLASSIFICATION

Professor Hoffmann, in his classic book Puzzles Old and New, described the problem of classifying puzzles as follows:

'The chief difficulties I have found in compiling the present collection have been nomenclature and classification. In view of the varieties of taste, some preferring a mathematical, some a mechanical problem - one person a trial of skill, another an exercise of patience - it seemed desirable to have as many categories as possible. On the other hand, the more numerous the divisions, the more difficult does it become to assign a given puzzle definitely to one or another. In many instances the same item might with equal propriety be classed under either of several categories'.

Professor Hoffmann's approach to classification has been modified and expanded, with the mechanical puzzles divided into categories based on what must be done to solve the puzzle and the form and material of the puzzle itself. The taxonomy or classification we have chosen is as follows:

1. PUT-TOGETHER PUZZLES - Putting the object together is the puzzle.
a) 2-dimensional assembly puzzles
b) 3-dimensional assembly puzzles

2. TAKE-APART PUZZLES - Opening or taking the object apart is the puzzle.

3. INTERLOCKING SOLID PUZZLES - Disassembly and assembly is required to solve the puzzle.
a) Figures
b) Geometric objects
c) 3-D jigsaw puzzles
d) Burr puzzles
e) Keychain puzzles

4. DISENTANGLEMENT PUZZLES - The puzzle is to disentangle and re-entangle the parts of the puzzle.
a) Cast iron and sheet metal puzzles
b) Wire puzzles
c) String puzzles

5. SEQUENTIAL MOVEMENT PUZZLES - The puzzle is to move parts of the object to a goal.
a) Solitaire puzzles
b) Counter puzzles
c) Sliding block puzzles
d) Rotating cube puzzles
e) Maze and route puzzles

6. PUZZLE VESSELS - Drinking or pouring a liquid, or filling the vessels without spilling is the puzzle.

7. DEXTERITY PUZZLES - Manual dexterity is required to solve the puzzle.

8. VANISH PUZZLES - The puzzle is to explain a vanishing or changing image.

9. IMPOSSIBLE OBJECT PUZZLES - The puzzle is to discover how the object is made.

10. FOLDING PUZZLES - The puzzle is to achieve a specified goal by folding.

Contents

The object of the Pigs in Clover Puzzle was to get the balls into the center 'pen'. It caught the imagination of the American public when it was sold in the late 19th century.

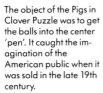

The Popular 15 Puzzle was the forerunner of the famous 14-15 Puzzle which was made by Sam Loyd in the late 19th century. Loyd offered a prize of $1000 to the first person to find the solution. His money was safe, however, because the 'puzzle' is impossible!

Interlocking wire puzzles enjoyed an enormous popularity during the first decades of the 20th century. They were often marketed in sets such as the Puzzle Parties collection shown below.

INTRODUCTION

Jerry Slocum

Jack Botermans

Jerry Slocum, co-author of this book, has one of the most comprehensive puzzle collections in the world. Jack Botermans is both a designer and maker of puzzles. He conceived and designed this book.

Even though mechanical puzzles have been around for centuries and have been made and sold all over the world, they were for the first time described at length in Professor Hoffmann's Puzzles Old and New, published in 1893 in London. Aside from a few smaller books on mechanical puzzles, some never translated into English, Hoffmann's book remained the only good source of information on the subject until Creative Puzzles of the World was published by Harry N. Abrams in New York (1978). The authors were two Dutchmen, Pieter van Delft and Jack Botermans (the latter is also co-author of the volume you now hold). Creative Puzzles is a marvellous compendium of art and information, but like Hoffmann's book it deals with puzzles of all varieties. The result is that it barely scratches the surface of the mechanical puzzle field. Now, and for the first time in history, we have in this book by SLocum and Botermans a comprehensive survey of the subject.

'Mechanical puzzle' is the term most widely used today for a puzzle made of solid pieces that must be manipulated by one's hands to obtain a solution. The degree of difficulty in solving a mechanical puzzle varies enormously. The two twisted nails, for example, can be solved by some children in a matter of minutes. Other puzzles such as Rubik's Cube (see page 138 of this book) may take an intelligent adult days or even months to solve, if ever.

Many require a vast amount of patience and a careful exploration of all possible manipulations. Some may require a computer program. A few years ago, a Japanese company brought out the Panex Puzzle. It is a fiendish elaboration of the ancient Tower of Hanoi (discussed on page 135), and it is so difficult that the smallest number of moves needed to solve it remains unknown. Several top mathematicians at the Bell Laboratories have been working on the theory behind this puzzle, but so far the best they have done is to prove an upper bound. Some of the traditional sliding-block puzzles (see page 126) are also unsolved in the sense that minimal-move solutions are not known. (Donald Knuth, the noted computer scientist at Stanford University, has a program for sliding-block puzzles that we understand will be discussed in the forthcoming Volume 4 of his famous series of textbooks

on the Art of Computer Programming.)

It is easy to see how combinatorial mathematics is involved in puzzles such as sliding blocks, Rubik's Cube, the Tower of Hanoi, the Chinese Rings, and hundreds of other puzzles designed to be solved in the smallest number of moves. In a broad sense, however, every mechanical puzzle has certain mathematical elements. It is true that many delightful mechanical puzzles seem non-mathematical because they are solved only by an 'aha!' insight that is unrelated to mathematics. Yet even such insights, mysterious though they be to a psychologist, are part of the kind of heuristic reasoning that is used by mathematicians when they discover an elegant proof of a theorem, or by scientists when a flash of insight leads to a fruitful theory. There is a sense in which both deductive and inductive reasoning can be viewed as formal logic, in turn a part of mathematics.

Quite aside from the role of logic, many puzzles that would not have been considered mathematical a century ago are now recognized as based on topology, an area of mathematics involving properties that remain the same when a structure is continously deformed. Knot theory, for example, is a flourishing branch of topology that concerns the properties of closed curves (modeled by cord or rope) when they are linked or knotted. Hundreds of string puzzles, many of which were first thought of by primitive cultures, are topological.

The story of mechanical puzzles is the least chronicled aspect of recreational mathematics. That probably has to do with the fact that many of these have not been widely available and cannot be made at home, and there is little incentive to write about a puzzle if the reader cannot work on it without owning one. Only if a puzzle is enormously popular for several years does it become worthwhile to discuss it in print. The most recent example was Rubik's Cube. Before the craze faded, dozens of paperbacks were written about the cube. In the 18th century the popularity of peg solitaire (see page 118) produced a similar flurry of books around the world. Even Leibnitz, the great German philosopher-mathematician, wrote about his enjoyment of this puzzle. But, as mentioned before, Professor Hoffmann, in Puzzles Old and New, was the

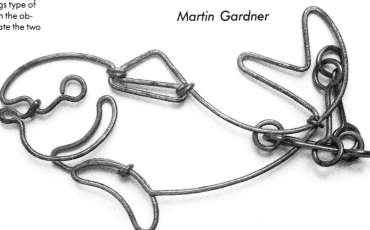

first to think mechanical puzzles in general of sufficient interest to devote chapters of a book to them. When Pieter van Delft and Jack Botermans first had the idea for this book they knew it could not be written without the collaboration of a number of collectors. That's where Jerry Slocum, co-author of this book, comes in. Since his youth he has been collecting mechanical puzzles and he now owns what is probably the world's largest collection (his closest rivals are Edward Hordern of England and Tom Ransom of Toronto). Most of the puzzle's shown in this book are from Jerry's collection. He has also done a massive amount of research on the puzzles and some of the results are included in this book. Unlike all previous books on the topic, this one aims to be complete by covering as many kinds of puzzles as possible within each category. Unfortunately, only a portion of the puzzles can be bought today. You must not suppose, however, that all the puzzles in this book must be purchased in order to enjoy them. The authors have included a large number of mechanical puzzles that can be made with scissors and cardboard, and suplies of such things as counters, strings, beads, and cubes. All the polycube puzzles are easily made by gluing wooden cubes together. Sliding-block puzzles and dissection puzzles are, of course, more fun to work on if you have solid tiles, but cardboard pieces do almost as well. If you are handy with tools, wire and metal, hundreds of other puzzles in this book can be constructed.

New mechanical puzzles are being invented and marketed every year and it will not be long before this elegant volume will be in need of updating. It is a good bet that it will go through many new editions and remain a classic reference for decades.

Martin Gardner

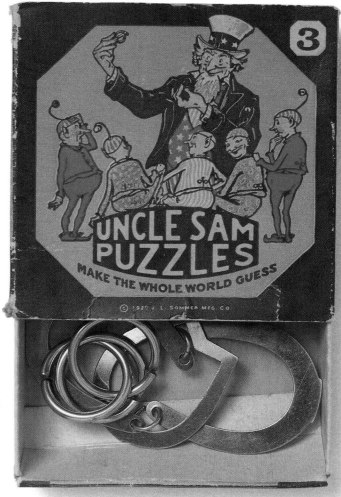

Here are four examples of puzzles in which the object is to assemble a number of pieces into the form of a cross. These puzzles were often beautifully made in ivory or hardwood.

Below center: During the last decades of the 19th century and the early decades of the 20th, puzzles of all sorts were widely used for advertising purposes. This example, an interlocking nail puzzle, was used to advertise a chimney sweeping service.

Below: Here are several examples of interlocking wooden puzzles, ranging from a kangaroo to a rocket. Almost any object can be the basis for such a wooden puzzle.

9

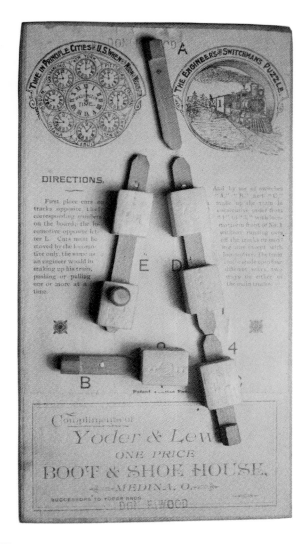

Puzzle locks of various types have been made for thousands of years. Several beautiful examples are shown on pages 80 and 81, where you will also find instructions on how to construct your own ingenious puzzle lock.

Shunting Puzzles can be found on pages 124 and 125. Puzzles have often been used for advertising purposes. This particular puzzle was used to advertise the Yoder & Lew Boot and Shoe House.

PREFACE

The writing - the last and probably the shortest stage in the development of this book - is now complete. The final stage of a process which began eight years ago, in 1978. Pieter van Delft and Jack Botermans, of ADM International, Amsterdam, had recently published a book called Creative Puzzles of the World which had proved to be enormously popular and which was translated into several languages and sold throughout the world. They received literally hundreds of letters from all four corners of the globe, and among them were many from puzzle collectors and designers. In 1979, Jerry Slocum, who has one the world's most extensive collections of puzzles, invited Pieter and Jack to Los Angeles to visit him and examine his collection. The following year, they returned to the United States to take part in one of Jerry's famous 'puzzle parties'. These parties are an annual event and give puzzle collectors and designers from all over the world the chance to meet, talk puzzles, swap ideas and exchange surplus items from their collections. Since 1980, Pieter and Jack have never missed a party, and through them have had an opportunity to meet everybody who is anybody in the upper echelons of the puzzle world. At one of the early parties, the idea was suggested of producing another book, this time based on one of the great puzzle collections, and it seemed logical to invite Jerry to take part in the project and use his puzzle collection as the primary basis for the book. Slowly the concept began to take shape. The authors decided on the categories of puzzles to be used, and then on the indivdual puzzles. Jerry undertook the research on the origin and history of the puzzles and collected and collated a lot of the background material. He primarily used his own extensive files and library of over 2000 books on puzzles and mathematical recreations. Jack commissioned the photographers to take the pictures and then put together the design, layout and drawings for each page of the book. Collaborating together on such a complex project is not easy, particularly when the two authors live more than six thousand miles apart. But in spite of the difficulties, everything was ready by mid-1985 and the text could finally be written. An eight-year journey had come to an end. One of the earliest problems facing the authors was

Carla van Splunteren

Tony Burrett

The two writers who turned a mass of background material in-to the finished text of this book.

how to classify the puzzles. Professor Hoffmann described the problem in his classic book Puzzles Old and New, which was published in 1893 (See Contents page). Since then classification has become even more difficult and the authors are aware that some puzzles in this book could just as easily be placed in a different section. The Chinese Rings Puzzle, for example, is in the chapter on disentanglement puzzles, but it could well appear in the sequential movement section.

Several well-known collectors and designers - James Dalgety and Edward Hordern, for example - submitted classifications and after a great deal of discussion the authors decided on the final classification. How were the individual puzzles chosen? Some classic puzzles, like the Tangram and the Chinese Rings, could not possibly be omitted and in effect chose themselves. Others were chosen because they were beautiful and elegant examples of their type; yet others, the box packing problems, for example, because their internal structures were of great interest. A few were chosen because the solution rather than the design of the puzzle itself was of interest. A good example of this is the 6-piece burr puzzle. Puzzles of this type usually have their solutions shown together with the puzzle. Most of the others are left to you, the reader, to solve. Solutions to most of these are given in the back of the book - but we strongly advise you not to spoil your enjoyment by giving in too quickly to the temptation to take a peek! A few of the puzzles have no solutions - leaving you at least something to puzzle over!

Of course, it is impossible to physically solve a puzzle until you have it in front of you, and therefore special attention has been paid to the 'How to make' sections. We have tried to keep the instructions as simple as possible and to suggest easily-available and cheap materials. Other materials may suggest themselves, of course, or you may have an idea to adapt or improve a puzzle. And you may find other solutions or come up with other excellent and fascinating puzzles which are not given in this book. If you do, please write and tell us. Finally, we hope very much that you derive as much pleasure and wonder from reading this book as we have derived from making it. Good puzzling!

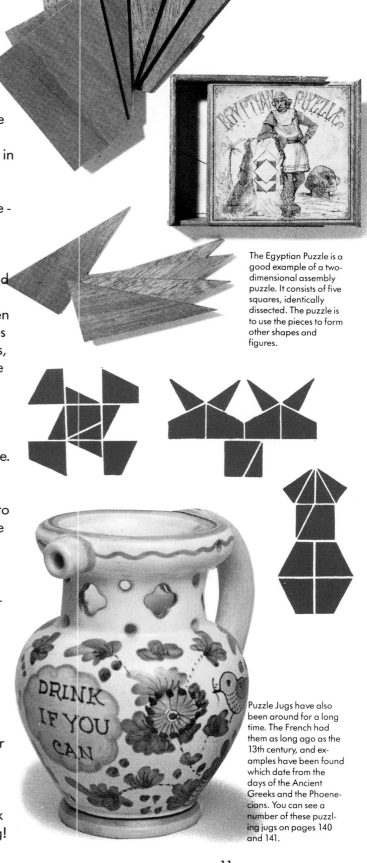

The Egyptian Puzzle is a good example of a two-dimensional assembly puzzle. It consists of five squares, identically dissected. The puzzle is to use the pieces to form other shapes and figures.

Puzzle Jugs have also been around for a long time. The French had them as long ago as the 13th century, and ex-amples have been found which date from the days of the Ancient Greeks and the Phoene-cians. You can see a number of these puzzl-ing jugs on pages 140 and 141.

A checkerboard puzzle, made in Germany for the Phenyo-Caffein Company at the beginning of this century. This puzzle was patented by H. Luers in 1880 in the U.S.A. (see page 14).

PUT-TOGETHER PUZZLES

The oldest and largest class of mechanical puzzles consists of those puzzles that are solved by assembly or by fitting pieces together. The most popular member of this class is the jigsaw puzzle, which was invented in about 1760 by the Englishman John Spilsbury. The first jigsaws were intended for use as educational toys and were made by gluing maps to thin sheets of mahogany and then cutting them up. Dissected puzzles of a completely different type were popular much earlier in Greece, and they appeared in the mid - 18th century in Japan, and at the turn of the 19th century in China. The object of this type of puzzle is to put together a given set of pieces to form a specified outline or figure. The earliest known example is the Loculus of Archimedes, or the Stomachion ('the problem that drives one mad'!). This appeared in the 3rd century B.C. and was a 14-piece dissection of a square. Sei Shonagon Chie No-Ita, an elegant 7-piece puzzle, first appeared in a book published in Japan in 1742, although it was probably invented several centuries earlier. The Tangram, another 7-piece puzzle, became popular in China about 1800, and by 1820 it had spread to Europe and the United States. It has remained popular to this day and is widely regarded as the most elegant and beautiful of the dissection puzzles. Towards the end of the last century, the German firm Richter began producing dissection puzzles using manufactured small bricks or stones.

These were known as the Anchor Stone Puzzles and were very popular during World War I, when they were used by soldiers on both sides to while away long boring hours in the trenches. Other interesting dissection puzzles are those obtained by cutting up crosses or letters. The best known is probably the 'T' puzzle, but Harry Lindgren created an elegant set of letter dissections, the pieces of each assembling into a square. The last class of puzzles in this section is that of Magic Squares, arrays of numbers where the sum of the numbers in each row, column and diagonal is the same.

The famous Bug House Puzzle, produced in the 30's by an American company. The 14 pieces are made out of cast metal.

Left: This wooden version consists of 12 pieces and was produced by Linie-Preben, Paarup, in Denmark.

Right: One of the original checkerboard puzzles. It was invented by H. Luers, patented Sept. 7, 1880, and produced by Selchow & Righter in New York.

Two checkerboard puzzles.
1) The famous Bug House Puzzle, produced by the Franco company of New York (around 1919), consists of 14 pieces of pewter.

2) This 14-piece checkerboard puzzle made from cardboard, was produced by the Unique Novelty Company, Los Angeles (1930-40).

Checkerboard puzzles

The first checkerboard puzzle seems to have originated in 1880, when a certain Henry Luers obtained a U.S. patent for a 'Sectional Checkerboard', consisting of fifteen differently shaped pieces of complete squares of a checkerboard. At first sight this type of puzzle may seem very easy to solve, but as Professor Hoffmann warned in 1893, 'any such idea soon vanishes when the matter is put to the test of experiment. The pieces drop into position with enticing facility till the board is about three parts complete, but at that point the neophyte usually finds himself with half a dozen segments still in hand, which absolutely decline to accommodate themselves to the spaces left for them'. Luers claimed that his puzzle offered 'much amusement and employment of time to those who have no better use for it'.

The continued popularity of the checkerboard puzzle is shown by the fact that more than 50 manufacturers designed at least 33 different 8 x 8 checkerboard puzzles since Luers' patent was issued.

How to make a checkerboard puzzle

Take a piece of cardboard, measuring 8 x 8 inches and divide it into 64 smaller squares measuring 1 x 1 inches. Color the squares, alternating black and red. Use a felt pen or glue squares of colored paper onto them. Now divide the checkerboard into pieces of different shapes, each shape consisting of a whole number of squares. A simple puzzle might consist of as few as eight pieces; fifteen is the maximum number which can be used to produce an attractive puzzle. When you have decided on your shapes, cut them out using a steel ruler and a sharp knife. The puzzle is simply to re-assemble the pieces into the original checkerboard.

A more durable puzzle can be made from balsa wood or plywood with alternate squares painted black or red. In this case you must plan your pattern on paper and then cut each piece separately, using a fretsaw. Another method is to glue together children's building blocks to form the pieces of the checkerboard puzzle.

Shown here is the 'The Broken Chessboard' puzzle, designed by Henry E. Dudeney in 1908. The puzzle consists of 13 pieces and has only four solutions.

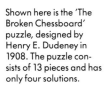

Polyominoes

The term 'polyomino' was coined by the puzzle-expert Solomon W. Golomb in an article in the American Mathematical Monthly, entitled 'Checker Boards and Polyominoes', written in 1954 when he was a young graduate at Harvard University. Polyominoes were first extensively discussed in Scientific American in 1957 and since then they have become an enormously popular mathematical recreation and countless polyomino puzzles and figures have been discovered. In recent years, the computer has enabled the study of polyominoes to be considerably extended and has resulted in many new solutions and proofs being found.

Golomb defined a polyomino as a 'simply connected set of squares'. By this he meant a set of identical squares joined along their edges. The simplest form of a polyomino is a single square and is known as a monomino. If we consider two identical squares, we can see that there is only one way in which they can be joined along an edge to form a domino. (You might think that there are two ways of connecting two squares along an edge - side by side or one on top of the other - but, mathematically speaking, these two shapes are identical, one being a rotation of the other).

The popular game of dominoes is played by young and old in homes, cafés and bars all over the world. It appears to have been invented in China many hundreds of years ago. Many elegant and interesting puzzles are based on a standard set of dominoes and the whole subject is extensively discussed in 'Creative Puzzles of the World' by Pieter van Delft and Jack Botermans.

There are only two different ways of joining three squares to form trominoes - the straight tromino and the right tromino. Again, mathematically speaking, asymmetrical pieces which give a mirror image when turned over are considered to be the same. Thus the 'L' and reverse 'L' of the right tromino are the same.

There are five tetrominoes, formed by joining four squares - the straight tetromino, the T tetromino, the L tetromino, the square tetromino and the skew tetromino. These are shown on the left and can be easily made from thick cardboard using a knife and a ruler. The pieces can be used to solve a number of simple but interesting problems.

For example, can the five distinct tetrominoes be used to form a rectangle, and if not, can you devise a simple proof to show why not? (Hint: Draw the two possible rectangles and color alternate squares of both the rectangles and the tetrominoes). Can a standard 8 x 8 checker board be covered by a number of similar tetrominoes and if so, how? What other shapes can be formed using a number of distinct tetrominoes or a combination of different tetrominoes? The number of distinct polyominoes is clearly a function of the number of squares in each and this rises rapidly. There are, for example, 12 pentominoes, 35 hexominoes and 108 heptominoes. Pentominoes are perhaps the most interesting of the polyominoes.

The five tetrominoes: the straight, the T, the L, the square, and the skew tetromino.

A checkerboard pattern decorates the inside of the box of this puzzle. This pattern will help to solve the problem of this homemade pentomino set.

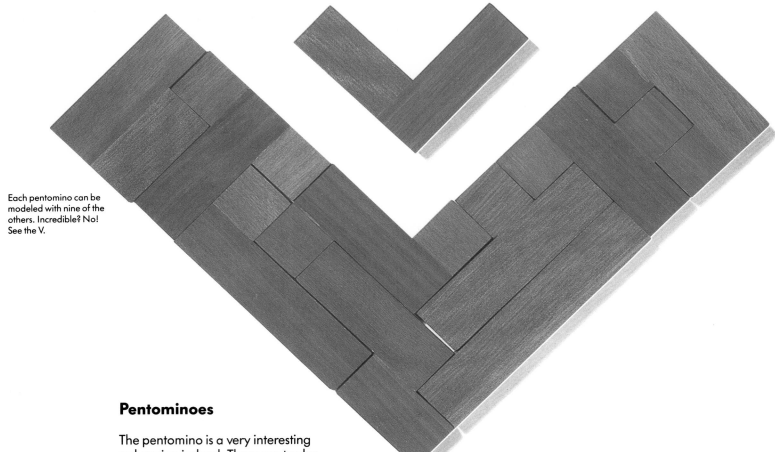

Each pentomino can be modeled with nine of the others. Incredible? No! See the V.

Pentominoes

The pentomino is a very interesting polyomino indeed. There are twelve 5-square pentominoes. The figures shown on the next page are to be covered with all 12 of them.(See below). Since each pentomino consists of five squares, each figure contains 60 squares.

The first five figures are 8 x 8 so-called chessboards. Each chessboard has four 1-square holes. The following figures are four rectangles constructed from 60 squares with unit dimensions of 3 x 20, 4 x 15, 5 x 12, and 6 x 10. The first of these is the most difficult; there are only two distinct solutions. Four more figures follow; of these, the cross is especially difficult. The last two figures are divided into congruent halves by a heavy line. This means that each of these figures can be assembled in such a way that it can be divided into two

halves. It is not essential to divide the figures thus, and many more solutions can be found if the line is ignored. Two other solutions for a different type of pentomino puzzle appear at the top of this page. Select one pentomino and try to make a model of it using nine of the remaining pieces. The result will always be three times as large as the original. All 12 pentominoes can be modeled this way. Many of the alternative solutions for pentomino puzzles are related; one can be generated from another by manipulating a few pieces. For example, on the left of the V above, the shape formed from the P and the T pentominoes can be exchanged for

the similar one at the right side of the V, which is formed from the F and the U pentominoes. You may consider every change of position of this shape as a solution. There are two different solutions to the puzzle when you include these changes of position. Whenever you spot a group of pieces that has a symmetrical outline, you can generate new solutions effortlessly. It is much more difficult to recombine a set of two, three or more pieces without changing their overall outline. Occasionally two groups in a pattern may have identical outlines. Exchange the groups and you again have two solutions instead of one.

The 12 pentominoes. It's quite obvious that they do resemble certain letters of the alphabet. But more importantly, each pento is made of five squares joined edge to edge to form different shapes.

      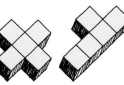 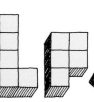

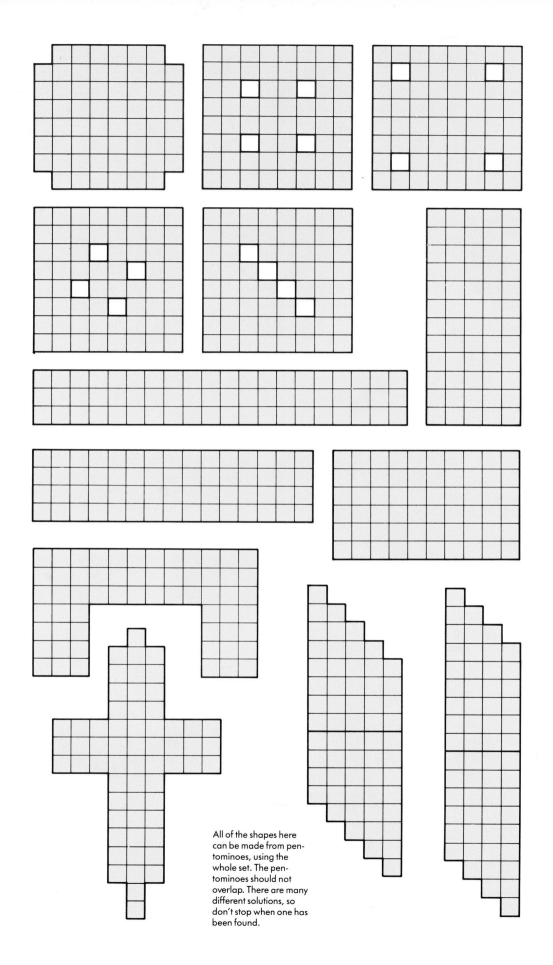

All of the shapes here can be made from pentominoes, using the whole set. The pentominoes should not overlap. There are many different solutions, so don't stop when one has been found.

How to make a pentomino set

There are two types of pentominoes. Shown on these pages is a two-dimensional pentomino set, but, as illustrated on page 40, there also exists a 3-D pentomino set. Page 40 features the beautifully designed set of Sabu Ogura.

To simplify matters, we have combined the instructions for making both sets on this page. For a two-dimensional pentomino set you need a piece of cardboard measuring 8 x 12 inches. With pencil and ruler, you divide this into 60 1'' squares. Using the examples at the bottom of page 16 you draw the shapes on the cardboard. Remember: each piece consists of five squares.

Cut out the pieces using a sharp hobby knife. After that, it's all up to your creative talents. A very nice result can be obtained by coloring the pieces with paint or by gluing colored paper onto them.

The three-dimensional pentomino set is made out of 60 (12 times five) wooden cubes. Saw these out of a piece of wood measuring ½'' square and approximately 34'' (30'' + 4'' for saw) long. By sanding the cubes carefully and gluing them together following the example shown here you will obtain an excellent three-dimensional pentomino set. To avoid problems while trying to solve the puzzle, make sure that the cubes are of exactly the same size.

The set shown below consists of 72 triangles glued together into 12 pieces.

these are the 3 x 4, 5, 6, 7, 8, 9, and 10 rhomboids, all of which have many solutions. The 3 x 11 rhomboid is difficult but possible. In all known solutions of the rhomboid the piece left out is G. Rhomboids of 4 x 6 and 4 x 9 (which uses all 12 pieces) are possible, and so is the 5 x 6.

Many other shapes, including hexagons, can be formed from hexiamonds. All symmetrical shapes formed by hexiamonds have threefold symmetry; they are symmetrical when divided along three different axes. Of course, it is possible to construct a wide variety of irregular shapes which are also pleasing. You might find it interesting to construct your own patterns using all twelve of the hexiamonds, draw around the outline and ask a fellow puzzle enthusiast to try to repeat your pattern - a stimulating exercise for the imagination!

How to make a set of Hexiamonds

Use a piece of cardboard (about 1 mm thick) of 10 x 15 inches and a ruler, pencil and hobby knife. Draw a pattern of equalateral triangles (1'' sides and equal angles) or buy isometric paper (printed with equilateral triangles). Glue your drawing or the isometric paper onto the cardboard and draw the shapes, as shown in the example. Cut these shapes out carefully and color them with a felt pen, paint or color pencils.

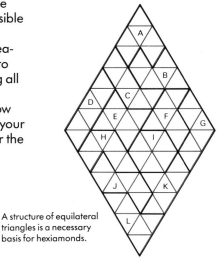

A structure of equilateral triangles is a necessary basis for hexiamonds.

Hexiamonds

In 1908, T.Scrutchin designed the first known example of a patented puzzle made up of a number of joined unit equalateral triangles. Golomb pointed out in his article on polyominoes in 1954 that a puzzle similar to polyominoes could be based on equalateral triangles. In 1961, the mathematician T.H.O' Beirne coined the word 'polyiamonds' to describe these triangle-based shapes. The most interesting of the polyiamonds are perhaps those consisting of six unit equilateral triangles, known as hexiamonds. By a pleasing coincidence there are exactly twelve of these - as many as the pentominoes discussed on the previous pages. These 12 hexiamonds are illustrated above. In addition to the solution shown in the diagram, there are scores of other ways of fitting the pieces together to form a 6 x 6 diamond. See how many you can find. Besides the diamond, a number of different rhomboids (parallelograms with oblique angles and unequal adjacent sides) can be formed by using some or all of the pieces. Among

Right: These examples of modern polyforms made by Tenyo, of Japan, are marketed under the slogan 'Beat the Computer'.

The Egyptian Puzzle

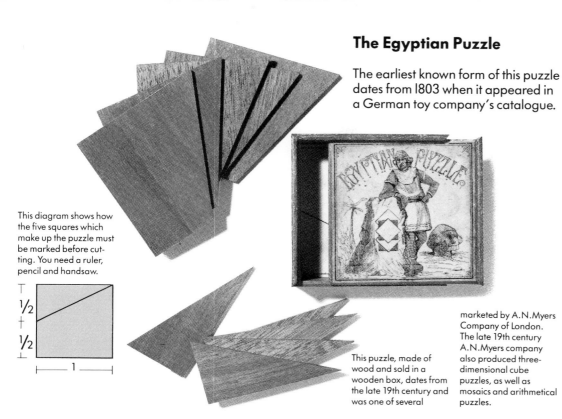

The earliest known form of this puzzle dates from 1803 when it appeared in a German toy company's catalogue.

The example shown here was published in the late 19th century by A.N.Myers Company of London. This company also manufactured the Arabian puzzle, the Chinese puzzle and the German puzzle. A booklet illuminating 72 problems and their solutions accompanied the Egyptian puzzle. According to this booklet, not only will 'a great amount of amusement be found', but 'the puzzle serves to illustrate some important facts and problems in Geometrical Science'.

This diagram shows how the five squares which make up the puzzle must be marked before cutting. You need a ruler, pencil and handsaw.

This puzzle, made of wood and sold in a wooden box, dates from the late 19th century and was one of several marketed by A.N.Myers Company of London. The late 19th century A.N.Myers company also produced three-dimensional cube puzzles, as well as mosaics and arithmetical puzzles.

How to make the Egyptian Puzzle
To make this puzzle you will need five squares of birch plywood, each measuring 4 x 4 inches. Mark each piece as shown in the diagram in the left hand margin and cut carefully using a handsaw. Sand each piece and either varnish or rub with teak oil. To complete your puzzle make a box for the pieces.

Use the simple triangles and quadrilaterals of the Egyptian puzzle to make the rather more complicated shapes shown here.

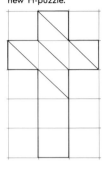

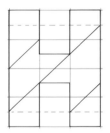

The Jeu de La Croix was made in France around 1890.

Cross Puzzles

There are many different cross puzzles - dissection puzzles in the form of a cross - and they can be made in many different sizes and materials. On this page three fine examples of this type of puzzle are illustrated.

The Ivory Cross

This beautifully-carved ivory cross, also sometimes known as the Latin Cross, is cut diagonally into five pieces and is Chinese in origin. It comes with a box to keep the pieces in. The earliest references to this puzzle can be found in the 'Magicians Own Book', published in 1857, and the first known examples, including the one shown on this page, date from the first half of the nineteenth century. The five pieces can be assembled into a rectangle and a number of other interesting forms.

More than one puzzle has been based on the Ivory Cross. A fine example of this is the T-puzzle on the opposite page, a very elegant letter puzzle and probably even more difficult and clever than the diagonally cut cross.

The Druids' Cross

Produced by the Edwards & Sons Company of London, this cross puzzle is also cut diagonally and is probably an adaptation of the Ivory Cross Puzzle. The puzzle consists of six pieces and is sold in an attractive looking box with a sliding cover. The example shown on this page dates from about 1855-1860. If you can make a rectangle from the Ivory Cross, you should not have any trouble in making the same rectangle from the six pieces of this puzzle. Try to make other forms.

Jeu de la Croix

This 'game of the cross' consists of seven pieces. On the left of this page there is an example of one that was made in France during the last decade of the nineteenth century. The earliest similar cross puzzle can be found in the Bestelmeier Catalog (a German toy catalog) of 1803. The box to hold the puzzle is made out of cardboard, the seven pieces (shown on the cover of the box) are of wood.

Below: The Ivory Cross, a beautiful piece of carved ivory from China, is cut diagonally and consists of five pieces. It dates from the first half of the 19th century.

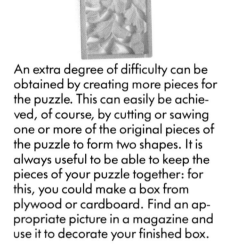

How to make a cross puzzle

This puzzle can be made out of thick cardboard or plywood. If you use transparent paper, it should not be difficult to trace the models shown on this page. Cut the pieces out with a hobby knife or handsaw. To make your puzzle as attractive as possible, sand the pieces and paint them in different colors. If birch or mahogany plywood is used, an attractive finish can be obtained with teak oil or by varnishing.

An extra degree of difficulty can be obtained by creating more pieces for the puzzle. This can easily be achieved, of course, by cutting or sawing one or more of the original pieces of the puzzle to form two shapes. It is always useful to be able to keep the pieces of your puzzle together: for this, you could make a box from plywood or cardboard. Find an appropriate picture in a magazine and use it to decorate your finished box.

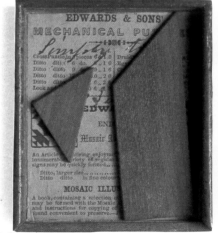

This Cross dates from 1855-1860 and consists of six pieces.

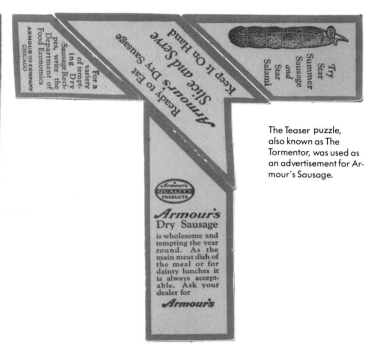

The Teaser puzzle, also known as The Tormentor, was used as an advertisement for Armour's Sausage.

Letter Dissections

There are no bounds to what the fanatical dissection puzzle enthusiast will try to dissect, so why not the letters of the alphabet? Cutting up the curved ones is a bit tricky, unless you use very distorted versions of the letters, but the straight-line letters are ideal for dissection.

Harry Lindgren created many fine letter dissection puzzles. The basic idea of his puzzles is to dissect a letter into a number of pieces which can then be arranged to form a square. However, in elegance and simplicity, the T-Puzzle has never been surpassed. Deceptively simple because it uses so few pieces, the puzzle is even more difficult and clever than the diagonal cross discussed on the previous page. The oldest 'T' puzzle found was an advertisement for White Rose Ceylon tea by Seeman Brothers, New York, N.Y., dated 1903. Another old reference to the T-puzzle appeared in 'Carpentry & Mechanics for Boys', published by A.N.Hall (1918).

The Teaser

This T-puzzle, consisting of four pieces, was used as an advertisement for sausages made by Armour & Co., of Chicago. All four pieces of the puzzle, which the company also called 'The Tormenter', were covered on both sides with texts proclaiming the superior quality of their product.

Below: A French version of the T-puzzle, called L'été. It dates from around 1920.

Above: La Hache Du Bourreau, a French version of the H-puzzle, consists of eight triangular pieces and was produced by N.K. Atlas, of Paris, around 1920.

L'été

This French T-puzzle was produced by N.K.Atlas of Paris around 1920. The T has been cut in the same way as the T-puzzle made by Armour & Co., shown at the top right of this page. The puzzle comes in a cardboard box.

This rather difficult H-puzzle, consisting of six pieces, served to advertise the products of the Hathaway Bread Company.

The new H Puzzle

This puzzle is an adaptation of the T-puzzle and consists of six pieces made of cardboard. Even though it doesn't look terribly complicated, it has proven to be quite a difficult puzzle to solve. It was used by the Hathaway Bread Company as an advertisement for their products.

The pieces of the puzzle were neatly wrapped in a paper bag and in this way distributed to the customers.

The Loculus of Archimedes

This two-dimensional 14-piece puzzle is essentially a super tangram. The Loculus (which means 'little box') is attributed to the Greek mathematician and inventor, Archimedes (3rd century B.C.). A 10th century palimpsest discovered in the Saint Sabba cloister in Jerusalem in 1906 describes the Method of Archimedes. The puzzle is sometimes known as the Stomachion ('the problem that drives one mad'). As with most two-dimensional geometric puzzles, each piece can be used either side up and, in addition to the shapes below, a variety of elegant human figures can be produced from the pieces.

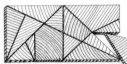

Above: This version of the Loculus of Archimedes has appeared in several books of puzzles, but is incorrect. Right: This is the correct dissection as shown in a 10th century manuscript.

Another name for this puzzle is the Stomachion - the puzzle that drives one mad! Try to make these figures using all 14 of the pieces.

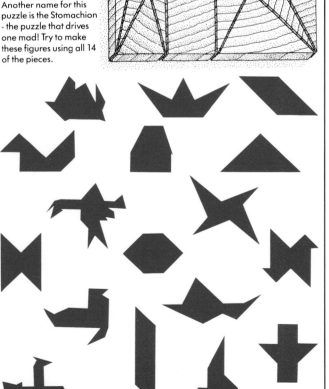

Sei Shonagon Chie No-Ita

This puzzle first appeared in a book published in Japan in 1742. It is thought the author may have been Fan Chu Sen, an author of math and magic books. (Translated, its name means: the ingenious pieces - or the plates of wisdom - of Sei Shonagon.) This 32-page book contains 42 patterns with answers - some inaccurate - and is one of the very few collections of early Japanese tangram-like puzzles. Sei Shonagon was a court lady at the end of the 10th and the beginning of the 11th century and was said to be one of the cleverest women in Japan. She is, perhaps, better known for her famous 'Makura no Soshi' (The Pillow Book), which is still in print.

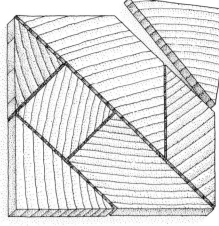

This is the earliest known example of a tangram-like puzzle.

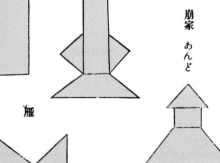

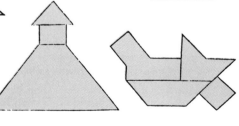

These are the original drawings from the book of Sei Shonagon, published by Kyoto Shobo in 1742.

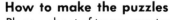

山形

色紙
組ちがへ、

紙船

時計

花生け

崩家
あんど

湯つぎ

雁

おし鳥

釘ぬき

蓮花

How to make the puzzles

Place a sheet of transparent paper over the illustrations and trace the pieces. Transfer your drawings to cardboard or plywood and cut or saw into pieces. Precision is essential here, particularly with the Loculus of Archimedes. As a finishing touch, paint the pieces, or decorate each piece with a Chinese or Japanese character. When you have solved the problems shown here, invent your own and try them out on your friends.

Tangrams

Dissection puzzles - plane or solid figures cut into various pieces - are among the oldest and most popular forms of recreational mathematics. There are hundreds of them, of varying degrees of complexity and elegance. The problem is always to fit the pieces together to make the original, or some other, figure. The Tangram is probably the most outstanding of all the dissection puzzles.

The charm of the Tangram lies in its subtlety. There are only seven pieces, called tans, and they are of the simplest possible shapes - two large, a medium-sized and two small triangles, a square and a rhombus (lozenge). Yet these seven simple pieces can be assembled in an extraordinary variety of ways. The figures can be geometrical - a triangle, trapezoid or parallelogram; they can represent letters or numbers; they can suggest the simple silhouette of a house, a church, or a bridge. But this is only the beginning. By using artistic skill and geometrical ingenuity an almost infinite number of human and animal figures can be formed from the tans. Such is the subtlety of the Tangram that the skilled puzzler can suggest the frantic energy of the Cossack dancer, the inscrutable face

of a Chinese Emperor, the superciliousness of a camel or the elegance of a bird in flight.

Oddly enough, little is known for certain about the origin of the Tangram or who invented it. Even the origin of the name 'Tangram' is obscure. The puzzle certainly originated in China; its earliest known reference is a woodcut from 1780 by Utamaro. This woodcut depicts two courtesans trying to solve Chi-Chiao (the Chinese name for Tangram, which translates 'The Seven Clever Pieces'). The seven pieces of Chi-Chiao were taken from the sun, the moon and the five planets of Mars, Jupiter, Saturn, Mercury and Venus.

The 'Chinese Puzzle Game' swept through Europe and America at the beginning of the 19th century and its popularity continues to this day. Although there is little factual evidence of the origin of the Tangram, there is a rich and detailed body of legend, largely due to the efforts of Sam Loyd, the great American puzzle expert, who devised a bogus history of the Tangram.

According to Loyd, the God Tan invented the puzzle 4000 years ago and described it in the Seven Books of Tan.(Each volume contained over 1000 puzzles which were supposed 'to illustrate the creation of the world

This beautiful book of Tangrams is undated but it was probably produced around 1800. The cover is ivory and the pages are made of silk.

The puzzles are printed in blue. Although there is no text, this 86-page book contains more than 333 problems and is a rare example of its type.

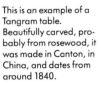

This is an example of a Tangram table. Beautifully carved, probably from rosewood, it was made in Canton, in China, and dates from around 1840.

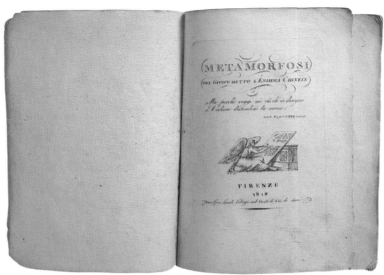

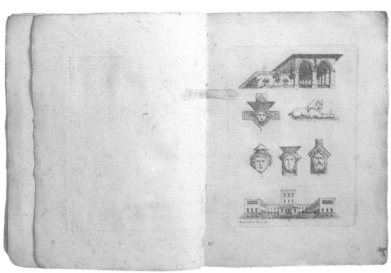

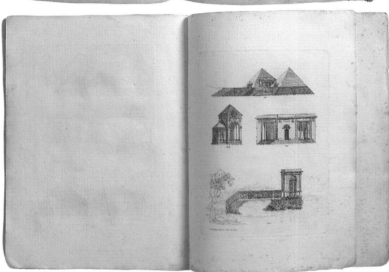

and the origin of species'.) Loyd, aided and abetted, probably unwittingly, by the English puzzlist H.E.Dudeney, succeeded in fooling a lot of people for a long time before it was concluded that it was an elaborate and scholarly spoof. Even though we know that the Tangram was not named after a god Tan, the origin of the name is open to some conjecture. The 'gram' - a common ending meaning something written or drawn - presents no difficulty. The origin of 'tan' is more in doubt. According to some, it is a corruption of the obsolete English word trangam, which meant a puzzle or trinket, and in the opinion of others it was derived from the tanka girls who entertained American sailors (although it strains one's credulity to imagine the crew of an opium clipper, after an arduous voyage, making tangram figures with ladies of pleasure!) The most likely explanation is that the word derives from the Tang dynasty, which was so famous that its name became synonymous with 'Chinese' in certain dialects. If so, then the Tangram is indeed the 'Chinese Puzzle'.

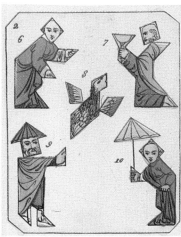

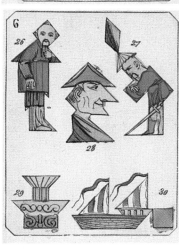
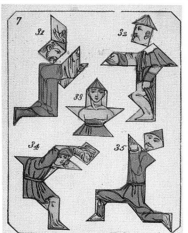
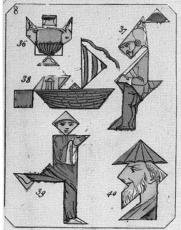

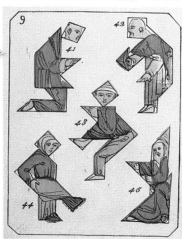
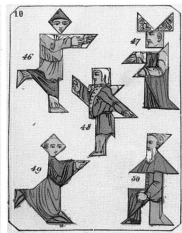

Nr. 3

Ei des Columbus

F. Ad. Richter & Cie. A.-G., Baukastenfabrik, Rudolstadt

Blitzableiter

Hromosvod.

Made in Germany.

The Wrath-Breaker
Der Zornbrecher
l'Apaise-Colère
De Toornstiller
Vrede-
stiller

104 Int. 5

Křižek

Made in Germany.

A "Puzzle Drive" with
ANCHOR STONE PUZZLES

17

KREISRÄTSEL.

Vejce Kolumbovo.

Made in Germany.

Quälgeist

Richters Unter= 18 Geduldspiel.

PYTHAGORAS.

Anchor Puzzles

Above: Dr. F. Adolph Richter, the German industrialist whose company produced the Anchor Puzzles.

Right: The castle in Rudolstadt, Thuringia, which was the home of the Richter family.
Below: The brochure showing the magnificent buildings which could be made with the Anchor Stone building blocks.

Here is a somewhat different puzzle to the ones mentioned so far in this book: What links a well-known 18th century educationalist, a German industrialist, a pioneer aviator, the inventor of the electric light bulb and a president of the United States? The answer to this seemingly insolvable conundrum: 'The Anchor Stone Puzzles'. The educationalist was Friedrich Froebel (1782-1852) who started the kindergarten movement in 1837. He was the first to use wooden building blocks as educational toys for the children. Some years later a friend of Froebel asked the industrialist, Dr. F. Adolph Richter, to manufacture better quality building blocks of many

Left: Booklets contained in the boxes of puzzles. They often carried endorsements from famous Americans.

Above: The trademark of the company which appeared on every puzzle box.

precisely related shapes and sizes. Richter searched for a suitable material and found it in a brick-making mixture of Kaolin clay from Bavaria, sand and linseed oil. This formula had been invented by Otto Lilienthal (1848-1896) who was also the first man to develop and successfully fly gliders. Richter bought the patent rights to the mixture and improved it and in 1882 began manufacturing Anchor Stone building blocks. By 1887 at least 23 different sets were being manufactured and the com-

pany had sales offices in New York and other American cities. In 1891, Richter produced a stone version of the Tangram which he called Der Kopfzer-brecher (literally the 'head cracker' but coloquially it refers to a difficult thinking problem). This was marketed in English speaking countries under the name of 'The Anchor Puzzle' and it became the forerunner of a whole range of different puzzles. And where, you may ask, do the inventor of the electric light bulb and a president of the United States figure in

this saga? All good conundrums, like all good puzzles, are just a little devious and this one is no exception! The answer is that both Thomas Alva Edison and President Grover Cleveland publicly endorsed the ingenious set of building bricks in the puzzle booklets which were enclosed with each set!
The Anchor Puzzle proved to be so successful that several new puzzles quickly followed. By 1899 Richter manufactured at least 11 different ones and this number soon increased

27

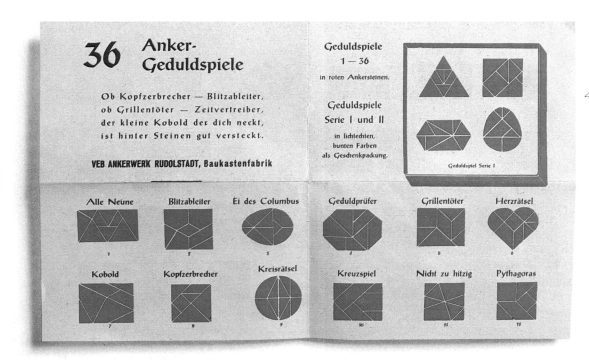

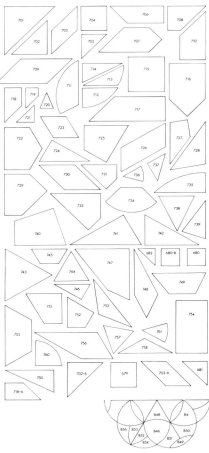

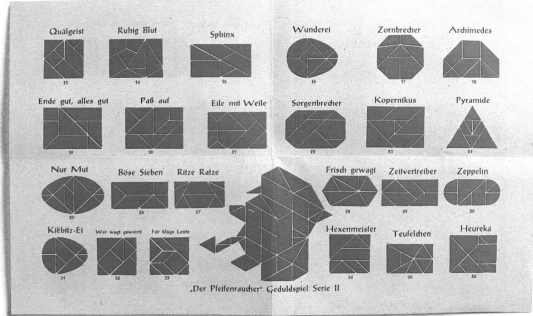

„Der Pfeifenraucher" Geduldspiel Serie II

These four pages of the brochure show all 36 puzzles made by the Richter Company. Eighteen of them had been produced by the early years of this century. The other 18 were designed during World War I in response to a demand for puzzles by the troops.

Above right: A complete set of the pieces which are needed to make all the Anchor Puzzles. Many of these pieces must be duplicated.

to 17 plus Das Sternratsel, the Star Puzzle. They were designed by a group of four artists who competed to produce the most elegant and difficult puzzles, sometimes wagering a round of beer on whether a new design was more difficult than the best of the old designs! These designs were based on a wide range of geometric shapes including the square, the rectangle, the triangle and the circle. Anchor puzzles reached the height of their popularity during the years of World War I. During that period, the com-

pany was ordered to produce large numbers of puzzles to occupy and entertain the troops in the trenches. Within a very short time 18 new puzzles were invented and produced, all using the old molds as there was not enough time to make new ones. A sad coincidence was that Allied troops, in the trenches opposite, were also whiling away the long hours with one of the same original puzzles which were produced under license in Great Britain at that time.

How to make the Anchor Puzzles

Making a complete set of Anchor Puzzles might at first seem a daunting task. But take heart! It is not quite as difficult as it seems. If you look at the shapes shown above and compare them with the puzzles you will notice that many of the pieces are duplicated. This came about for two reasons. First it was expensive and difficult to make the molds and so the designers tried to duplicate wherever practicable. The second reason was that at the beginning of World War I there was a great demand for new puzzles. The company was asked to design 18 new puzzles and there was no time to make new molds.

Enlarge the shapes to a reasonable size (we should not really suggest this, but a copy center will do this for you). Glue the copies onto a piece of cardboard or plywood and cut or saw out the shapes, duplicating where necessary. Paint or varnish the finished shapes in order to produce an attractive and durable set of puzzles.

The Egg of Columbus

Above: This diagram shows the dissection of Richter's Egg of Columbus puzzle.

Right: This puzzle is one of the most beautiful in the collection. Here you can see the box, the problem booklet and the puzzle itself.

Below: The figures shown in the booklets were often decorated. This puzzle was later reissued under the name 'The Magic Egg', and it is possible to make 106 different birds, using the same pieces.

The earliest known example of this puzzle dates from September, 1893. It was later reissued with a booklet containing a completely new set of puzzles in the form of birds. Today there are many modern copies in both plastic and cardboard made and sold in both Eastern and Western Europe.

How to make the Egg

A very attractive puzzle can be made (or laid!) from birch plywood. You will need a ruler, a pencil, a fretsaw, a handsaw and a rasp. The first step is to enlarge the diagram in the left-hand margin to a reasonable size - we suggest about 6 inches (15 cm) high. Trace the shape onto the plywood and carefully cut out the egg using the fretsaw. Smooth the edges with the rasp and sandpaper until you have a

perfect oval shape. Mark out the dissection lines and cut the egg into nine pieces using the handsaw. Sandpaper the edges. A coat of clear varnish or teak oil adds a professional finishing touch to this most attractive puzzle. Use your finished puzzle to make the shapes shown below. When you have succeeded, try to find some of the 106 birds.

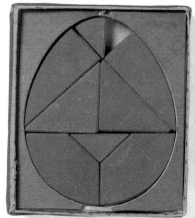

The Sphinx

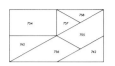

The Sphinx Puzzle was one of the many puzzles produced and marketed by the Richter company in Germany. The earliest known example dates from September, 1899. The puzzle was later produced under license by the Lotts Brick Company, in England, who marketed the it under the name Butterfly Puzzle. During the early years of World War 1, British troops found this puzzle to be an ideal way of passing the long, often boring hours spent in the trenches. The same puzzle, Richter's Sphinx Puzzle, was used by the German troops to while away their time.

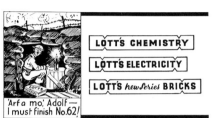

The dissection for the Sphinx puzzle. Follow the general instructions on page 28.

Above right: Here we have two identical puzzles marketed under different names. On the right is Richter's original Sphinx Puzzle together with its accompanying solution booklet. On the far right is the same puzzle produced under license by Lotts Brick Co. in England and marketed under the name of the Butterfly Puzzle.

The advertisement on the right appeared in newspapers and magazines in the weeks prior to Christmas 1914. Soldiers on both sides found that stone puzzles were an ideal means of whiling away boredom in the trenches.

Some of the many different shapes that can be made using the seven pieces of this puzzle. When you have discovered how to put these together, try to make new shapes of your own. There are many possibilities.

LOTT'S CHEMISTRY
LOTT'S ELECTRICITY
LOTT'S *new Series* **BRICKS**

'Arf a mo,' Adolf —
I must finish No.62!

XMAS PARADE

LOTT'S TUDOR BLOCKS AND BUILDEC

Not only the Sphinx Puzzle, but all the other Anchor Stone Puzzles became very popular among the German troops. The company received a great number of cards from soldiers in the field praising the existing puzzles, suggesting ideas for new figures and ordering new puzzles.

One of the designers of the Anchor Puzzles, Richard Moeller, has written that it was primarily the postcards which the company received that caused the designers to develop 18 additional puzzles in the shortest possible time. He also mentioned that designs for new puzzles were received from the field and that the 'trench puzzle' really was created in the trenches. This is a miniature puzzle, similar to the Zoo and Piccolo puzzles and easy to carry in the vest pocket. The task of creating so many new puzzles in such a short time placed great demands on the designers, since they had to design the puzzles in such a way that they were composed of pieces which could be formed using the existing molds.

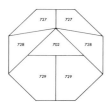

The dissection for Richter's Zornbrecher Puzzle. Make it in the same way that you made the other Anchor Puzzles, described earlier.

The illustrations show, respectively, the box cover, the problem booklet which accompanied the puzzle and the puzzle itself.

When you have made the pieces, use them to try to make some of the figures shown here. With a little imagination and ingenuity perhaps you can discover some of the dozens of other figures which can be made with the stones.

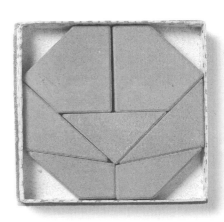

The Zornbrecher Puzzle

The earliest known example of this puzzle dates from June, 1892 and there have been at least four different box cover designs over the years. The Zornbrecher Puzzle is based on an octagon - a regular eight-sided figure.

One of the greatest problems in the manufacture of the Anchor Stone Puzzles was in the casting of the clay mixture. Each piece not only had to be exactly the right shape, it was also essential to ensure that the corners were sharp. Dr Richter improved the original mixture after he bought the patent from Otto Lilenthal. The pieces were made by placing a specified amount of the mixture in a steel mold. The bottom of the mold consisted of an airtight piston held in an exact location while a top piston was depressed to compress the clay mixture. To do this the operator rotated a crank and pushed a foot lever to eject the 'stone'. Then the stones were placed on trays and baked in gas-fired ovens. The compression pressure was determined by the amount of material in the mold and it required some skill on the part of the operator to ensure that no air was trapped and compressed in the stones. If this happened the stone would explode on baking. A skilled operator could produce about 100 stones an hour for which, in 1910, he was paid about 2 cents.

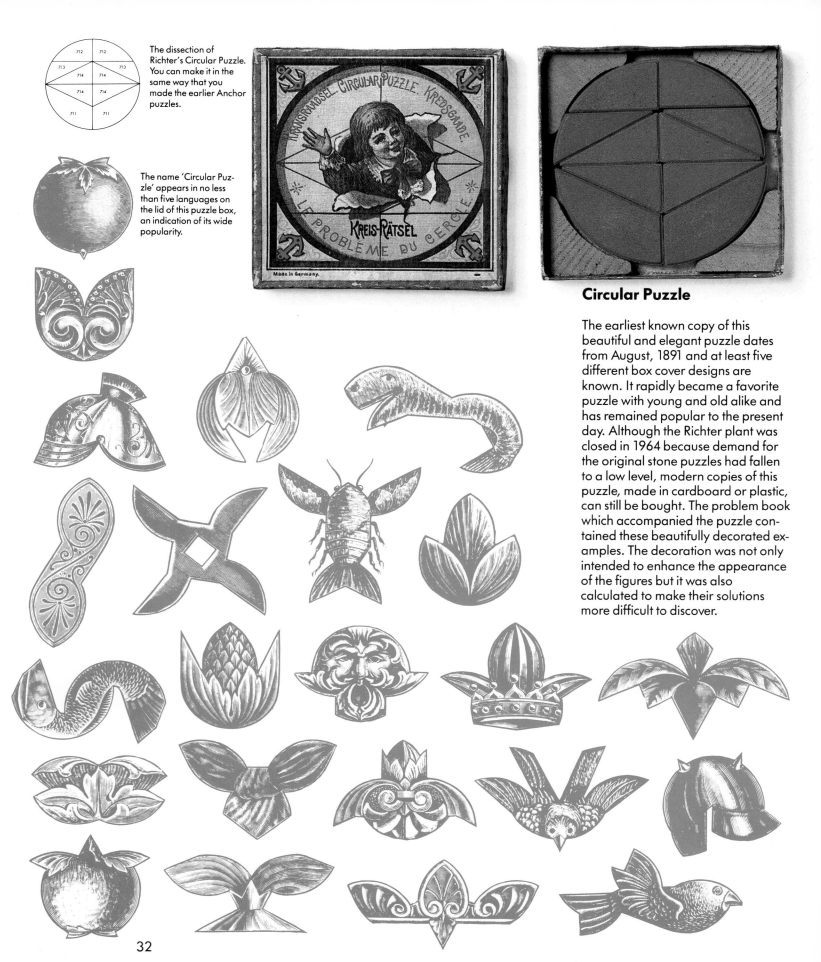

The dissection of Richter's Circular Puzzle. You can make it in the same way that you made the earlier Anchor puzzles.

The name 'Circular Puzzle' appears in no less than five languages on the lid of this puzzle box, an indication of its wide popularity.

Circular Puzzle

The earliest known copy of this beautiful and elegant puzzle dates from August, 1891 and at least five different box cover designs are known. It rapidly became a favorite puzzle with young and old alike and has remained popular to the present day. Although the Richter plant was closed in 1964 because demand for the original stone puzzles had fallen to a low level, modern copies of this puzzle, made in cardboard or plastic, can still be bought. The problem book which accompanied the puzzle contained these beautifully decorated examples. The decoration was not only intended to enhance the appearance of the figures but it was also calculated to make their solutions more difficult to discover.

32

Sam Loyd's Trick Mules Puzzle

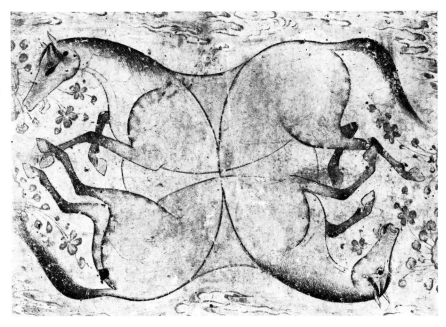

Over the years, a great number of advertising puzzles have been based on the original Trick Mules Puzzle. The earliest version of this puzzle was devised by the great American puzzlist, Sam Loyd, who for half a century until his death in 1911 was the undisputed puzzle king of the United States. During this time he produced several thousand superb puzzles. Most of them were mathematical and many of them retain their popularity until this very day.

This puzzle looks deceptively easy until you try it! The idea is to cut the puzzle along the dotted lines and arrange the three resulting rectangles (without folding) so that the two jockeys ride the two mules. When the rectangles are arranged correctly the weary-looking mules miraculously break into a frenzied gallop.

Loyd sold this puzzle to the great American showman P.T. Barnum, who marketed millions under the name 'P.T. Barnum's Trick Mules', and it is said that Loyd earned $10,000 in a few weeks - a fortune in those days. In 1872, Barnum advertised the puzzle in the Advance Courier together with a warning which stated: 'Unprincipled parties have infringed upon this patent puzzle. Business men are cautioned against using or paying for cards not having the imprint of the inventor, S. LOYD.'

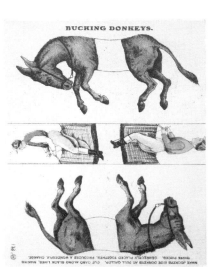

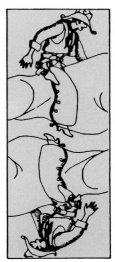

Cowboy and Bull Puzzle This puzzle is based on Loyd's original. The problem is to fit the two pieces together without bending, folding or tearing in such a way that the cowboys sit on top of the bulls. At first sight this appears to be an impossible task. There is a solution, but you will have to exercise considerable ingenuity to find it!

How to make The Trick Mules Puzzle

Making this puzzle presents a real challenge to your artistic ability. You need a sheet of tracing paper, thin white or colored card and scissors or a hobby knife. Carefully trace the outlines of the mules and the jockeys. Transfer your tracings to the card. This is where your artistic ability comes in! Use colored pencils or paints to make the mules and their jockeys as lifelike as possible. Now try to solve the puzzle. The Cowboys and Bulls Puzzle, shown on the left, can be made in the same way.

Question du Lapin

This beautifully elegant silhouette puzzle was first produced by Watilliaux in Paris around 1900. It provides an excellent example of the kind of puzzles which at first sight appear to be deceptively simple, but which in practice turn out be diabolically difficult.

The puzzle consists of five colored octagonal (eight-sided) cards. Each card has a cut out silhouette of respectively: a horse's head, a Grecian flower vase, a cat's head, a bluebell and a tortoise. The puzzle is to superimpose the five cards so that the silhouette of a rabbit appears. A little thought will show that the order in which the cards are superimposed is not important.

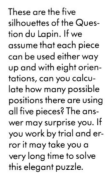

The box in which the original puzzle was marketed in the early years of the century.

How to make the Question du Lapin.

This puzzle would make a delightful gift for your friends. To make it you need five pieces of thin card, each piece of a different color, a sheet of tracing paper, two pencils (one soft and one hard) and a sharp hobby knife. First trace five octagons, one on each of the five pieces of card, and cut them out. Trace the silhouettes illustrated below using the soft pencil. Turn your tracings upside down and retrace each silhouette onto a separate octagon using the hard pencil. Cut out the silhouettes carefully with the hobby knife. To complete the puzzle find a small box and decorate it with a sixth silhouette - the rabbit. If you are very skillful with a fretsaw you could make the puzzle in plywood.

These are the five silhouettes of the Question du Lapin. If we assume that each piece can be used either way up and with eight orientations, can you calculate how many possible positions there are using all five pieces? The answer may surprise you. If you work by trial and error it may take you a very long time to solve this elegant puzzle.

The solution

We could not be so sadistic as to leave you to discover the solution without a little help. The diagram below shows the correct position of each piece. When the pieces are superimposed the silhouette of the rabbit will appear. Or will it? Maybe that is a little too easy! In fact, only four of the pieces are in the correct positions. Can you find the 'odd man out' and so solve the puzzle?

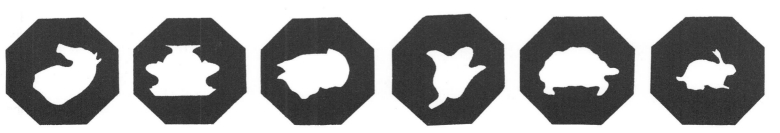

'Grandpa's Wonder Puzzle' by A.K.Rankin, patented in 1911, was used to advertise soap. It was a variation of Thurston's puzzle: the object was to arrange the cards so that there were four different colors in each center circle and two different colors in each half circle.

The diagram below is the basic pattern of the Heads and Tails Puzzle. If you are artistically inclined you can make a wide variety of attractive puzzles with animals, faces, signs of the Zodiac or even with cars or sailboats. The capital letters A,B,C and D represent the 'tails' and the small letters a,b,c and d represent the 'heads' of the objects you wish to depict. These objects appear in the same positions as the letters (see the Calumet Puzzle below left). It is even possible to make puzzles which show four different objects and in this case they do not need to be color coded. The a-A-Heads-Tails formula must still be followed, however.

This is the original Calumet Puzzle used as advertising material by the Calumet Baking Powder Co. of Chicago. The solution was found by matching the colors and the four sizes of baking powder cans.

Heads and Tails Puzzle

Heads and Tails puzzles belong to the family of matching puzzles in which a number of cards must be arranged so that their corners or sides match. The first puzzle of this kind was patented in 1893 by E.L.Thurston. It was used by the Calumet Baking Powder Co., Chicago, as an advertisement. Several other advertising versions were produced in the early 1900's and in more recent years KLM Airlines and the Los Angeles Olympic Games have been similarly advertised. The puzzle has been analyzed by the Japanese puzzler Kiyoshi Takizawa, who showed that there are several possible variations of the basic pattern patented by Thurston. This pattern is shown below and we will use it to make the puzzle.

How to make the puzzle

You need a square of thick cardboard measuring 6 by 6 inches, a ruler, a pencil and a hobby knife. Divide the cardboard into nine two-inch squares. Further divide each small square into four triangles by drawing diagonal lines. Your puzzle is now ready to be decorated. You will see in the diagram that each triangle is marked with a letter: 'A', 'a', etc. Color the triangles as follows: All triangles marked either A or a must be the same color, those marked B/b are in a different color, as are C/c and D/d. When you have colored the triangles, mark each with its appropriate letter 'A', 'a', etc. Cut the large square into nine cards, shuffle them and try to arrange them into the original pattern. A more durable puzzle can easily be made from birch plywood.

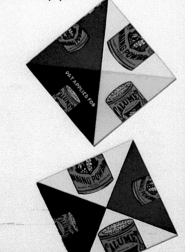

THE CALUMET PUZZLE
DIRECTIONS
The solution of this puzzle is the perfect matching of the color squares and the four different sizes of the Calumet Baking Powder Cans. The completed puzzle is a square as shown.
CALUMET BAKING POWDER CO.
4100-4128 Fillmore Street
CHICAGO, ILL.

(THIS IS KEY TO PUZZLE)

The problem of the eight queens

The Octo Puzzle was produced by Parker Brothers, Salem, Mass. and dates from about 1900. The problem is to place the eight counters on the 8 x 8 board so that no two counters lie on the same line, either in a horizontal, vertical or diagonal direction. As the slogan on the box says: 'it is hard to do, but it can be done'.

The N & F Puzzle was patented in 1886 by A.W. Butterworth and marketed by Nichols & Frost. This puzzle is solved by placing six pins in the 6 x 6 board so that no two pins line up in any direction. In fact, there is only one possible solution to this puzzle.

Jeu des Manifestants was manufactured by Jeux et Jouets Francais in about 1900. The puzzle is to arrange eight cards so that only one colored mark is in each row, column or diagonal line.

All these puzzles are commercial versions of the problem usually known as 'the problem of the eight queens'. It was first proposed by Max Bezzel in 1848, who asked: 'What is the largest number of queens that can be placed on a chess board in such a way that no queen is attacked by another?' In other words, so that no two queens are in the same row, column or diagonal. It was soon shown that the maximum number of queens is the same as the number of squares on one side of the board (as long as the number of squares is greater than 3) and therefore eight queens can be so placed on a standard chess board. The next step was to discover in how many different ways this can be done. In fact there are 12 unique solutions to this problem and they were first published in 1850 by Franz Nauck. A proof that these 12 solutions exhaust all the possibilities was finally obtained by the English mathematician J.W.L.Glaisher and published by him in 1874. What mathematicians call 'rotations and reflections' are not considered to be different solutions. If they were, the number of solutions to this puzzle would soar to 92!

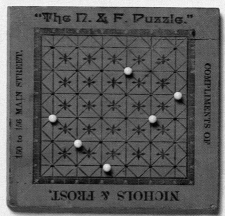

How to make the puzzles

For the N & F Puzzle you need a block of hardwood 6 x 6 x 1 inches, six 1" lengths of ½" dowel and a drill. Mark the block in squares and divide each square by drawing diagonal lines. Drill holes ½" deep at each point where the diagonals cross.
To make the Jeu Des Manifestants you need a piece of 8 x 8 inches cardboard. Mark it exactly as shown in the diagram. Cut along the red lines to produce eight cards. Shuffle the cards and try to arrange then so that no two stars are in the same row, column or diagonal. How many solutions can you find?

Instant Insanity

About 20 years ago, Franz O. Armbruster, a California computer programmer, designed a puzzle consisting of four plastic cubes, each face of each cube having one of four colors. The problem is simply to arrange the cubes in a straight row so that all four colors appear on each of the row's four sides. He called his puzzle 'Instant Insanity' and it was an instant success for Parker Brothers, its manufacturers. Armbruster's puzzle has, in fact, been around in many forms for over 80 years. The original version was designed and patented by Frederick A. Schossow of Detroit in 1900. His puzzle consisted of four cube blocks decorated with one of the

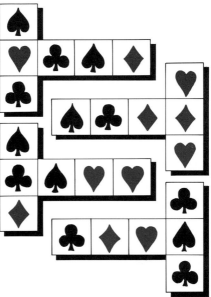

four suits of cards - club, diamond, heart, or spade. (Reference: o'Beirne.)

How to make the puzzle

You will need a large sheet of thin card, a hobby knife and glue. Carefully draw these shapes on the card. Add tabs on each side of both arms of the 'T' and at the foot of the 'T', so that you can glue the cubes together. Decorate as shown in the diagram, using symbols cut from an old deck of cards. Gently score along the lines and along the edges where the tabs are, being careful not to cut through the card. Cut out the shapes and fold along the scored lines. Glue to form four cubes. You can use wooden blocks instead of card.

Second from the top: Schossow's original puzzle. It was marketed as the Katzenjammer Puzzle.

Third and fifth row: World War I puzzles with flags of nations as decoration.

Below is another example of how puzzles have often been used for advertising. The cubes must be arranged so

that each of four different products (soup, cream, custard and gravy) appears on the row of four cubes.

Right: These diagrams show you how to make the four cubes and where to place the symbols.

38

Magic Squares

Magic squares have exercised an almost mystical fascination over mathematicians and laymen alike since they were first discovered more than 4000 years ago. They have been endowed with religious, occult and even diabolical properties. Even today they are still seen on amulets worn in the Far East and India and in fortune bowls and medicine cups in Tibet. On large passenger ships a magic square even forms the pattern for games of shuffleboard.

What is a magic square? It is simply a beautifully balanced square array of numbers in which each row, column and diagonal adds up to the same total. According to Chinese legend, the first magic square appeared to the mythical Emperor Yu while he was walking beside the Yellow River. He saw a turtle and noticed that its shell seemed to be marked in squares and that each square contained a number of dots. The Emperor's curiosity was aroused and he picked up the turtle and examined it carefully. To his astonishment he found that when he counted the dots he arrived at the same total for each row, column and diagonal marked on the turtle's shell. The turtle became famous and spent the rest of its life at the Emperor's court. Lo-Shu, as the array was later called, soon began to appear on charms and magic stones. To the Chinese, the even numbers of the Lo-Shu represented yin, the female principle of the universe, and the odd numbers represented yang, the male principle.

Lo-Shu is a magic square of order 3, because there are three cells on each side of the square or nine cells in all. The numbers in each row, column and diagonal add up to 15, which is the constant. If we discount rotations and reflections, we find that Lo-Shu is unique - it is the only possible third-order square. If we consider magic squares of a higher order, however, things are rather different. There are 880 fourth-order squares and several million fifth-order squares. To find the constant of a square of any order is quite easy using the formula: ½ x (order cubed + order). For example the constant for a fourth order square is ½ x (64 + 4), which is 34. That of a fifth order square is ½ x (125 + 5), which is 65. If we add, say, three to every number in the Lo-Shu, the square still remains 'magic' although its constant is obviously increased. A magic square remains magic when all its terms are increased, reduced, multiplied or divided by the same number - thus magic squares composed of fractions are possible. However, only squares containing integers (whole numbers) 1 thru n squared are considered to be pure magic squares.

As we mentioned earlier, magic squares have fascinated people all over the world for centuries. From China news of the squares spread to Japan and India, where studies were made long before the first century A.D. The first recorded instance of a fourth-order square appeared in an inscription in Khajuraho, India, and dates from about 1100 A.D. Magic squares also appeared in both Hebrew and Arabic writings at around the same time. Magic squares were not introduced into the West until the early part of the 15th century when they soon became associated with alchemy, astrology and the occult. In 1514, Albrecht Durer constructed a fourth-order magic square which had the date '1514' in the two center bottom cells. This square appeared in his famous engraving Melancholia and has since been the subject of much discussion among mathematicians and philosophers. The real study of magic squares, however, only began in France in the 17th century and since then they have been a favorite subject for study by professional and amateur mathematicians all over the world.

Right: The 15 & 34 Patience Puzzle marketed by Thomas De La Rue & Co., London. Besides the third-order Lo Shu, hundreds of 4th order magic squares can be made. Can you make a square so that not only the rows, columns and diagonals add to 34, but the four corner numbers, the four central numbers and each of the four corner groups also add to 34? An additional problem is to find a square in which any four adjacent numbers forming a 2 x 2 square add to 34.

Right, bottom: The New Puzzle- Marvelous 26 - is based on the magic square principle. The object is to place the discs to obtain the maximum number of runs-lines, angles or geometric figures-each having a total of 26. More than 30 runs can be found in one arrangement.

Below: Lo-Shu is usually given in the form shown here, which is a 90 degree clockwise rotation of the array shown on the turtle's shell. Question: How many other rotations and reflections are there? Note: Magic squares of any order and how to create them are discussed in great detail in 'Creative Puzzles of the World' by Pieter van Delft & Jack Botermans, published by Harry N.Abrams, New York, in 1978.

8	1	6
3	5	7
4	9	2

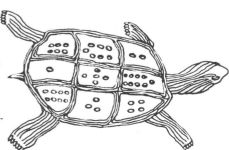

This is the array of dots which by legend the Emperor Yu discovered on the shell of a turtle as he walked by the Yellow River more than 4000 years ago. This array became known as Lo-Shu and it is the only 3rd-order magic square.

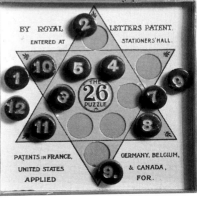

Three-Dimensional Assembly Puzzles

The earliest three-dimensional assembly puzzles were dissected ivory cubes cut into ten irregular pieces. These pieces were to be reassembled into an ivory box. They were made in China and often included with twenty or more other ivory puzzles in lacquered chests. During the first half of the 19th century, these chests were brought to Europe and the United States on clippers transporting tea. In New England the chests of ivory puzzles were called 'Sunday Boxes' because

the church had no rule forbidding playing with them on Sundays. This meant that everybody could enjoy the puzzles together, as Sunday was the only day when the whole family was at home.

Although Piet Hein invented the Soma Cube in 1936, it was not until the late 1960's, when Parker Brothers distributed a plastic version, that it became really popular. Piet Hein also invented the first ball pyramid puzzle, in 1970, and this in-

spired a wide variety of similar puzzles. Anyone who has packed a suitcase knows how difficult it can be to cram a number of 3-dimensional objects into a specified space! If you think that is tough, try your hand at the packing puzzles on page 43. That may drive you crazy: then relax by making one of the beautiful 3-dimensional jigsaws on pages 44 and 45. Or try your hand at the puzzle ring on page 47.

The figures below are models of three of the solid pentominoes. Each model uses all the pieces. If you think building blocks are kid's stuff, try to build them! Can you build the other pieces in the set? There is only one way to make the 'F' and two are impossible - which?

Far right: This beautiful 3-D pentomino set was designed by the Japanese teacher Sabu Oguro.

The solid pentominoes

When you have made a set of solid pentominoes (see page 17), your first problem is to pack them away neatly. The easiest way to do this is to build the pieces into one of the three rectangular solids shown in the top row of the diagram below. Try the 3 x 4 x 5 solid. It should not prove too difficult - there are 3940 different ways of building it.

The solution to the middle puzzle is rather interesting. It consists of two 5 x 6 rectangles which can be laid side by side to form one 6 x 10 rectangle. Both the staircase and the hollow rectangular solid shown in the middle row are formed using all 12 pentominoes. The pyramid uses only 11 pentominoes. Can you find which piece is omitted and so discover the solution?

How to make this puzzle
This beautiful pentomino set was designed by the Japanese teacher, Sabu Oguro, and is now produced commercially by U-Plan, Japan. The 12 pieces are based on the animals and birds of the Japanese year cycle. To make it, trace the shapes onto a piece of birch plywood (thickness one unit as width unit) and cut them out carefully with a fine fretsaw. This is a difficult task but highly rewarding if you succeed.

The Soma Cube

The Soma cube was devised in 1936 by the Danish poet and puzzle inventor Piet Hein. Since then it has been a source of both fascination and frustration to young and old alike; it must be one of the few puzzles in the history of puzzledom to have inspired its own newsletter! The seven Soma pieces represent all the ways in which three or four cubes can be arranged other than in straight lines; in elegance and versatility it is the 3-dimensional equivalent of the Tangram. There are literally thousands of geometric and representational forms which can be built from the seven simple pieces. The name 'Soma' is derived from the drug in Aldous Huxley's Brave New World, a drug which transported its user into a dreamlike trance. So, before you work on this puzzle, remember - You have been warned!

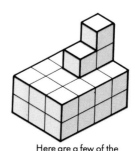

Above: The dark version of the Soma Cube is made from hardwoods and produced by Skjude of Skjern, Denmark. Piet Hein developed the elegant checkered Soma in 1970 by coloring alternate blocks in each piece.

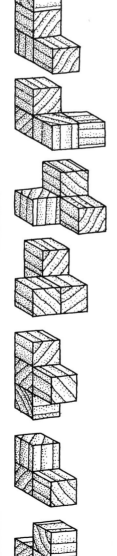

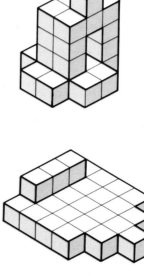

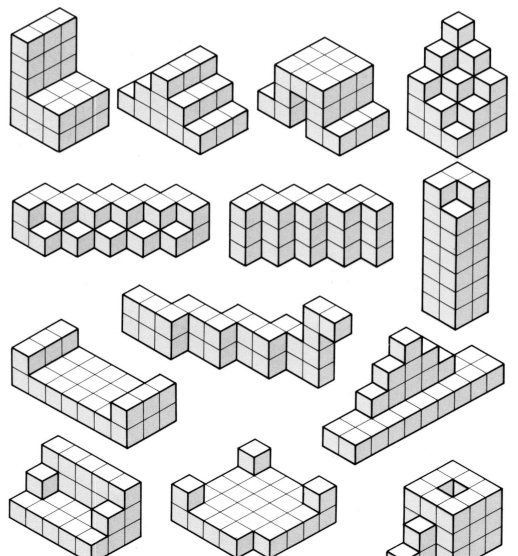

Here are a few of the shapes which can be built with the Soma pieces. When you have succeeded in making these, devise forms of your own. Before long you will see why the newsletter was called the Soma Addict!

Stewart Coffin's Setting Hen and four-piece Pyramid Puzzle.

Pyramid Puzzles

Now your appetite has been whetted by puzzling with solid pentominoes and the Soma Cube, you should be ready to set your teeth into some other difficult three-dimensional problems. Both the puzzles shown on the left were designed by Stewart Coffin. The first, the Setting Hen, consists of 14 rhombic dodecahedra which are joined to make four puzzle pieces. They can pack into a cubic box and build either a square or a rectangular pyramid. Each piece of the second puzzle, the four-piece Pyramid, is non-symmetrical and dissimilar, and is made of five rhombic dodecahedra, interlocking in one way and in one order only to produce a tetrahedron.

The Vanishing Space

This 35-ball Giant Pyramid was designed by Len Gordon. It has nine pieces and assembles with great difficulty into a five layer tetrahedron. The first ball pyramid puzzle, known as the Pyramystery Puzzle, was invented in 1970 by Piet Hein. It had only 20 balls arranged in six pieces.

Based on Coffin's Pyracube, this puzzle calls for the fitting of five shapes - formed from 14 spheres - into a small cubic box. The shapes can them be placed so that the box is filled with only 13 spheres. Where has the 'missing' space gone?

This variation of Coffin's Pyracube was made with spheres by Jack Botermans, one of the authors of this book. It was first published in Creative Puzzles of the World.

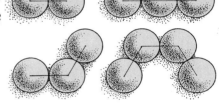

How to make this puzzle

You need 14 wooden spheres each 1'' in diameter, 1/8'' dowel and glue. Drill holes, 1/2'' deep, in the directions marked in the diagram. (Note: Care must be taken to ensure that the holes are drilled both at the correct angle (90° or 120°) and at the center of the spheres). Cut nine 1'' lengths of dowel and glue in place to produce the pieces shown.

The easiest way to make the box is from five 2½'' squares of cardboard, taped along the edges. Unfortunately this conceals the pieces and makes the packing problem even harder than it already is. Why not try to make a box using five squares of acrylic? The most difficult part of the job is to bevel the edges to a 45° angle, but this can be achieved with a little ingenuity.

This is a smaller version of the Giant Pyramid. Can you make it and assemble it?

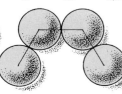

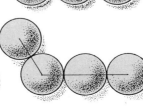

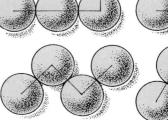

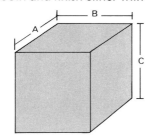

Above: This is Trevor Wood's elegant answer to Hoffman's Box Packing Puzzle. Each of the 27 pieces measures 18 x 20 x 22 millimeters. Question: Do the 27 pieces fill the box exactly?

Hoffman's Packing Puzzle

In a complex industrial society, all kinds of problems arise involving the packing of three-dimensional objects into a specified space - a so-called box packing problem. Every time a warehouse manager takes delivery of a consignment of goods or a ship's mate loads a cargo, he is solving such a problem. During recent years several mathematicians have devoted thought to the matter. Dean Hoffman proposed this problem to a conference at Miami University in 1978: 'Fit 27 blocks, measuring A x B x C, into a cubic box of side A + B + C. A, B and C must be different and the smallest dimension must be larger than (A + B + C)/4'. In Trevor Wood's solution, each block has the dimensions of A = 18, B = 20 and C = 22 mm. (1 1/8 '' x 1 1/4 '' x 1 3/8''). The 27 blocks must be packed into a box measuring 60 x 60 x 60 mm. (3 3/4 '' x 3 3/4 '' x 3 3/4 ''). This is a fascinating puzzle and one which is quite easy to

make. Try to figure out how to pack the pieces in the box before you look at the solution given.

How to make Hoffman's Puzzle

You need about 65 cm. (30'') of wood with a cross-section of 18 x 20 mm. (1 1/8 '' x 1 1/4 ''). Cut 27 pieces, 22 mm. (1 3/8 '') in length. Sand each piece smooth and finish either with teak oil,

varnish or paint. The box should measure 60 x 60 x 60 mm. (3 3/4 '' square), but make it a little larger so that the pieces can be packed easily. It can be made out of cardboard but it is not too difficult to construct an attractive wooden box to complete the puzzle.

Kolor Kraze

This puzzle was designed and first manufactured by House of Games, Canada, in 1970. Its object is to pack the 13 pieces to form a cube so nine colors show on each face. Sounds simple enough - until you try it!

How to make the Kolor Kraze

This puzzle can be made as large or as small as you wish, but we suggest that pieces of 1'' cross-section are ideal. If you choose this size you will need about 30'' of 1'' x 1'' wood and the smallest available cans of nine different-colored paints. The model shown here used white, green, blue, yellow, red, black, pink, brown and orange. Cut twelve 2'' pieces and one 3'' piece from the length of wood. Sandpaper each piece smooth and seal the sawn ends so they will not absorb too much paint. Now comes the tricky bit! You will see that in the diagram below that each block is numbered. Each number represents a particular color of paint. Make a table (1 = white, 2 = green, etc.) and follow it carefully while you are painting the blocks. When the blocks are finished make a box to keep them in.

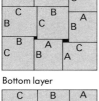

Top layer

A C	C	B
A B	B A	A C
A B	A	B C

Middle layer

B A	C A	A C
C B	B C	A B
B C	A B	A C

Bottom layer

C B	B A	A B
A C	A C	B C
A C	C B	A B

Above: Here is a solution to Wood's example of Hoffman's puzzle, layer by layer, viewed from above. The letters A, B and C represent the dimensions and show how each piece must be placed.

When the pieces are assembled correctly nine colors show on each face of the cube.

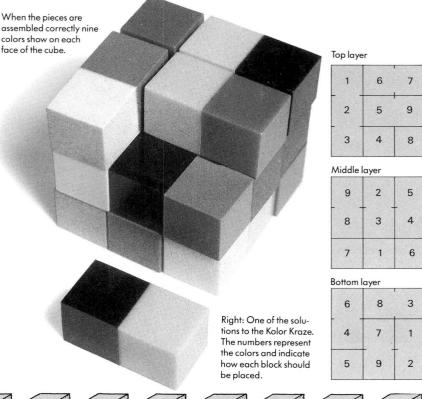

Right: One of the solutions to the Kolor Kraze. The numbers represent the colors and indicate how each block should be placed.

Top layer

1	6	7
2	5	9
3	4	8

Middle layer

9	2	5
8	3	4
7	1	6

Bottom layer

6	8	3
4	7	1
5	9	2

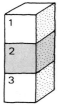

This very attractive three-dimensional jigsaw was sold as a souvenir at the Chicago World Fair in 1934. It is a fine example of a type of puzzle which was first sold in England in the late 1870's.

SCRAMBLED EGGS

TRADE MARK REG.   PAT. PENDING

The Three Dimension Puzzle

EVERY PIECE A PERFECT FIT

When properly matched they will slide together easily.

How the Egg Can Be Unscrambled

By taking your time and fitting the pieces together carefully.
By having patience and perseverance.
By NOT FORCING the pieces together.
{If they stick or bind they do not match.}
By only putting pieces together when they slide easily, but sometimes in one direction only and not in the other.
POSITIVELY DO NOT FORCE PIECES TOGETHER.

SUGGESTIONS

A new and novel prize for bridge and other parties. A pleasing relaxation after the game.
An appropriate gift for the invalid or convalescent. {It can be put together in the lap—a table is not necessary.}
An ideal way to keep children quiet in the evening. {Make them constructive instead of destructive.}

Give a Scrambled Egg Party

Here is the new idea the popular hostess has been seeking.
Use SCRAMBLED EGGS for prizes to the best unscramblers. Serving scrambled eggs for refreshments would add to the novelty.
In fact, it is one of the most interesting and fascinating forms of entertainment for any and all members of the family.

Manufactured and Distributed Solely by

SCRAMBLED EGGS INCORPORATED

121 W. WACKER DRIVE   CHICAGO, U. S. A.

PRINTED IN U.S.A.

Three-dimensional jigsaw puzzles

These puzzles first appeared in the form of rectangular blocks in England at the end of the 1870's, literally adding a new dimension to jigsaw puzzles. A jigsaw cut ball was patented in the U.S. in 1881 and Furniture Puzzles, sawed out of a block of wood, were on sale by 1919.

The maple leaf puzzle dates from the 1930's. The maple leaf is the national symbol of Canada. Can you design a puzzle using the national symbol of your own country?

This fish puzzle also dates from the 1930's. It also represents Pisces, one of the signs of the Zodiac. Design your own puzzles, based on other animal or bird forms or make one for your birth sign. Or better still, design one for the birth sign of a friend or member of your family and present it as an unusual and very personal gift.

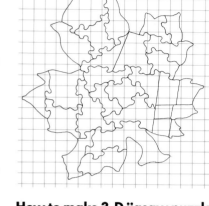

How to make 3-D jigsaw puzzles

This is work for a craftsman and to make a good job of it you need a bandsaw. Use the blue grids to enlarge the drawings and transfer them to a piece of hardwood (teak, mahogany or walnut, for example) of about 1'' in thickness. Cut out the pieces on the bandsaw. Now recut each piece edgeways, moving it from side to side while cutting. Sandpaper each piece smooth and finish with teak oil or varnish. If this task is too much for you, try making the same jigsaws in two dimensions. This is much easier. The pieces can be sawed from a piece of plywood using an ordinary fretsaw. Sandpaper and finish as before.

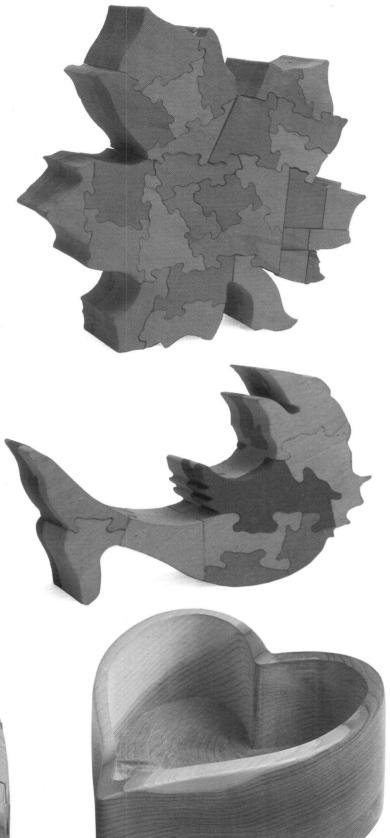

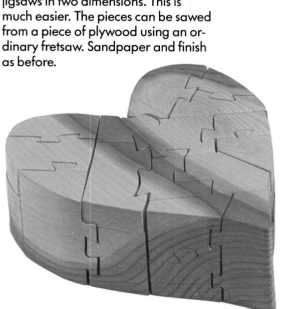

This beautiful heart puzzle was made by Peter Stocken in 1978.

Pyramid Puzzle

This put-together puzzle consists of two identical pieces and at first sight it seems too easy to include in a serious puzzle book. However, appearances can be deceptive and this apparently simple puzzle has frustrated many a self-confident individual. It consists of a tetrahedron (a triangular pyramid) cut into two equal pieces and was first patented by E.T.Johnson in 1940. A plastic version was widely sold by FUN Inc., of Chicago, starting in 1956.

How to make this puzzle
You need to make two pieces using the grid below.Trace the diagram and transfer your tracing onto a piece of thin card. Score along the dotted lines being careful not to cut through the card. Cut out and fold. Glue each tab to the inside of its respective face to form the solid. An even more difficult 4-piece puzzle can be made following the second diagram illustrated, of which two are mirror images.

This puzzle was originally published in Wonders in Wood by E.M.Wyatt, in 1946. This apparently simple puzzle is more difficult than one would expect.

This elegant 4-piece variation of the Pyramid Puzzle was made by Richard Appel. Each of the two like pieces of the original puzzle has been further dissected into two like pieces.

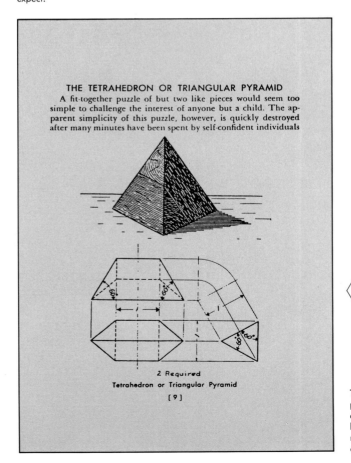

THE TETRAHEDRON OR TRIANGULAR PYRAMID
A fit-together puzzle of but two like pieces would seem too simple to challenge the interest of anyone but a child. The apparent simplicity of this puzzle, however, is quickly destroyed after many minutes have been spent by self-confident individuals

2 Required
Tetrahedron or Triangular Pyramid
[9]

The two pieces of the puzzle are made according to this grid. A larger version can be made by doubling the dimensions.

A 4-piece version can be made using the 'half' grid. Two of these smaller pieces fit together to form one of the pieces of the original puzzle.

Puzzle Rings

A puzzle ring consists of a number of pieces of wire ingeniously bent and intertwined so that they appear to form a single indivisible ring, even though the pieces can be separated into independent hoops. Puzzle rings developed from gimmal rings which derived their name from the Latin gemelli, 'twins'. These rings consisted of two or more linked hoops which fitted together. Miniature hands were sometimes mounted on the loops which would clasp when the ring was put together. Gimmal rings were used both as betrothal and wedding rings.

Some were made in such a way that the pieces could be worn separately by the betrothed couple and symbolically joined together during the wedding ceremony. There was frequently an inscription running along the facing halves of the hoops which would only be visible when they were separated. 'Quod Deus conjunxit Homo non separet' - 'What God hath joined, let no man put asunder' - was, not surprisingly, a popular inscription.

Most surviving gimmal rings were made in Italy during the Renaissance although some are of English or German origin.

How to make a Puzzle Ring
This is not as difficult as it might appear to be at first sight. You need six lengths of thin silver or copper wire. Weave them carefully following the pattern below. The wires must be laid as close together as possible and the woven pattern should be about ¾'' in length. When the pattern is complete, hammer the wires flat. Bend the flattened wires around a rod the size of your finger. Cut off the surplus wire and solder each hoop. If you have followed the pattern exactly, your ring will fall into six interlocking separate loops which reassemble into the ring.

To make your ring, weave the wires carefully, as shown in the diagram.

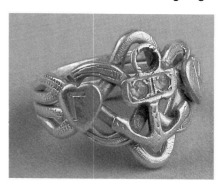

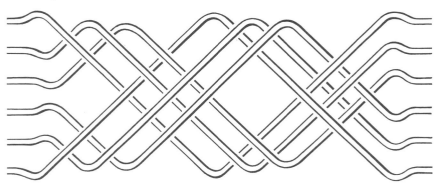

Several European museums have fine examples of 16th and 17th century gimmal rings, some of which are made of gold and set with precious stones. The simplest consists of two interlocking hoops, but rings of four, five or even six hoops were common.

Puzzle rings were popular as early as the beginning of the 15th century and were often used as betrothal and wedding rings. The Protestant reformer, Martin Luther, had such a wedding ring. In Turkey, it was customary for a soldier to give his wife a puzzle ring before going to war. If it was apart when he returned it meant that she had taken it off.

The popularity of gimmal rings is shown by the fact that they are described in works by the poets Herrick and Dryden. William Shakespeare also mentions them in Act II of Twelfth Night.

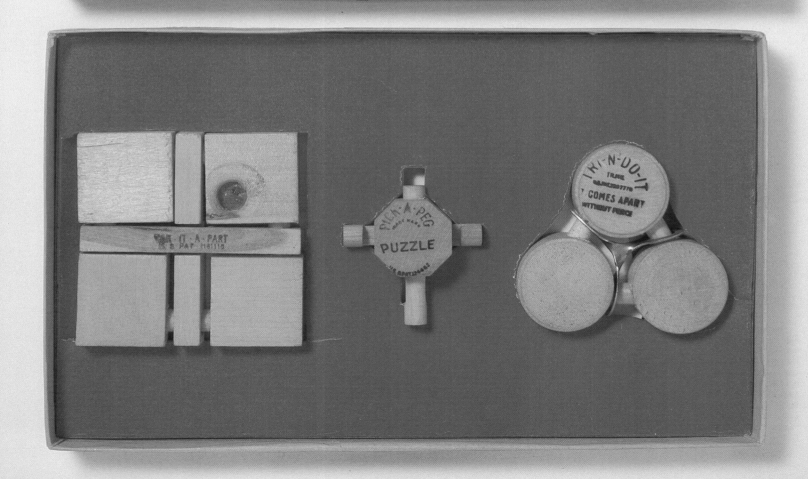

TAKE APART PUZZLES

Opposite page: These three puzzles were attractively boxed and sold under the name The Masterpiece Puzzles.

The TAKITAPART puzzle, patented by J.D.Boyle in 1939, is so difficult that some puzzlers have resorted to X-rays to help them solve it. Tri-N-Do-It was also patented by Boyle, in 1940. The object of Pick-A-Peg is to get the pegs out and get them back in.

Puzzle locks were used in several countries in the early 17th century and puzzle purses were popular in the United States and Europe in the 18th century, but the 'Golden Age' of secret opening puzzles was the period from 1879 to 1895. Famous stores such as Marshall Field of Chicago, Peck and Snyder of New York and Hamleys of London sold a variety of very clever secret opening puzzles. These were beautifully made of polished boxwood, ebony, brass or nickel plated steel. The name of Professor Hoffmann (actually the pseudonym of the Englishman, Angelo Lewis) has long been renowned among puzzlers. In his Puzzles Old and New, which was published in 1893, he describes more than 40 secret opening puzzles and there were probably at least twice that many available at that time.

Some of these puzzles were used to carry matches, rings, snuff and even drugs such as cocaine, but the object of most of them was to amuse and puzzle. Often the puzzle was to remove an object such as a marble or a ring from a barrel, a tower or a cannon. More complex are the Japanese puzzle boxes which have been exported to the West since before 1920. These require several sliding panels to be moved in a specific order before the box can be opened. During the last few years, Japan has again become known for the quality of its puzzle boxes and a number of new and extremely clever secret boxes have been designed by Akio Kamei. Produced from the finest and rarest woods, the craftsmanship of these secret puzzle boxes is matched only by the ingenuity of their design.

Above: Professor Hoffmann was not only a writer on puzzles and a skilled magician and conjuror, but also a lawyer. He used a pseudonym because he feared for his professional prospects if it were known that he possessed so great a familiarity with the arts of deception. Or so he claimed!

Right: A few of Hoffmann's Puzzles from the Hordern Collection. From left to right they are the New Castle Moneybox, the Barrel and Ball, the Lighthouse, the Zulu Box and, in the foreground, the New Persian Puzzle.

The Dice Box, which dates from between 1880 and 1890. It is 2'' (48 mm.) in length.

L.E.Hordern has one of the world's finest puzzle collections. The Hoffmann puzzles shown on these pages are all from this collection. Edward Hordern has also produced a beautiful compendium of Hoffmann Puzzles, unfortunately in limited edition and not generally on sale.

The Barrel and Ball also dates from between 1880 and 1890. It is a little smaller than the Dice Box, being 1¾'' (45 mm.) in length.

Hoffmann's Puzzles

In 1893, a book was published called Puzzles Old and New. It was written by Professor Louis Hoffmann (1839-1919), who was an British lawyer and whose real name was Angelo John Lewis. This book is so well illustrated and contains such a wealth of detail that it has become almost 'the Bible' for collectors of old mechanical puzzles. In fact, puzzles which appear in his book are often referred to as 'Hoffmann Puzzles'. All the puzzles shown on these pages first appeared in Chapter II of the book, a chapter which Hoffmann called 'Mechanical Puzzles dependent on some trick or secret'. The problem is to extract a marble or other small object from some outer receptacle which has no visible opening large enough to allow it to pass, or which cannot be opened unless you know the secret... or can figure it out!

The Dice Box This puzzle is in the form of a miniature barrel; the bung and spigot are removable ebony plugs. The barrel contains three dice which must be removed.

The Barrel and Ball This boxwood barrel contains an ordinary marble, which is considerably larger than the hole in the top of the barrel. An ebony pestle rests in the hole. The problem is: How do we get the marble out of the barrel?

The Cannon and Ball The cannon also contains a small marble which must be extricated. The breach can be removed but the cavity revealed has no connection with the part which contains the marble. No, the answer isn't to fire off the cannon!

The solution to the Dice Box puzzle is much simpler. The bottom is simply a slightly tapered plug which is held in place only by friction. It can be released by tapping the barrel smartly on a flat surface. The bung and spigot have nothing whatever to do with the solution and are there to lead you astray!

The secret of the Barrel and Ball puzzle is that the bottom is a plug screwed into the body. This is not at all obvious because of the way in which it is sunk below the edge of the barrel. To unscrew the end, the barrel is held with the thumb on the bottom and the forefinger on the pestle. When pressure is exerted, the pestle, ball and plug are pressed together and the bottom may then be unscrewed clockwise, releasing the ball after a few turns.

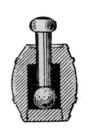

The Cannon and Ball is an ingenious puzzle. The removable breech is in two parts, one screwing into the other. When the pieces are taken apart, a small square stud is revealed. Now if the puzzle is examined closely, it can be seen that the opening is surrounded by an incised circle, apparently decoration. Not so! It is, in fact, a circular plug screwed into the muzzle. The stud serves as a key to unscrew this plug and release the ball.

The Cannon and Ball is beautifully made in boxwood. It dates from the same period as the other puzzles shown here and is approx. 5'' (125 mm.) in length.

The Ebony Puzzle Balls These are sometimes known as 'Indian' Puzzle Balls. They are made of unpolished ebony, beautifully ornamented with rose cutting and often with delicate patterns of inlaid veneers. The ball

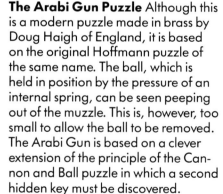

The ebony balls were small, the largest only measuring just over 2'' (55 mm.). The solution is clever. A tiny depression, no bigger than the head of a pin, indicates the position of a tapered plug. This can be forced out by sharply rapping on the table. The mechanism was so perfect and the opening so cleverly masked by the rose cutting, that the secret was quite difficult to discover.

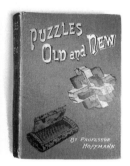

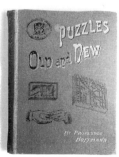

Above: These are two of the covers of Professor Hoffmann's books.

Far right: The principles of the Hoffmann secret opening puzzles have been used by many designers to make similar puzzles. These are made of brass by Doug Haigh in England and are much smaller than the original wood models. Hoffmann's Arabi Gun measured 5t'' (139mm.) and his Cage and Ball (see bottom far right) measured 4'' (110mm.).

appears to be absolutely solid, even the keenest eye failing to detect any sign of an opening. Yet they can be opened by someone who knows the secret. Inside there is a receptacle large enough to hold several coins.

The Arabi Gun Puzzle Although this is a modern puzzle made in brass by Doug Haigh of England, it is based on the original Hoffmann puzzle of the same name. The ball, which is held in position by the pressure of an internal spring, can be seen peeping out of the muzzle. This is, however, too small to allow the ball to be removed. The Arabi Gun is based on a clever extension of the principle of the Cannon and Ball puzzle in which a second hidden key must be discovered.

The Cage and Ball Puzzle The puzzle shown is also made in brass by Doug Haigh. This is a little different from the other Hoffmann puzzles described here. The ball is confined in a cage consisting of five 'bars' which join the cylindrical top and base. The problem is to extract the ball.

Professor Hoffmann described more than 40 puzzles of this type in his book Puzzles Old and New. He was, however, a collector and writer, not an inventor of puzzles. It is rather sad that the actual inventors of these ingenious puzzles are condemned to remain anonymous.

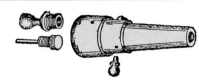

First the knob at the breech is unscrewed. This is in two parts, e and d, which must also be unscrewed. The trunnion, f, is then removed.

The pin, e, is inserted and locks the inner core. The barrel can now be unscrewed and the ball released.

Right: One of the four 'bars' of Hoffmann's 'Cage and Ball' is movable. When it is turned on its axis, it will sink about a sixteenth of an inch out of the socket at the oppsoite end and the bar may then be completely removed.

51

The Author's Puzzle

These methods of locking two pieces of wood were devised by Jerry Slocum, co-author of this book. In the first mechanism there are two steel pins in a horizontal hole. When the puzzle is spun rapidly, centrifugal force pushes these pins to the sides, the middle piece then falls and the top piece can be removed. In the second mechanism there is a hidden magnet in the lid which holds a locking pin in a locked condition. When the puzzle is tapped firmly on the table the pin will be released momentarily. If the lid is pushed at the same moment as the puzzle is tapped, it will slide open.

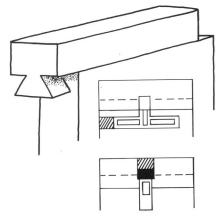

The two ingenious locking mechanisms devised by Jerry Slocum. Based on very simple principles, they still prove very difficult to solve unless you happen to know the trick.

This take apart puzzle was made for Jerry Slocum by Vernon Wood. The mechanism used to lock the two pieces together was developed by Jerry in 1955.

The TAKITAPART Puzzle

This is a wooden puzzle patented in the United States. It consists of four square blocks, two interlocking bars and four pins or dowels. The object is to take the puzzle apart. You get a penny back when you do. TAKITAPART was very popular for many years and a version of it is still made by Pentangle of England.

The TRI-'N'-DO-IT Puzzle

This puzzle consists of three disks held together with three dowels. The problem is to dismantle the puzzle and then put it back together.

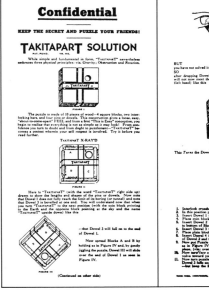

These puzzles were invented by J.D. Boyle and patented at the start of World War II.

The published solutions to the two puzzles TAKITAPART and Tri-N-Do-It. The first is very difficult and to find the solution it is necessary to use the three principles of gravity, rotation and obstruction. Truly a 'mind-bending' task. The solution to Tri-N-Do-It is rather easier to find and involves working the dowel pegs with the thumbs until they lie in a certain way at which point the puzzle comes apart and the metal ring assembly is released.

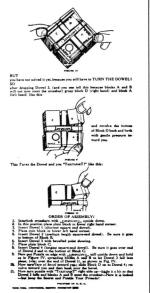

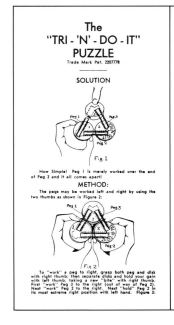

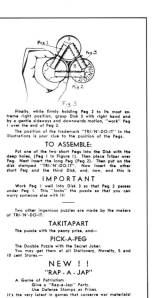

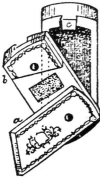

The secret opening book was probably made in Britain and dates from about 1900. It uses the same principle as the Psycho Match-box. The problem is to open the box.

Hidden Keyhole Boxes

There is a two-fold mystery connected with these puzzles. First there is a secret compartment in which the key is kept. This compartment must be found, and the proper slide moved to open it. A key is not much use without a keyhole to put it in and its dicovery is the the second part of the mystery. When the correct sections of the box are moved, one 'book' slides revealing the keyhole and allowing the box to be unlocked. Jewelry was often kept in secret boxes, presumably on the assumption that a would-be thief would be discouraged by the difficulty in opening them.

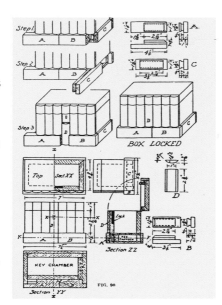

Hoffman's Psycho Match-box Puzzle. This example, made of wood, usually measures 3'' x 1¼'' x ¾''. The apparent lid is a dummy and the true lid seems to be an integral part of the box.

Maybe you had a 'secret' pencil box at school? If you had, it was probably based on the same principle as the Psycho Match-box. The false lid can easily be moved. But then what? The answer is to turn the box upside down. This releases an internal 'pin' which in turn allows the true lid, b, to be pushed forward. In its new position it just clears the stop, c, which previously held it fast. Then the box can be turned right side up and now opens easily.

'How to Make a Secret Opening Box', taken from Puzzles in Wood, by E.M.Wyatt, which was first published in 1928. As Wyatt remarks ''None but an A-1 workman should undertake to make this piece''. Maybe you are brave enough to take on the challenge?

Souvenirs of Sorrento and Napels in Italy, possibly dating from the 1920's and 1930's. Beautifully made in the form of books, these secret opening boxes were popular souvenirs. A typical solution would be to slide a piece in the base in order to release a second part and so allow the key to be removed. The base slides backward and one 'book' drops down to reveal the keyhole.

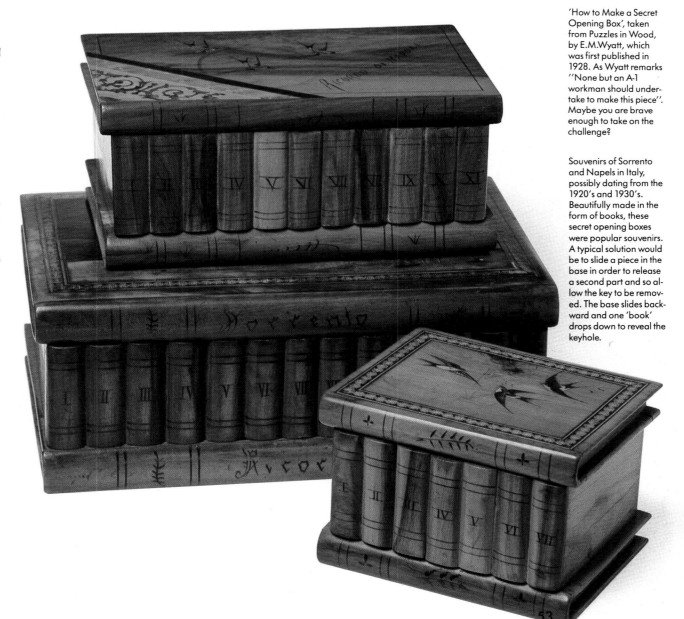

Japanese 'Trick' Boxes

Japan has exported secret opening boxes to the West since before 1920. They are often complex, requiring many 'moves' to open them. One or more sliding parts in one end are moved, allowing the end to be moved slightly. This partially unlocks a side panel, which allows other pieces to be moved. These, in turn, partially unlock the top or bottom. This method is continued, moving around the box, until the top panel can slide, opening the box.

The boxes were often beautifully lacquered or veneered. The elaborate wood mosaic is called 'yoseki', a craft practised for centuries in Japan. It uses the natural grain and texture of a wide variety of woods. Woods of many colors are selected - spindlewood for white, Katsura for black, sumac or mulberry for yellow, camphor for brown, American walnut for purple, Japanese cucumber for blue, Chinese cedar for red, etc.

Oblong rods of the desired cross sections are selected and glued together to form the geometrical pattern required. Subsequently, the sectional surface is sliced into very thin sheets of veneer which can be glued onto the surface of the box. the box is then glazed and polished.

By choosing wood of different cross sections - squares, regular and irregular hexagons, etc. - and of different colors; it is possible to design patterns of great beauty and complexity. These serve not only to decorate the boxes; they also play an important role in concealing the sliding pieces which must be moved in order to open them.

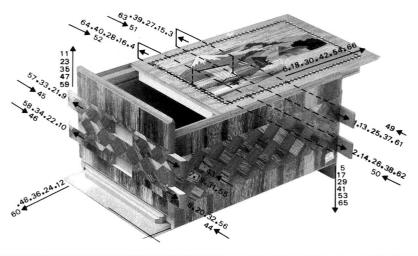

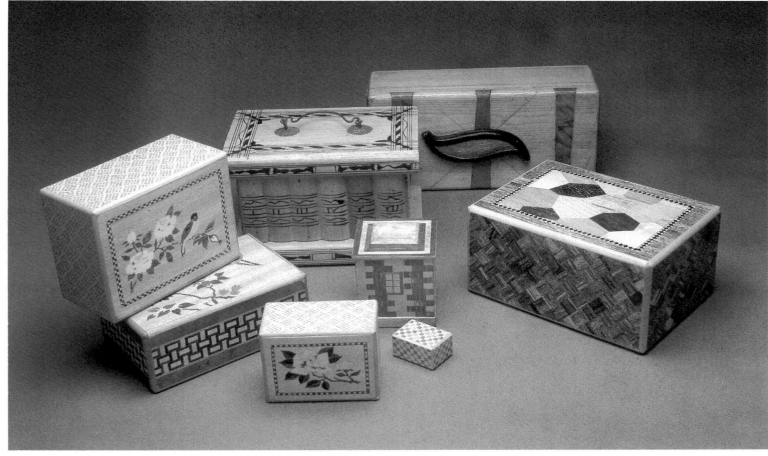

These three Japanese puzzle boxes are made in the form of houses. They were first sold in the United States in 1937.

How to make a secret box

This is a formidably difficult task for most of us but it can be done. To describe how to make one of the boxes on this page would probably take the rest of the book - and we decided that the space could be better used to show you a lot of other interesting puzzles! However, if you study the diagram on page 53 carefully, you will see the general principle of the simpler hidden key box and may be able to build one.

This Japanese secret opening box is a fine example of its type. It was made around 1960 and requires no less than 66 moves to open it.

Interlocking Name Puzzle

This puzzle consists of a box, containing a number of letter shapes, which are cut in such a way that they can are locked into the box by several pins and keys. The unlocking of the puzzle requires a series of moves of the pins, keys and letters. Finally, the central key can be withdrawn and the last of the letters released.

The rear puzzle box was made in England, the one in front of it in Italy. The others are from Japan. The tiny box in front center requires 10 moves to open it. Some of these types of puzzle boxes were on sale in the United States by 1919.

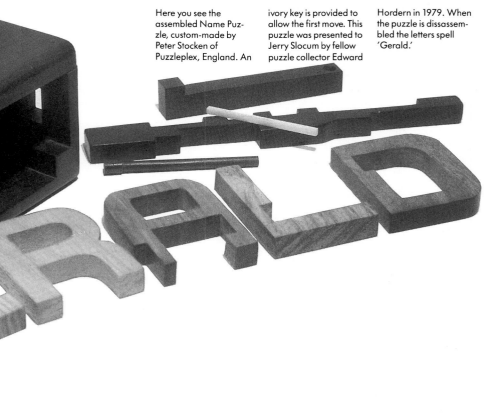

Here you see the assembled Name Puzzle, custom-made by Peter Stocken of Puzzleplex, England. An ivory key is provided to allow the first move. This puzzle was presented to Jerry Slocum by fellow puzzle collector Edward Hordern in 1979. When the puzzle is disassembled the letters spell 'Gerald.'

The Kamei Secret Boxes

Akio Kamei, the Japanese craftsman who designed the beautiful puzzle boxes shown on these pages. Mr. Kamei also invented clever new methods of locking and opening the boxes.

The beautiful Hakone district of Japan is famous for its centuries-old tradition of craftsmanship in woodworking. This tradition has been enhanced in recent years by Akio Kamei, who has invented a whole series of new secret opening puzzles which incorporate highly ingenious new methods of locking and opening. Each puzzle is handmade and the hardwoods from which they are built are carefully selected so that the cutting is hidden in the grain. Many of the puzzlers who have managed to open the boxes still cannot figure out some of the techniques behind Kamei's work, because the locking devices are so ingenious that they are still hidden even when the boxes have been opened. Looking clockwise from the left you see:

The Barrel ''Roll out the barrel'' is a famous old London pub song, and it gives you a clue as to how this puzzle is opened. The barrel is rolled on its side in a clockwise direction and the inside section pushed to one end. It is

Above: The Barrel Box, which is opened by rolling it first one way, then the other. If this were a beer barrel, you would be very thirsty by the time you discovered its secret!

The Tortuous Box has indeed a tortuous solution. Perseverence is called for before the box reveals its secret compartment.

''You can't make an omelette without breaking eggs'', said Napoleon. Break this egg and see what its secret is.

The Love Box conceals its secret by hiding the joint in the grain of the wood. This lovely box measures 15cm x 15cm x 4.5cm. (6'' x 6'' x 1¾''), and could be used as a jewelry box.

The genius of Kamei lies in the logic of the locking devices of his puzzles. How else do you open an egg but by cracking it? And what else is the bow for but to open the gift box?

then rolled in a counter-clockwise direction and the inside pushed out far enough to release an end lid. Once released, this lid slides off and a secret comparment is revealed.

Once you realize that the pips do not add up, you are half way to solving the puzzle of the Die box.

The Egg This puzzle is opened just like any other egg! It must be struck on the side and pulled apart. Inside is a wooden baby chick.

The Tortuous Box Rated 'moderately difficult', this box is opened by rotating the panels on the sides in the correct sequence until finally one of them can be removed.

The Die The clue here is that the pipes on opposite sides do not add up to seven as they do on an ordinary die. The die is placed with one pip on the upper face, then turned so that 2, 3, 4, 5, and 6 pips appear on the upper face consecutively. One side then slides open far enough to allow a second side to open.

The Top Box First, the box is turned upside down and spun. The bottom panel can then be moved and one side slid downward. This allows the top to slide off, revealing a hidden compartment.

The Gift Box This box is opened by moving the bow sideways which allows one bottom section to move. The bow is then moved in the opposite direction so freeing the second bottom section. It is then centered releasing one section and revealing one compartment. The bow is again moved to its second position. This releases the other section and reveals a second compartment.

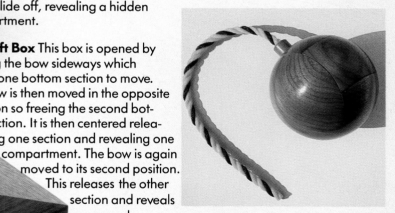

The Maze Box looks exactly like the Top Box. It has an entirely different but equally clever locking device. The Top

Box has a steel ball hidden in a maze in one side panel. When the ball is moved by centrifugal force, the bottom panel slides out a little, freeing the other side panel which in turn slides out and frees the top.

Above right: The Pentagon Puzzle has an ingenious solution. The cover is removed and reveals what seems to be a sliding lid. But however hard you try, the lid refuses to slide out. The secret is to place the cover upside down, place the box in it. Hidden magnets then push locking pins aside, releasing the lid which now slides up just enough to slide the top piece sideways through a slot, revealing the compartment.

Center right: When the fuse is pushed in, the bomb 'explodes' with a loud click. A hidden drawer then jumps out.

The Love Box (far left and above) The two halves of the top of the heart must be separated. This reveals a secret drawer which can be partially opened. The 'broken' heart is then 'mended' by pushing the two halves together. The drawer can now be pulled out completely.

57

Other secret opening objects

So far we have introduced you to Hoffmann's elegant puzzles, complex wooden puzzles like TAKITAPART and Tri-N-Do-It, and beautiful Japanese puzzle boxes. But virtually anything can be designed in such a way that it is impossible to open until the secret is discovered. On these pages you can see objects as diverse as a penknife, nuts and bolts, and a pair of pants, all of them locked until you find the secret key which allows them to be opened.

Puzzle Pocket Knife Most pocket knives have a notch so that they can be opened with the thumbnail. Not so this knife! The question is: How do you open it? Another Hoffmann puzzle to tantalize the uninitiated!

Nuts and bolts puzzles We can all probably agree that removing a nut from a bolt can be difficult - you never seem to have the right-sized wrench or the darned thing is rusted solid. But

Three nuts and bolts problems. In the first the nut in the middle of the shank must be removed. In the second the nut and washer must be removed. The third puzzle is most ingenious. The nut can not be removed, but the washer can!

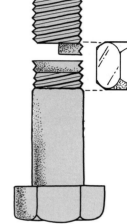

This cross-section shows how to make a nut and bolt puzzle. It is quite easy to make and baffling to those who do not know the secret.

the three puzzles shown here are difficult for other reasons. When you try to unscrew the nut in the conventional way you find that it is impossible. To remove the nut in the top puzzle, the head of the bolt must be held and the thread end turned counter-clockwise. The bolt separates revealing an internal threaded bolt which holds the two pieces together. The middle puzzle, patented by E.Stancliffe in 1894, is somewhat different. The bolt is in two pieces which bind if you try to unscrew the nut. The trick here is to hold the bolt by the threaded section at the end. The third nut and bolt puzzle, patented by W.E.Watkins in 1914, is solved by holding the bolt vertically and spinning the nut. Ball bearings roll into holes inside the nut and allow it to be unscrewed far enough to reveal a groove in the bolt. The washer can then be removed.

The Hello Puzzle. The original Hello puzzle consisted of an octagonal piece of leather with seven holes and two half way holes punched in it. The one we show is of tough plastic. A wire spiral runs through the holes. The ends of this wire overhang each other by about three-eighths of an inch, so the wire can be twisted round from one hole to another. It cannot, however, be freed because the overlapping ends will not allow it. Nevertheless, the spiral can be freed. But how?

How to make a nut and bolt puzzle

You need a hacksaw, file and vise to clamp the bolt. Buy a large brass nut and bolt. Clamp the bolt in the vise and cut it through the threaded section as shown. Now cut sections from the two pieces as indicated in the diagram. The section removed from the top part is half the diameter of the bolt and two threads deep. The section removed from the other piece is somewhat less than ¾ of the cross section and also two threads deep. Now file the cut sections smooth. Put the two parts together and screw on the nut so that it covers the cut. Amazingly, if you now try to unscrew the nut, you find that it cannot be done! The cut parts of the bolt bind together and act as a brake. To open it you must hold the nut while you unscrew the end of the bolt. Use brass nuts and bolts and make a few of these simple but fascinating puzzles as gifts for your friends.

The pocket knife is kept closed by a catch on a spring. One side of the knife is fixed to the free end of the spring. The catch is withdrawn by sliding the thumb along the side. The knife then opens easily. When open the blade is held fast by a second notch on the catch. The knife is closed by repeating the opening operation.

This puzzle is opened by twisting the spiral until one end is in the central hole and the other is in the top hole. In this position the spiral can be twisted sideways. The spiral is elastic enough to allow the polished ends to slip past the edges of the holes and slide out.

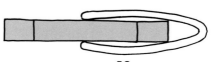

The Scotch Purse & Trousers Puzzles

The much maligned Scots have always had an undeserved reputation for being shy when it comes to paying for the drinks. Hence the Scotch purse which contains coins but is seemingly impossible to open. The secret lies in one of the inside seams which is sewn in such a way that it can be pulled apart. The Trousers Puzzle works in exactly the same way. One of the inside seams allows the cloth to be pulled apart so that the balls inside can be removed. These puzzles are still sold today.

Puzzle purses

Puzzle purses were described by Ozanam as long ago as 1735, and one was included in Bestelmeier's toy catalog in Germany in 1803. Folding Pennsylvania Dutch puzzle purses were used in the United States at the end of the 18th century. These were made of heavy paper and the folds were designed to conceal love poems and colored designs, often of the thistlefink bird. They were usually presented as Valentines and today they are collector's items.

The Card and Key Puzzle

This was patented by J.L.Kellogg in 1902. Like so many puzzles around the turn of the century it was intended for advertising purposes. The puzzle is to separate the pieces "without the slightest injury". It is solved by folding the card and inserting the thin section through the key. This allows the red piece to be removed, thereby releasing the key.

The Three Ring Puzzle

The puzzle here is how to remove the rings without bending the bar. It was used to advertise Tom Keene's 5-cent-cigars and patented in 1892. Can you figure out the secret?

The secret of the Scotch Puzzle Purse is revealed in the diagrams below. The trousers are opened on the same principle.

Fig.1 LOCATE IRREGULAR SEAM BY PULLING SIDES AS ABOVE

Fig.2 GRASP TOP CLOTHS ON BOTH SIDES AS SHOWN ABOVE

Fig.3 GRIP FIRMLY AND GENTLY PULL SEAM APART

Above: An original pair of Puzzle Pants and the paper wrapping in which they were sold.

Below these three take-apart puzzles are based on three very different opening principles.

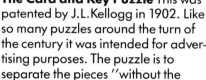

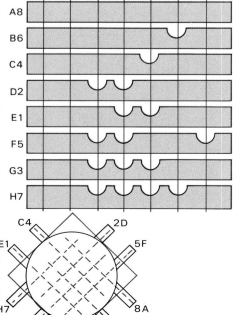

The Sputnik Puzzle, copyrighted in Japan in 1958, is guaranteed to send the puzzler into orbit. Of course, the problem is how to take it apart. The Sputnik is based on the general principles which we will discuss in detail in the following section. Eight dowel rods, seven of them having one or more grooves, are interlocked into the body of the Sputnik in such a way that they seem impossible to remove. The secret lies in the order in which they are taken out. The rods are not difficult to make if you trace the diagram. Drilling out the wooden disc is more of a problem, but it can be done with a little ingenuity. Finish the puzzle by painting it black and drawing the Sputnik's fiery trail.

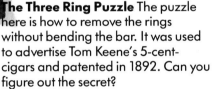

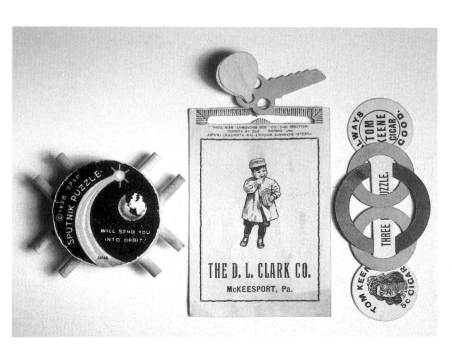

Puzzle Locks

Locks of various types are very much a part of our everyday lives and we might be forgiven for thinking that they are a comparatively recent invention. Nothing could be further from the truth, for locks have been around for about four thousand years. The Ancient Egyptians guarded their temple treasures with large wooden pin locks. These worked on the principle of gravity. When a bolt was pushed into the body of the lock,

Dick Hess is both a designer and a collector of mechanical puzzles. The locks shown on these pages form part of his collection.

60

a number of pins dropped under their own weight into corresponding holes in the bolt. The craftsmen of northern India have been making complex puzzle locks in iron and brass for many centuries. These were often in the form of a fish or a scorpion. The keyhole was hidden in the body of the lock. Sometimes there was no keyhole at all, and the lock was opened by pressing various parts of the decoration to release the locking pin. Puzzle locks were also produced in Iran as long ago as the 17th century. Often the lock was concealed in a shell which had to be twisted in a certain way to remove it so revealing the keyhole.

In Britain, brass letter locks were being produced by the beginning of the 17th century. These had four cylinders containing letters. The lock was opened by arranging the letters to spell a word such as 'AMEN'. In the late 19th century, small brass locks with no key whatsoever were being made in England. They had a hidden lever which had to be moved in order to open the lock. Some of the 20th century Indian locks shown on these pages are opened by pushing one or more rivets which appear to be only for the purpose of holding the body of the lock together.

How to make a Puzzle Lock

The puzzle lock shown in the diagram below is based on the principle of gravity and its 'key' is concealed inside the body. It is quite easy to make in wood. First you need two pieces of thin plywood and a thicker piece for the center section. Clamp the three pieces together and shape them using a saw and a wood rasp. Draw the labyrinth on the thicker piece and cut it out with a fretsaw. Also cut away the corner so that the locking arm can be fitted. Glue on the back panel. The locking arm is shaped from a piece of plywood a little thinner than the piece used for the center section. Drill holes in each end. One is for the pivot and runs from the front to the back. The other is for the locking pin and runs from the inside to the outside. Now cut five lengths of dowel and lay them in the labyrinth as shown in the diagram. Make sure that they move freely. Add the ballbearing. The next step is to glue on the front panel. Drill a hole through both front and back panels so that the dowel which forms the pivot for the locking arm can be glued in. Sandpaper the whole lock smooth and varnish it.

By this time you will have seen how to unlock your puzzle, but your friends will have no idea when you challenge them to open it! When you turn the lock upside down, the ball falls. Turning the lock on its side releases the first dowel. Subsequent moves release the other four dowels in turn so unlocking the puzzle. It is locked by reversing the procedure.

These are a few of the puzzle locks in the Dick Hess collection. The small brass locks are late 19th century English. The large iron locks are 20th century Indian in origin.

INTERLOCKING SOLID PUZZLES

A burr puzzle designed by Bill Cutler. It is 30 cm. high and built from 30 square rods. If you look carefully you will see that the ends of the rods on each face are in the form of a pentagon and that there are twelve sides to the model. Such a figure is known mathematically as a dodecahedron.

The sculpture of the Spanish sculptor Miguel Berrocal can be taken apart like an interlocking puzzle. This piece is his David.

This spherical puzzle uses eight notched 'corner' pieces. It shows the transition from the original 6-piece burr to solid interlocking shapes such as the barrel shown with it.

At some time or other most of us have been baffled by one of those puzzles made of pieces so cleverly interlocked that they seem almost impossible to separate. And once they have been taken apart they are often even more difficult to put back together again. There is usually a single piece, called the key, which must be removed first in order to disassemble the puzzle. In many such puzzles the pieces must be replaced in a certain sequence and the key is always inserted last to lock the other pieces in place. Almost nothing is known about the early history of these puzzles but they were certainly being produced in both Asian and European countries as early as the 18th century. The 1803 catalog of Bestelmeier, the German toy manufacturer, included illustrations of two interlocking puzzles, the 6-piece 'Small Devil's Hoof' and the 24-piece 'Large Devil's Hoof'. It was not until 1857, however, that details of the pieces were illustrated in The Magician's Own Book. Our old friend, Professor Hoffmann, included two interlocking puzzles in his Puzzles Old and New, published in 1893.

Puzzles of this type used to be known as 'Chinese' puzzles, but nowadays they are commonly known as burr puzzles, presumably because of their resemblance to a seed burr. During the 19th century, the 6-piece burr evolved into solid, interlocking puzzles such as cubes, balls and barrels. How this transition came about is not known for sure, but a puzzle discovered several years ago in the Netherlands may provide a clue. This spherical puzzle used eight notched 'corner' pieces. By 1870, these pieces were glued to other pieces to make solid interlocking puzzles like the barrel shown below. Puzzles of this type were mainly produced in Germany, but by the late 1930's the market had been largely captured by Japanese manufacturers. They not only produced traditional burrs but designed many new interlocking puzzles in the form of animals, vehicles, and weapons. In recent years, designers such as Stewart Coffin and Bill Cutler have created dozens of new and very complex burr puzzles based on abstract forms. Some of Coffin's beautiful designs can be seen on pages 84 and 85.

Interlocking Figure Puzzles

This 7-piece puzzle dog was designed by Jack Botermans and Kurt Naef. It became the mascot of a puzzle exhibition organized by the Craft and Folk Art Museum of Los Angeles, an exhibition which in the coming years will be seen all over the United States and Europe. Produced in pear wood by Kurt Naef in Switzerland, this puzzle dog is sold in gift shops throughout the world.

The ancient Japanese skills and techniques of joining wood without nails to make buildings and other wooden structures were first applied to making interlocking puzzles in the Hakone district of central Japan during the Edo period. These puzzles are called kumiki and the first kumiki maker was reportedly Mr. Tsunetaro Yamanaka (1874-1954), who began producing interlocking models of traditional Japanese houses, pagodas, towers and gates in the 1890's. Later his interest turned to the design of ships, cars and airplanes. His sons carried on the tradition, producing new kumiki puzzles based on architectural and animal forms. Today there are six small companies producing kumiki puzzles in Hakone. They employ some 35 skilled craftsmen, and sales amount to almost $500,000 a year.

Most kumiki puzzles are made of cheek wood because it is easy to work with and does not warp. Cherry and zelkova are also used. The four techniques of kumiki are oshi, mawashi, kendon and sayubiki. Oshi means 'push', and kumiki based on this principle have a key piece which must be pushed out to disassemble the puzzle. In kumiki using the mawashi principle one piece must be rotated to release the other pieces. In kendon a piece is removed by an up-down or left-right move while in sayubiki there are two key pieces which must be removed simultaneously. Whichever principle is used, the key piece is always skilfully hidden.

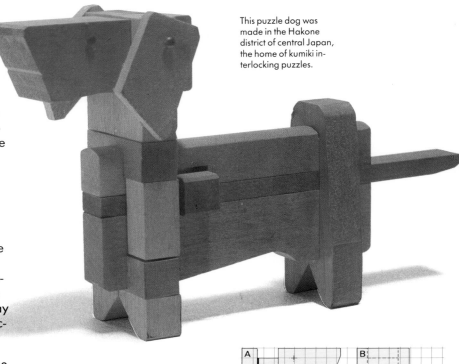

This puzzle dog was made in the Hakone district of central Japan, the home of kumiki interlocking puzzles.

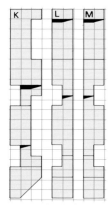

The grid for the front legs of your dog. Note that one is a mirror image of the other. K is the cross-section. The template made from it can be turned to give the cross-section of the second leg.

How to make a kumiki dog

This elegant Japanese dog can be made out of a hardwood such as oak or mahogany. The pieces are shown on the blue grids. These give you the relationship between the dimensions but the actual size of the unit square is optional. If you choose, for example, a unit square of ¼'', your finished dog will be 4¾'' tall. The first step is to draw the shapes on gridded paper and cut them out to make a series of templates. The body sections are all two units wide and the cross-sections of the head, the back legs, and the two pieces which lock the front legs are shown respectively as B, F and H in the diagram. The front legs are shown separately in the diagram on the left. You will notice that one is a

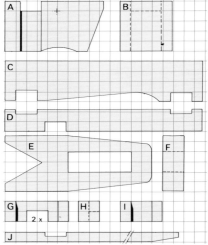

mirror-image of the other. K shows the cross-section. Special care is needed when making these pieces because each leg has two potentially weak points. The best thing is to choose a piece of wood with a fine, straight grain. The tail, J, can be as long as you like and the design of the ears is also left to you so that you can add a personal touch to your dog. When you have made the templates, transfer the drawings to the wood and cut each shape out with a fret-saw. Use a small square file and sandpaper to smooth each piece. Finish with varnish or teak oil. The exploded diagram on the left shows you how to assemble the pieces to produce the finished dog: a puzzle you will be proud of!

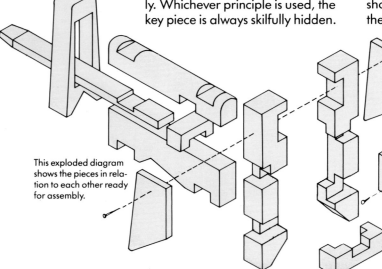

This exploded diagram shows the pieces in relation to each other ready for assembly.

Middle Right: These are the unit dimensions of each piece of the puzzle dog. You can make the basic unit as large or small as you wish. You must make two of piece G. Piece I is the key which locks the puzzle.

Every single model on this page is assembled from a number of pieces of wood which interlock with each other without glue or nails. Known as kumiki puzzles, they were first made in the Hakone district of Japan by Tsunetaro Yamanaka in the 1890's. He began by applying ancient building techniques to making models of traditional Japanese structures such as towers, gates and pagodas. His sons and grandsons carried on the family tradition, designing many objects including weapons of war (airplanes, tanks and ships), vehicles (cars, trains, even a Western covered wagon) and a range of animal figures and abstract forms. Today, there are several small companies producing kumiki puzzles in Hakone and the craft is also practiced in other parts of Japan.

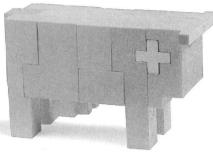

Wooden Burr Puzzles

According to Bill Cutler, designer of a number of beautiful and complex puzzles, a burr can be described as an interlocking geometrical puzzle which is composed of notched rods of wood and possesses a high degree of external symmetry. The 6-piece burr (illustrated below) is without doubt the best known and often forms the basis for many larger and more complex puzzles. Such a burr is made of three pairs of interlocking wooden pieces. Each pair is at right angles to the other two pairs and they are arranged so that there is usually no empty space at the center of the puzzle. The pieces which originally are blocks of equal length with a square cross section, have a number of cut outs made by removing cube-shaped volumes of wood, each with sides equal to half the width of the piece. Most people have come across one of these fascinating puzzles at some time or another, but few realise that there are so many different burrs. They may all look the same but often their internal structures are quite different. Mathematicians had realised for many years that there are hundreds of different pieces which can be used to make up thousands of different burrs. But the problem was not completely analyzed until 1975, when Bill Cutler programmed a large computer to do this. It was determined that there are no less than 369 different usable pieces from which a total of 119,979 burrs can be assembled, each of them having a distinct different internal structure. The results of his analysis were published in a classic article, The six-piece burr, in the Journal of Recreational Mathematics (1978).

How to make a 3-piece puzzle

This puzzle is easy to make and shows you the underlying principles of this type of puzzle. You need three lengths of wood, each 5'' in length and 1'' square in cross section. At the center of each piece seven-eighths of the wood is cut away for a length of one inch, leaving the remaining eighth in the form of a triangular prismatic section. This is rather difficult to visualize but the diagram below will help. The pieces lock with a diagonal and simultaneous movement; you cannot lock two pieces and then interlock the third.

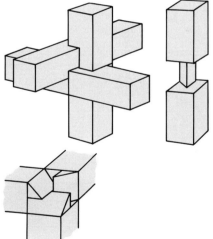

De Boer's Burrs

The Dutch mathematician J.H.de Boer made a detailed study of burr puzzles and produced his own set of pieces. In determining the patterns of the pieces, he first drew all the possible shapes on paper. He then cut out the pieces and also their mirror images. The next step was to group the pieces according to the quantity of wood that had been cut from them. He gave each piece a number, the first figure of which referred to the group to which the piece belonged. Thus, for example, all the pieces whose numbers started with 2 contained the same amount of wood, which was less than the wood in pieces having a number starting with 3. In this way, de Boer arranged his pieces into six groups. He then sorted the pieces within the groups according to the positions of the notches, each figure representing a different placement of one unit notch. The simplest of all the pieces with the least wood in it, has the code number 000, while more complex pieces were given numbers starting with 5 or 6. The pieces were arranged in boxes for easy reference. Having made the pieces to his designs, de Boer then set about determining the number of possible combinations that could make up a burr. (In most construction puzzles a key piece is needed to secure the interlocking pieces, and the key in de Boer's burrs is always a solid, uncut piece.) Each burr therefore is made of one solid piece and five of the notched pieces. During his spare time over ten years and with great perseverence, de Boer established that there were 2906 possible combinations, excluding mirror images.

The Red Cow Puzzle, made in Switzerland by Spiel Naef. It unlocks by pushing its eye - the white cross - through and lifting its horns.

Believe it or not, this tiny 3-piece burr, made by Allan Boardman, actually comes apart.

This 3-piece interlocking puzzle first appeared in Scientific American in the late 1890's. It has internal voids as you can see from the cutaway section which shows how the pieces interlock.

These elegant 6-piece burrs are produced by the family firm of Yamanaka Kumiki, in the Hakone district of central Japan.

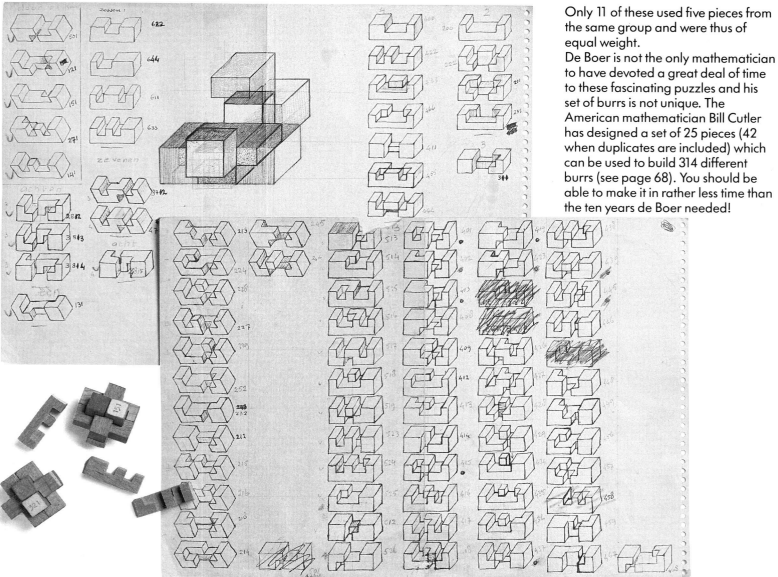

Only 11 of these used five pieces from the same group and were thus of equal weight.

De Boer is not the only mathematician to have devoted a great deal of time to these fascinating puzzles and his set of burrs is not unique. The American mathematician Bill Cutler has designed a set of 25 pieces (42 when duplicates are included) which can be used to build 314 different burrs (see page 68). You should be able to make it in rather less time than the ten years de Boer needed!

Two pages from the original notebook of J.H.de Boer. Groups of five carved pieces and a solid piece interlock, as in the diagram just above. De Boer arranged his pieces in groups according to how much wood had been removed and laid them out in boxes for easy reference.

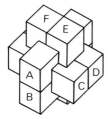

Bill Cutler's Set of Burr Pieces

Bill Cutler designed a set of only 42 pieces which can be used to build 314 different 6-piece cross burrs. There are only 25 different notchable* (see margin) pieces, but some are duplicated; two (J and Y) are triplicated. A high degree of craftsmanship is not required for the making of these pieces, but it does need care and patience. But then again, the one thing a puzzler has in abundance is patience!

How to make Bill Cutler's Puzzle

Piece A is the solid locking key and the grid shows you the method you must follow when marking and cutting the pieces. Each piece is 2 x 2 x 8 units (we suggest ½' x ½'' x 2'') and the cutting is done from the central 2 x 2 x 4 section. You will probably find it easier to work if you mark several pieces on one length of wood and saw it into unit lengths after the notches have been cut. Mark the pieces out following the diagram (the number after the code letter tells you how many of each is required). The first cuts should be made with a fine-toothed handsaw. The wood is then cut out using a small, sharp chisel. It is important that the pieces should be made to the exact measurements, otherwise they will not fit together properly to make the burrs. File and sand each piece smooth, then mark them according to the letter code for easy reference. You are now ready to begin finding the 314 solutions! A small clue: 158 of the solutions use the solid key (A) and 156 do not.

Each piece has a code letter A thru Y. The letters indicate the pieces which interlock to form a solution to the puzzle. In the example here, pieces A, B, C, D, E and F are used to form three so-called 'direction sets'. The 314 solutions are given at the back of the book.

Bill Cutler is an American mathematician and systems analyst and has had a lifelong interest in puzzles. He is particularly interested in burrs and box-filling puzzles. Although he has designed many himself, Bill doesn't consider himself a good puzzle solver and when faced with a tough one he prefers to write a computer program to solve it.

The grid shows how the pieces should be cut. All cutting is done from the middle 2x2x4 section of the piece. The easiest way to draw the cutting lines at first is to mark the complete grid and then shade the cubic sections which must be removed. Once you have made a few pieces, you'll get the hang of visualizing the cuts three-dimensionally.

*Note: Puzzle experts make a difference between notchable and non-notchable pieces. Notchable pieces are those which can be notched with a table saw, rather than those which have blind corners and inside edges which must be chiseled out. Further, only pieces which can be asembled into a puzzle with no internal empty space are considered. There are 25 pieces which fulfil both these conditions.

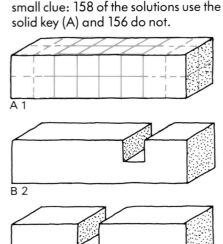

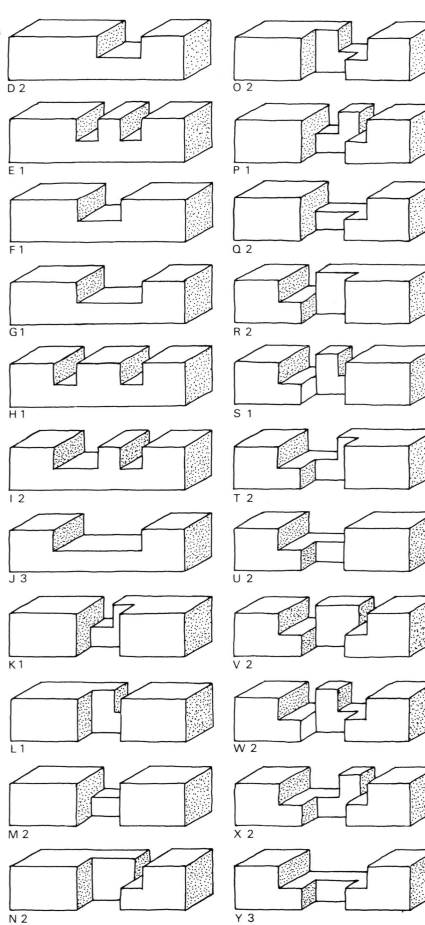

Bill Cutler also designed this unique hexagonal porcupine. It is a extension of a puzzle designed independently by Bill Cutler and Stewart Coffin. Coffin's version was patented and sold under the name HECTIX and 'Hexsticks'. It is formed by four sets of 12 parallel hexagonal rods. There are only three different types of notched rod used in the porcupine but the notching is complex. Bill uses the phrase 'non-trivial' to indicate the degree of difficulty of this puzzle and trivial it certainly is not. Fiendish is one word which springs to mind. Basically, the pieces of the type he calls 'C' pieces are manipulated until one will come all the way out, at which point the remaining 11 'C' pieces can be removed. The 'B' pieces are then freed and the 'A' pieces come apart easily. Simple, huh? Well no, not really. The well-known French mathematician, Fermat, once wrote that he ''had discovered a most wondrous proof which, however, the margin was too small to contain''. It was thus lost to us and since then mathematicians have labored in vain to rediscover the proof of what is now known as Fermat's Theorem. We know how Fermat must have felt. Bill sent the authors a 10-page explanation of how his 'wondrous' porcupine is designed and disassembled and we can't fit it into the margin either.

Flexible Burrs

Puzzles are as old as man himself. In Ancient Egypt the Sphinx puzzled the finest brains of the day and it is written that Alexander the Great, after making several attempts to untie the Gordian knot, finally drew his sword and slashed through it. Now we do not advocate such a drastic method of disassembling the flexible interlocking puzzles shown here, but we would have sympathy with anyone who did resort to heavyhanded methods after attempting to take apart these puzzles. Although they are made from a number of interlocking pieces, they do not actually come apart. The reason for this is that they were made from green unmatured wood or wet wood which shrinks as it ages and dries. Their origin is not entirely certain, but it is thought that they were probably made in Britain by prisoners of war captured in the Crimea. They date, if this theory is correct, from about 1854. Each joint contains a piece of lead shot which presumably was meant to rattle when the pieces were moved. (All of these flexible burr puzzles are from the collection of L. Edward Hordern.)

A chair and table made of interlocking pieces of green or wet wood. Once locked the pieces dry and shrink and the wretched thing doesn't come apart. Their origin is uncertain, but they were probably made in the 1850's by Russian prisoners of war from the Crimea.

This elegant walking stick is made on the same principle as the chair and table. (Both the chair and table and the walking stick are from the Hordern Collection.)

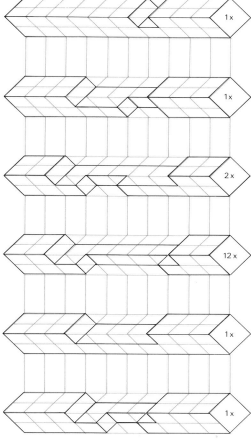

To cut the notches first saw through half the thickness of the piece, using a backsaw. This cuts the sides of the notches. Small pieces can be cut with a sharp hobby knife.

Turn the piece over and chisel out the excess wood. Tap the head of the chisel gently with a light hammer so that the wood is chipped out without splitting the piece. It is better to score the lines with a knife before chiselling. This helps to prevent splitting.

File the rough edges with a fine file. Make sure that the angles of each notch are 90° and that the width of each notch is exact. Adjust by careful filing along the sides of the notch if necessary.

18-piece Burr Puzzles

As mentioned earlier, burr-like puzzles with large numbers of interlocking pieces have been known for a long time. A 13-piece burr in the National Museum in Helsinki, Finland, dates from about 1910, and in that country very old 18-piece puzzles have also been found. Burrs consisting of several hundred pieces have been made.

Here you can see how to make an 18-piece burr. Several different designs have been produced, using different notches on the pieces. When you have made the pieces the problem is to put it together. The photo gives you a hint as to how to take it apart. Work backwards, you might think! Yes, but still a tricky puzzle to assemble.

How to make an 18-piece burr

The pieces for your 18-piece burr are made following the methods described on page 68 (the design is of 1951). Each piece measures 2 x 2 x 10 units. Mark out the cutting lines indicated on the blue grid in the diagram. Cut out the notches, file and sand smooth. This is a perfect puzzle to make to a

The pieces required to make the puzzle are shown in the top diagram. You will notice that not all the eighteen pieces are different. You can make them as small or as large as you like using the grid under the drawing. The photograph above gives you a clue to help find the solution.

large scale, say a unit size of 2″ which gives a 20″ high model. Oiled or varnished, or painted like the kumiki burrs on page 66, this puzzle should look lovely on your coffee table and is guaranteed to provide a never-ending topic of conversation for visiting friends.

The Altekruse Puzzle

This is an unusual puzzle and it has many variations. It was originally patented in 1890 by W. Altekruse, an American of German- Austrian origin. The actual origin of the puzzle is unknown, but the name 'Altekruse' means 'old cross' in German. This may, however, be just a coincidence.

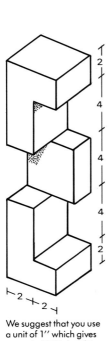

Apparently, when he drew up the patent, Altekruse was only aware of the simplest one-axis solution. But there are, in fact, three solutions, depending on whether the mechanical action of assembly (which is quite unlike any of the other common burrs) occurs along one, two or all three axes. If minor variations of the first two are counted, there are six distinctly different solutions. The original puzzle consisted of twelve pieces, but Stewart Coffin discovered 14, 36, and 38 piece variations. This family of puzzles is unusual in that all the pieces of each puzzle are identical. This makes these puzzles comparatively easy to make.

We suggest that you use a unit of 1'' which gives a puzzle 16'' in height. The pieces can be cut from solid pieces of wood which measure 4x4x16 units but you may find it easier to construct them by gluing five pieces, each of which measures 2x2x4 units.

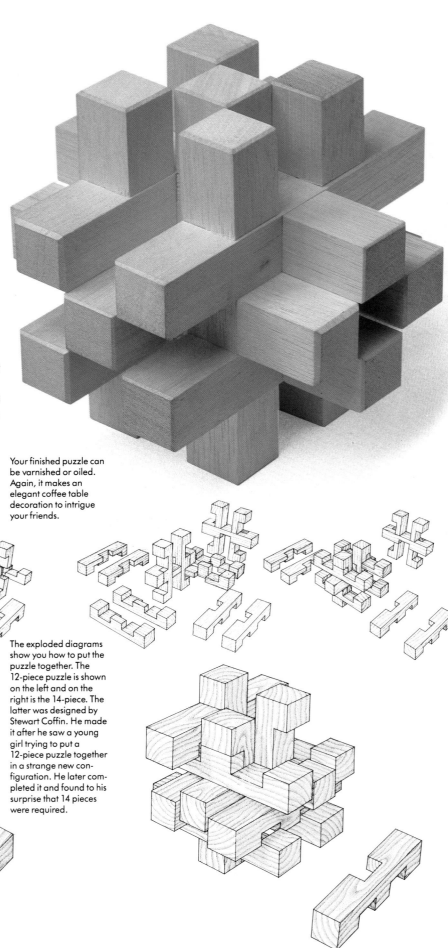

Your finished puzzle can be varnished or oiled. Again, it makes an elegant coffee table decoration to intrigue your friends.

The exploded diagrams show you how to put the puzzle together. The 12-piece puzzle is shown on the left and on the right is the 14-piece. The latter was designed by Stewart Coffin. He made it after he saw a young girl trying to put a 12-piece puzzle together in a strange new configuration. He later completed it and found to his surprise that 14 pieces were required.

The pieces for this puzzle should be made following the method shown previously for six-piece burrs. The unit dimensions are those on piece e. The dotted lines mark two unit blocks and the number of times each piece must be duplicated is shown above each piece.

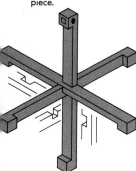

Interlock the three longest pieces. The remaining pieces should be laid out in the order given. They are added to the central cross, starting with the left-hand a. The order of placing and the positions of the pieces are given in the diagrams on the right and arrows indicate the direction the pieces should be moved. A cross in a circle indicates that the bar should be moved away from you. Each number refers to a different move - adding either one piece or several pieces in symmetrical positions.

The Great Pagoda

Also called Japanese crystal, the Great Pagoda is one of a family of similar burrs of which the simplest has only three pieces. Such burrs have been popular in Japan for many years and may well have originated there. As pieces are added, the puzzles have successively 9, 19, 33, 51, 73 and 99 pieces. The one shown here has 51 pieces. Each piece has been carefully cut so that the pieces can interlock to make a symmetrical, multifaceted structure with a solid core. Once assembled, no single piece can be pulled out of place to take the puzzle apart. As with many construction puzzles, the key lies in turning one particular piece, and this piece is difficult to discover for the surface cubes hide the internal differences of the pieces. In fact, the locking piece is the shortest one and lies directly below one of the six points of the octahedron. Once discovered, it is twisted until it can be lifted so releasing the two pieces below it. The other bars can now be lifted and removed until the puzzle is finally dismantled.

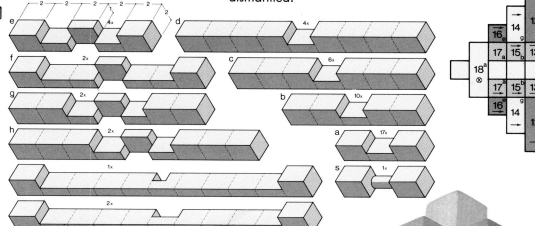

aeaafbbaaddfeshhccccggbbbbeeaaaaaaddccbbaabbaaaa

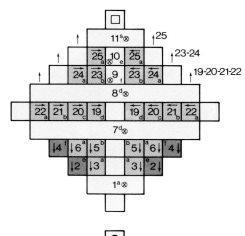

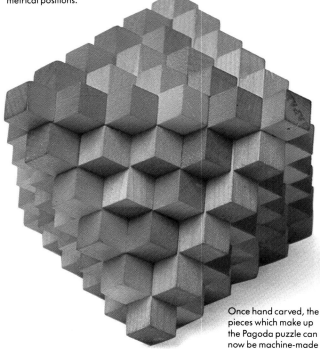

Once hand carved, the pieces which make up the Pagoda puzzle can now be machine-made

with great accuracy. They are often made of the lightest and most beautiful hardwoods. You can buy one, but it's much more fun to make your own.

Chuck Puzzles

The original chuck puzzle was based on an extension of the 6-piece burr and it was patented by Edward Nelson in 1897. The design was improved by R.F.Cook and subsequently developed by Paradox Engineering, England, who are the producers of the Pentangle Puzzles. The company produced a series of chucks in which a given number of simple bridge-like pieces and one or more key pieces could be built into a variety of self-sustaining three-dimensional shapes. This property is unique to chuck puzzles. The simplest puzzle in the series is the Baby-Chuck which consists of only six pieces, including one key. The Woodchuck has 24 pieces, the Papa-Chuck has 54, and the Grandpapa Chuck has 96. The pieces can be used in a variety of ways to build forms other than the octagonal shapes. Many intriguing constructions

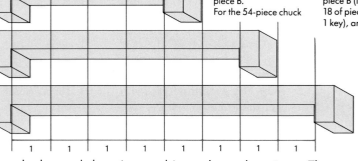

To make the chucks:
For the 6-piece chuck you need 6 of piece A (including 1 key).
The 24-piece chuck requires 18 of piece A (including 2 keys) and 6 of piece B.
For the 54-piece chuck are needed 30 of piece A (including 2 keys), 18 of piece B, (including 1 key) and 6 of piece C.
For the 96-piece chuck you need 42 of piece A (including 2 keys), 30 of piece B (including 1 key), 18 of piece C, (including 1 key), and 6 of piece D.

The exploded diagrams illlustrate the general principles which must be followed to put the chuck puzzle together.

can also be made by using combinations of pieces other than complete sets.

larger key pieces. These are exactly the same in form but based on the 5 and 7 unit lengths with respectively 3 and 5 units cut from the edge.

The first thing is to decide what sized chuck you want to make. The caption above tells you how many of each piece are required. These can be cut out with a bandsaw because cutting by hand with a fretsaw is a tedious and difficult business. A simpler method might be to glue blocks, 1 unit square by ½ unit thick to each end of 2, 4, 6 and 8 unit blocks, 1 unit by ½ unit in cross-section. Use quick drying glue and small clamps. Finish the pieces   with clear varnish.

How to make a Chuck Puzzle

The diagram shows the bridge-like structure of the pieces. Each piece is one unit square in cross section. Their lengths are respectively 3, 5, 7 and 9 units and the cut-outs are all half a unit in depth and 2, 4, 6 and 8 units in length respectively. The basic three unit key piece is shown on the right. You will notice that it is the same as the smallest bridge piece but with an extra one unit piece cut from the edge. The 54 and 96-piece chucks need

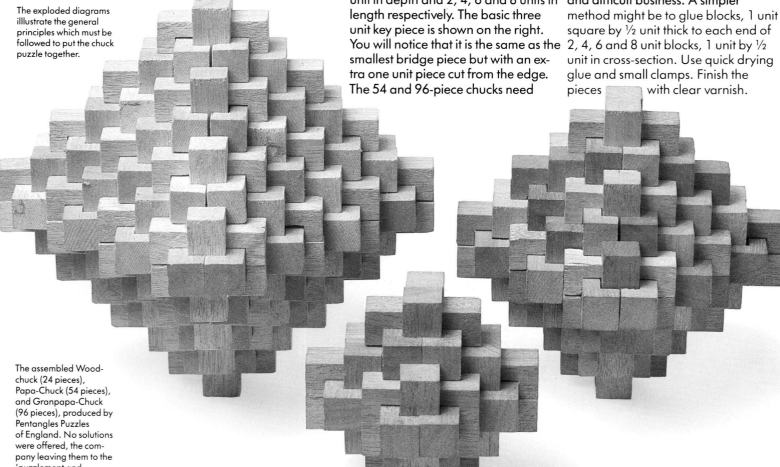

The assembled Woodchuck (24 pieces), Papa-Chuck (54 pieces), and Granpapa-Chuck (96 pieces), produced by Pentangles Puzzles of England. No solutions were offered, the company leaving them to the 'puzzlement and diligence' of the puzzler.

Arjeu Burrs

During the last few years, a range of more than fifty various wooden puzzles has been produced in France by the firm of Arjeu. These include versions of many of the puzzles described in this book, including the Pagoda and the Altekruse burrs. Clockwise from top to bottom you see:

Pluton 32/90: This stellation is built from 32 spheres and 90 rods (30 long and 60 short). Locked in the center is a larger sphere. The designer was Jean-Paul Pierlot.

Oursin: This wooden burr is formed with 20 spheres and wooden rods. Inner rods form five interlocking tetrahedrons. Oursin was also designed by Jean-Paul Pierlot.

Etoile Tetraedrique: Yet another Jean-Paul Pierlot puzzle. This one includes 20 spheres and 30 rods that form five interlocking tetrahedrons.

Triple Cross: This elegant 15-piece burr will prove to be a challenge.

Carpenter's Cross: Another burr, this one consisting of 12 pieces.

Cubix: The pieces of this difficult puzzle first assemble into three sections. The sections must then be locked together.

These are a few of a variety of puzzles produced by the French company of Arjeu in St.Priest, just south of Paris. Besides making many of the puzzles shown in this book, they also make packing puzzles and disentanglement string puzzles. Arjeu was started by Xavier Grandvaux in 1979. The name Arjeu comes from 'Art Games' in French.

Philippe Dubois, the Israeli designer of the puzzles shown on this page.

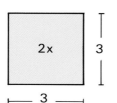

Your box should be made according to these dimensions. The letter a represents the thickness of the wood.

This diagram shows you the basic cutouts of ten of the pieces you need for your puzzle. The other two pieces are mirror images and have the center cut on the opposite side.

Gaby Games

The beautiful and ingenious puzzles shown on this page are the work of Philippe Dubois, born in Switzerland but now living in Jerusalem, Israel. He calls them Gaby Games because he started making puzzles and games for his daughter, Gabriel, before he became a professional designer and maker of puzzles.

How to make one of Gaby's puzzles. *(Designed by D. Feldman)*

This puzzle consists of twelve pieces, ten of which are the same and two of which are mirror images of the other ten. The twelve pieces are built into an interlocking form which encloses a cubic space in which a secret box can be enclosed. You need twelve pieces measuring 1 x 1 x 7 units. Ten must be marked and cut according to the net shown at bottom left. The other two differ in that the center section is cut from the opposite side. These are shown bottom right. The twelve pieces are cut with a fretsaw and chisel following the general method described on page 68. To assemble the puzzle you should take two of the ten identical pieces and lock them into a cross. Then six of the other identical pieces are interlocked in pairs to form three similar crosses. The four crosses should then be interlocked. The last cross must be positioned diagonally so that it slides in, twists and locks. You now have a free standing form with four 'legs'. To complete the puzzle, take the mirror image pieces and lock each with one of the remaining standard pieces to make two more crosses. These are now slid in diagonally and locked to complete the puzzle. The secret box should be made following the diagram in the margin. Its finished dimensions are 3 x 3 x 3 units. Inside you can conceal some small object such as a ring. Put the box inside the puzzle before locking it with the last cross. Now challenge your friends to open the puzzle and find the hidden object.

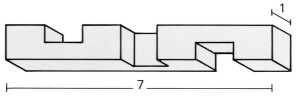

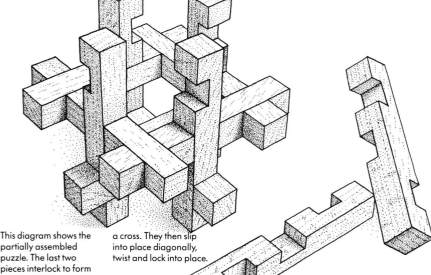

This diagram shows the partially assembled puzzle. The last two pieces interlock to form a cross. They then slip into place diagonally, twist and lock into place.

The dimensions for the draftsman's dream are: A = 3″, D = 2¼″, E = ¼″, B = ⅛″ and C = ½″. Actually, it wasn't our draftsman who had the dream. E.M.Wyatt first published this puzzle in Wonders in Wood in 1946.

The Draftsman's Dream

Our draftsman had a strange dream the other night. The result can be seen in the diagram on the left. It is a box made of six interlocking panels. Of course, it is impossible to build. Only a draftsman, or an artist like the Dutchman, Escher, could dream up such a construction. And then only on paper! It doesn't matter which panel you begin with, all six panels are alike and are held in place identically. But wait a moment. Maybe there is a way to make it. Or even more than one way! The first step is to make the six panels. The dimensions are given in the caption beside the grid. Mark out the pieces on ¼″ (8 mm.) plywood and cut them out with a fretsaw. Mark the grooves as shown and cut them out with a handsaw and chisel. These grooves should be half the thickness of the plywood. It is very important to cut them to exactly the right size, otherwise it really will be impossible to

assemble your puzzle. Now comes the tricky part! How on earth do you get the thing together? Actually, it's so easy, we're almost ashamed to spoil your fun by telling you. Suppose the six pieces were laid inner face down in water until they warped and expanded a little. Wouldn't they go together then? Another way would by to use thin hardwood instead of plywood. If the panels are cut so that the grain runs lengthwise and not crosswise and the 2¼″ dimension is made a little scant by shaving off one piece after another, the pieces can be forced together quite easily. This will make a rickety assembly, rather like a dried out wagon wheel. So treat your 'dream' like a farmer treats a loose wagon wheel. Soak it in hot linseed oil until the pieces swell tight. The oil will oxidise and leave the pieces fitting as tightly as the draftsman drew them. How to get it apart? We don't have a clue. The draftsman woke up before he got that far.

Money boxes (from the Hordern puzzle collection) made in the form of burr puzzles and having sliding panels between the bars. The one in the foreground is from Japan. The one top left was given by Franklin Reynolds to his sister in 1892. The third box also dates from the 1890's.

The design for this 24-piece Chestnut Burr appeared in Wyatt's Wonders in Wood which was published in 1946. A 6-piece 'Star' diagonal burr was sold as long ago as 1875. The modern one shown in the photograph is sold by Pentangle under the name The Snowflake.

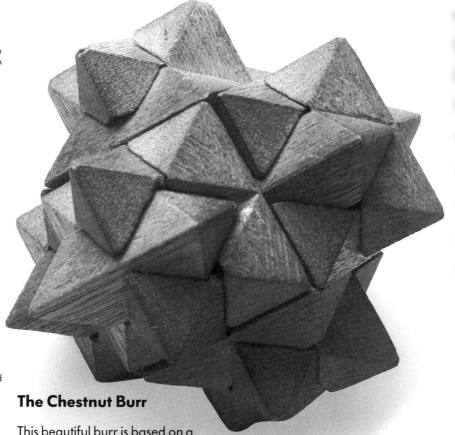

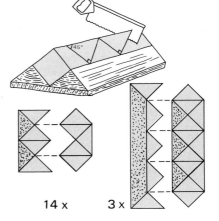

These three attractive burr puzzles are made of pieces which are similar to the pieces used to make the 24-piece Chestnut Burr.

The diagram to the left shows how you must mark each piece before cutting. In the center you can see the device we designed to position the wood for handsawing the pieces.

The Chestnut Burr

This beautiful burr is based on a stellated rhombic dodecahedron and has no fewer than 144 triangular facets on its exterior. It first appeared in Wyatt's Wonders in Wood in 1946, and the author noted that the puzzle was difficult to make without the use of precision machinery. However, we have devised a simple method of positioning the wood to enable you to cut the pieces using an ordinary handsaw.

How to make the Chestnut Burr

You position the wood by gluing and screwing two lengths of wood of triangular cross section to a base. The easiest way to obtain these is to ask your hobby shop to cut a length of 1'' x 1'' wood lengthwise along its diagonal axis. As you can see in the diagram at the foot of the page, you need to make 24 pieces of 6 different dimensions and cuttings, all made

from wood with a cross-section of 1'' x 1''. You need 18 three-inch and 6 six-inch lengths. Cuts are always measured from the center of the piece. Mark the triangles on one side, turn the wood and mark on the second side. Position the piece in your holding device and cut out the sections as marked. Cuts are made at 45° to the axis - not the corners - but just follow your pencil lines carefully. After one or two trial attempts, you will soon get the hang of it. It is not strictly necessary to cut the corners of the pieces; your puzzle will just look like a diagonal burr.

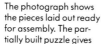

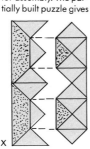

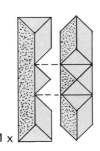

The photograph shows the pieces laid out ready for assembly. The partially built puzzle gives you a clue how you must arrange the pieces in order to make it.

1 x   3 x   14 x   3 x   2 x   1 x

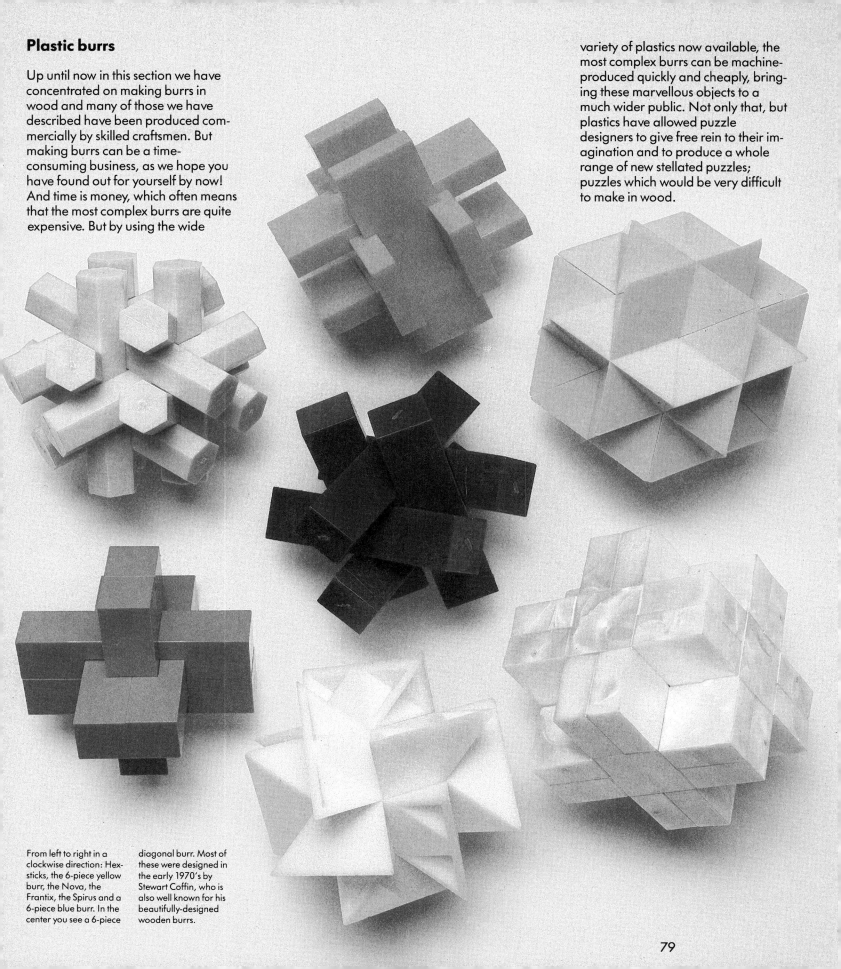

Plastic burrs

Up until now in this section we have concentrated on making burrs in wood and many of those we have described have been produced commercially by skilled craftsmen. But making burrs can be a time-consuming business, as we hope you have found out for yourself by now! And time is money, which often means that the most complex burrs are quite expensive. But by using the wide variety of plastics now available, the most complex burrs can be machine-produced quickly and cheaply, bringing these marvellous objects to a much wider public. Not only that, but plastics have allowed puzzle designers to give free rein to their imagination and to produce a whole range of new stellated puzzles; puzzles which would be very difficult to make in wood.

From left to right in a clockwise direction: Hex-sticks, the 6-piece yellow burr, the Nova, the Frantix, the Spirus and a 6-piece blue burr. In the center you see a 6-piece diagonal burr. Most of these were designed in the early 1970's by Stewart Coffin, who is also well known for his beautifully-designed wooden burrs.

79

The Third Dimension

The main problem with the Third Dimension puzzle is that you need four hands to assemble it. Those of you who don't have four hands can use elastic bands instead. But you only need two hands to make the 60 rods from which the puzzle is built. 59 of these rods are identical and an example is shown above.
The last piece, the key, differs only in that it has one dowel instead of two. The rods should be 1 x 1 unit in cross section. The exact length is not important but each rod should be at least 14 units long. The distance between the two dowel pegs is nine units. Mark each rod and drill the holes. These should be ½ unit deep. The dowel pegs are 1 unit in length. Glue the pegs in place. That's it! Making this puzzle is child's play after the tackling the complexities of the Chestnut Burr on the previous page. The last step is to varnish or oil the pieces. Well, not quite the last step. You still have to put the thing together!

Van Deventer's Matchboxes

Many a practical joke has been played with matchboxes and you probably played yours for the first time way back when you were a kid. It goes like this: Slide the cover with the picture side down over a box filled with matches and turn the picture side up again. Now wait till someone needs a match. Your unsuspecting victim will obviously open the box with the picture side up. The result - to much merriment on your part - will be that all the matches drop on the floor. Although Van Deventer's puzzle also has an amusing aspect to it, it's quite a bit more complicated than the trick described above. While playing around with empty matchboxes, he had a brilliant idea for a puzzle. It's subtle and quite amusing at the same

Far right: Van Deventer's matchboxes. The sample shown here is a beauty, made by the inventor of very thin wood and attractively painted.

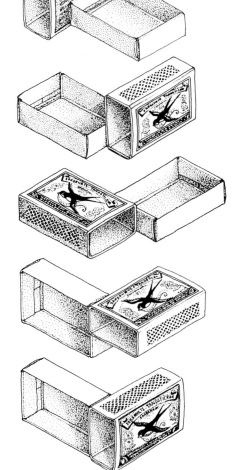

The matchbox puzzle is very easy to make. All you need is five matchboxes and good quality glue.

time and only five matchboxes are needed for it. The object of the puzzle, he announced in the puzzle column of a local newspaper with almost sadistic glee, was just as simple as it was difficult: CLOSE ALL THE BOXES.

This is a very easy puzzle to make. All you need is five matchboxes and good quality glue. The length-width-height proportions have to be 3:2:1 and you will find that many small matchboxes fit the bill. Glue the boxes together as shown on this page.

There are actually three different ways to solve this puzzle. To get you off to a good start we are giving you one, shown below. It would be even better, of course, if you cover it up and try to find it yourself first. You'll be fiddling with it for quite some time. Unless you have been pushing and twisting those rather fragile little boxes into their covers in a way we don't even want to think about. Solutions obtained like this are NOT VALID!

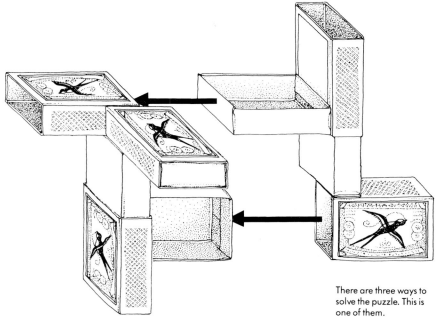

There are three ways to solve the puzzle. This is one of them.

The Cuckoo Nest Puzzle and related puzzles

The American puzzle designer Stewart Coffin has invented numerous ingenious puzzles, many of them seemingly simple - until you try to do them, that is! The two interlocking puzzles on this page, the Cuckoo Nest and the Locked Nest, fall into this catagory. The Cuckoo nest consists of only six hexagonal sticks and six lengths of dowel. In each stick, three holes have been drilled. The puzzle is to lock the sticks together with the dowels to form the nest. This puzzle is an interesting variation of the Locked Nest. In this nest twelve sticks are used, each with five holes drilled through it. These holes are all at an angle of 70½° and are equally spaced. Spacing is determined by trial and error so that the sticks just rest against each other. If you want to make this puzzle, or the simpler Cuckoo nest, we suggest using ¾'' hexagonal birch sticks and 7/16'' dowels. The holes should be 15/32''. Drilling the holes to the exact angle is the most difficult part but it can be done. Six dowels are attached to six sticks to make what Coffin calls 'elbow' pieces, leaving six plain sticks and six dowels. The elbow pieces, sticks and dowels are then assembled to build the nest. Stewart Coffin calls this 'a fairly hard puzzle', which means, for most of us, it is well-nigh impossible! In fact, you could call it 'The Locked Nest Monster'!

Above: The Cuckoo Nest and Locked Nest puzzles were both designed by Stewart Coffin in 1976.

Right: Coffin also designed the Three-Piece Block puzzle. It was created in 1980 for an advertising agency.

Far right you can see the top (above) and front (below) elevations of the three pieces of the Block Puzzle.

The Three-Piece Block Puzzle

Glue ten blocks together into three pieces to make this very difficult interlocking triangular pyramid. Common sense tells you that this is impossible, but common sense is wrong in this case. This amazing little puzzle has baffled experts. The drawings below contain all the information you need to make it. Top view and front views are shown. Glue 1'' cubic building blocks together to make the three pieces. Then drive yourself crazy trying to figure out how the pieces fit together to make the pyramid. When you have figured it out, drive your friends crazy.

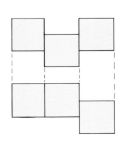

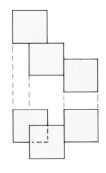

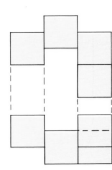

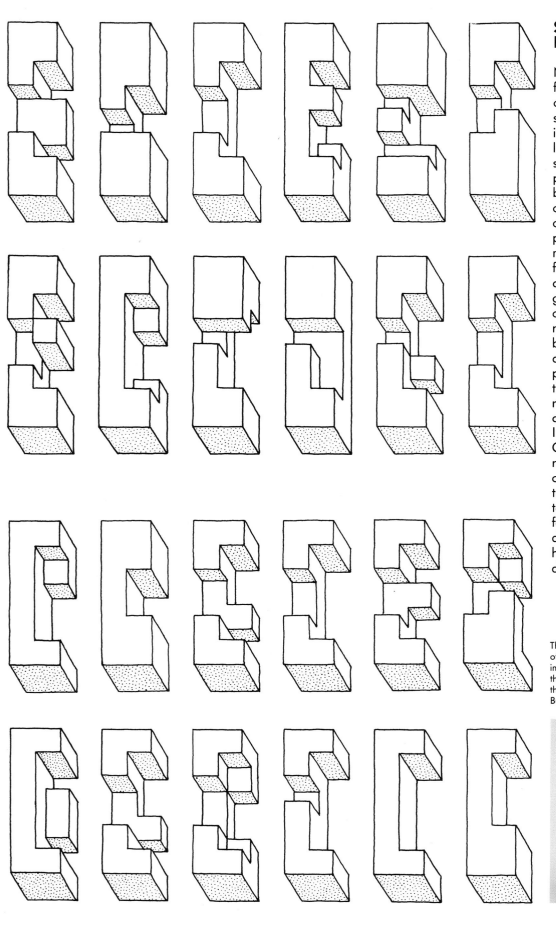

Super Burrs - The Fearsome Four

Now back to 6-piece burrs, which we first introduced on page 68. All the ones we have discussed so far are solid burrs, which means they have no internal voids, and can be called level-1 burrs, meaning that in the first step of disassembly, one or more pieces slide straight out. However, burrs with voids can be much more complicated, interesting and challenging than those without. In particular, the first step of disassembly may involve the shifting back and forth of one or more pieces within the assembly before the first piece or group of pieces is released. Bill Cutler coined the term 'level' to indicate the number of shifts required. The first burr here is Coffin's Improved Burr and is level 2-3, meaning that the first piece is removed with two shifts, and three more shifts are required to release the next piece. The second, also designed by Stewart Coffin, is the Interrupted Slide of level 3-2-2. Bill Cutler recently discovered a superb new burr design of level 5 which he calls Bill's Baffling Burr. In 1985 an extremely clever burr design (the bottom one on this page) of level 7-4 was found in Israel by Philippe Dubois and doubtless someone, somewhere, is hard at work looking for a level 8 design.

The lengths of the pieces of solid burrs are not so important as long as they are not less than three times the width. But the lengths of the two lower burrs here must be exactly three times the width. If they are any longer the puzzles cannot be assembled.

The puzzle designer, Stewart Coffin, the most outstanding designer and builder of interlocking puzzles the puzzle world has ever seen.

Coffin's Puzzles

During one of the first craft shows at which he showed his work, Stewart Coffin was asked: "How did you ever think of that?" Since that moment, Coffin has tried to make puzzles which would cause people to ask the same question. He recalls the remark in his book Puzzle Craft, and goes on to say that this casual comment got him started in 'polyhedral' designs. He called them 'AP-ART, the sculptural art that comes apart'.

Who is this man whose name has come up more than once already in this book? Quite simply, Stewart Coffin is the most outstanding designer and maker of interlocking puzzles that the world has ever seen. He has more than 80 original designs to his

name and although a few of them have been commercially manufactured in plastic he continues to produce his favorite puzzles only in the finest woods. His enthusiasm for this material is clear from the comment he once made to a journalist: "I never used to know anything about wood at all, but now, look at these. That bright yellow wood is Osage orange. It's used for fence posts in the Mississippi Valley. And the bright purple is purple heart. It's a hobby wood from Brazil. And here's some pau rosa - that's an Argentine rosewood - with all of those lovely streaks. And that beautiful red wood is from a breadfruit tree." The only wood Stewart Coffin never uses is pine because "it gums up tools". And if he isn't sure what a wood is, he simply smells it. He reckons he can distinguish hundreds of different hardwoods in this way.

Coffin's most elaborate puzzle is the one he describes as a 'dissected castellated triacontahedron', which he called Jupiter. This consists of sixty separate pieces of wood glued in five places to make twelve identical puzzle pieces. To produce the effect he wants, he uses six woods with contrasting colors or grains. Although he is the world's foremost puzzle designer, Stewart Coffin has his feet firmly on the ground.

He is of the opinion that designing very sophisticated puzzles can become an end in itself, which may bring a great deal of satisfaction to the inventor, but to no one else. He says his most popular puzzle is simply a stick of wood with a hole at one end and a loop of string through it. "You put it in someone's buttonhole and try to get it off". In his book Puzzle Craft, Stewart describes mechanical and geometrical puzzles, burrs and polyhedral puzzles, woodworking techniques and it includes a compendium of 80 of his original puzzle designs.

Coffin at work in his workshop at his home in Massachusetts, in the United States.

These are three of Coffin's puzzles. The top one is called the Four Corners Puzzle. It consists of six identical pieces and the assembled puzzle has tetrahedral symmetry. Far right is Scorpius, another 6-piece puzzle. It feels solid when you pick it up but it can be slid apart into two halves along any one of four axes. If you toss it into the air (with a spin) it flies apart. The last of these three puzzles is the Second Stellation of the rhombic dodecahedron. It has six pieces, all different and quite tough to solve.

This puzzle-sculpture is called Jupiter. The Scorpius family of puzzles leads directly by analogy to an arrangement of 60 triangular half sticks surrounding a hollow center in the shape of a triacontahedron. The sticks are joined in fives to make twelve identical symmetrical pieces. There are six sliding axes and, just like Scorpius, Jupiter flies apart when you toss it into the air with a spin.

These photographs show the half assembled puzzle and how it comes apart along one of its six sliding axes. Coffin makes Jupiter in six different hardwoods so that when it is correctly assembled the arms of the same colored wood are mutually parallel.

85

Keychain Puzzles

Most of us have probably owned one of these little novelties at some time or another during our lives. They are quite like the interlocking wooden puzzles described at the beginning of this chapter, the most important difference being that they are made of plastic. Plastic is an easily-molded material which means that the designer is not so limited in the shapes he can use to build his puzzles. Keychain puzzles seem to have originated in 1939. During that year the World Fair was held in New York. The theme of The World of Tomorrow had as its symbol a 700 ft. high obelisk, called a Trylon, and a 200 ft. ball-like structure, called a Perisphere. Irving Steinhardt patented a small plastic puzzle which represented the Perisphere with the Trylon sticking out of it. The piece representing the Trylon was soon replaced by a keychain and

the puzzle became quite popular. By the mid-1950's, dozens of different keychain puzzles were on the market and sold in drug stores and dime stores everywhere. They have been popular ever since and are currently made in several Eastern European countries, Germany, Japan and Hong Kong. Because of their variety and relative cheapness, keychain puzzles have become quite popular with collectors.

Here are just a few of the wide variety of plastic keychain puzzles, some of which are still being made. As you can see, plastic is such an easily worked material that virtually any object can become the basis for a keychain puzzle.

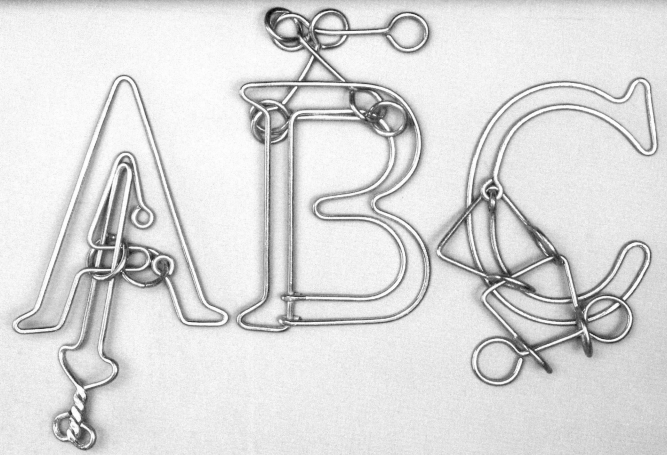

DISENTANGLEMENT PUZZLES

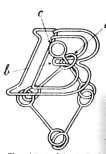

Above, below, and opposite page: Three examples of wire Puzzles: the A, B, C wire puzzles, made in Hong Kong by I-Chee Manufacturing & Trading. The puzzles date from around 1950.

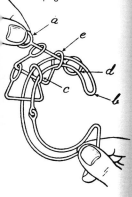

The object of the A, B, C puzzles is to detach the object from the letter. In the case of the A, this is a dagger. The B puzzle is very similar to the Fish on page 99.

This Super Puzzles set was made by Sherms, from Bridgeport, Connecticut and dates from around 1940. The box cover aptly illustrates the frustration and confusion felt when trying to solve these 'twisted, tangled and perplexing puzzles'.

Disentanglement puzzles deal with the problem of freeing (or attaching) a part of the puzzle, usually a ring or a handle. They are made of various materials such as cast iron and sheet metal, wire, and string.

The most famous disentanglement puzzle is probably the Gordian Knot, which is named after Gordius, a simple farmer, who by his extreme cleverness became King of Phrygia. It is told that when he assumed power he tied his former implements in such a peculiar way that the knots could not be unfastened. The oracles proclaimed that whoever could untie them would become emperor. Alexander the Great, or so the story tells, made many ineffectual attempts to untie some of the knots, but finally became so enraged at this lack of success that he drew his sword and cut the cord. (Hence the expression: 'I have cut the Gordian knot!)

The Bent Nails Puzzle has been popular for a long time and it still is played. As long ago as the first half of the 17th century, a bent nails puzzle existed. Another well-known metal puzzle is the Horseshoe puzzle (see page 99). On page 98, the Puzzle Hobble is discussed. It was used by cowboys in the early West in the United States to tie the front two feet of their horses together so they couldn't run away and wouldn't be stolen.

The Chinese Rings Puzzle, a type of Ingenious Rings, is by far the oldest puzzle we know that's usually made of wire. These puzzles often consist of beautiful figures or shapes and a good example of this is the butterfly on page 104. According to legend, the puzzle was invented in the second century by Hung Ming, a famous Chinese hero. It became popular in China around 800 years ago, and was viewed as a kind of wisdom game, condusive to the training of intelligence.

Through the ages, wire puzzles have been very popular with people who liked to play with puzzles to be distracted and at the same time used them to keep their mind supple and sharp. Two famous fans of these puzzles were the physicist Albert Einstein and the American author Jack London.

Many wire puzzles have been available from Germany, France, and England since the 1880's. The German puzzles are usually very well-made of heavy wire and many are still in excellent condition today. The French generally used thin wire for their puzzles and so a lot of them have rusted; however, many of the beautiful color lithographs on the boxes that contained the puzzles are still in excellent condition today.

Right: Le Canon, a French wire puzzle. The object is to free the shell. To do this, pass the point of the shell A under the ring B, as shown; then pass the ring B and the wheel along the inside of the shell.

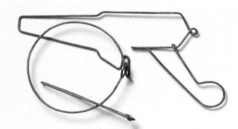

Puzzle Parties, one of the attractively boxed puzzle sets so popular at the beginning of the 20th century. The one shown was made in 1911 by Mysto Mf'G Co., later called the A.C.Gilbert Company, of New Haven, Connecticut.

Ozanam's book Recreations Mathematiques et Physiques, published in 1735, included the illustrations of a seven-ring Chinese Ring Puzzle and five string puzzles. All of these puzzles were made of beautifully carved ivory in the early 19th century and have been popular ever since. They are still available today.

Like so many other puzzles, string puzzles have often been used for advertising, some of them with great success. The best example of this is probably the Sam Loyd Buttonhole Puzzle, made for New York Life Insurance Company, to help their insurance agents sell insurance by attaching the puzzle to the lapel of their clients' coats.

The beginning of the 20th century saw a boom in wire puzzles, then considered suitable family entertainment. Elaborate boxes of them were produced. The French especially produced very attractive boxes. However, the quality of the French puzzles was often less than that of the German and English wire puzzles, as the French tended to use thin wire.

Above: Le Dragon, another example of a French wire puzzle. Here the object is to free the helmet. To do this you must pass the point of helmet A through ring B; then pass ring C through the helmet.

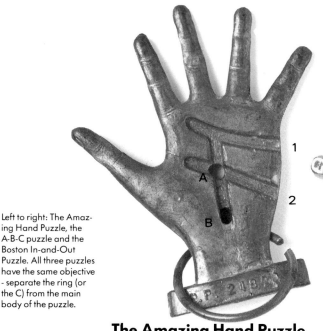

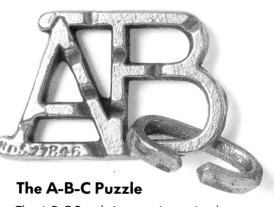

Left to right: The Amazing Hand Puzzle, the A-B-C puzzle and the Boston In-and-Out Puzzle. All three puzzles have the same objective - separate the ring (or the C) from the main body of the puzzle.

The Amazing Hand Puzzle

The object of this puzzle is to remove the ring from the hand by turning and sliding it through the holes and sleeves. The hand carries the initials J.W.L., possibly the initials of the manufacturer. It dates from around 1900. From the Hordern Collection.

The Three Nags Puzzle is made in metal. This puzzle cost 15 cents when it first appeared in the Johnson Smith catalog in 1929.

The Three Nags Puzzle

This puzzle consists of an iron bar on which three horse's heads are suspended. There are two smaller rings, one at each end of the bar. It seems almost impossible to take the center horse off the bar without breaking it apart. But it is very simple once you know the secret. And just as easy to put it back on again.

The A-B-C Puzzle

The A-B-C Puzzle is not quite as simple as A,B,C, but it is not especially difficult. If you go about it the wrong way, however, you will get it badly tangled up. This puzzle was first registered in the United Kingdom in 1911 by Sydenham and McDustra. In 1929 it appeared in the Johnson Smith mail order catalog - the price? 15 cents (postpaid)! It was one of hundreds of puzzles and novelties which were advertised in this catalog.

How to make an A-B-C puzzle

This puzzle can be made from a piece of plywood measuring ½'' x 12'' x 8''. Divide it into the same number of squares as there are in the grid below. Trace the letters carefully and cut them out. To cut out the insides of the letters, first drill holes and then use a keyhole saw. Use a triangular wood file to round off the wood at the points indicated by the arrows. These show the route that must be followed to solve the puzzle. It is important that the opening of the C should be the same width as the wood at these points, otherwise the puzzle won't work. File some 'fake' sleeves to confuse the would-be solver. Finally, varnish or oil your finished puzzle.

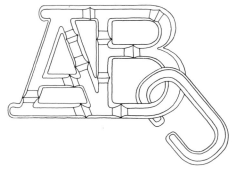

The Boston In-and-Out Puzzle

The medal has five holes in it, and the puzzle is to work the ring from hole to hole until it is finally detached from the medal. This puzzle was sold by Hamelys of London as long ago as 1879. It has appeared under different names at different times. It was sold as The Queen's Jubilee Puzzle (Queen Victoria) in 1887, and appeared as The Conjurer's Medal in Hoffmann's Puzzles Old and New in 1893. The Boston In-and-Out puzzle is from between 1880 and 1895.

How to make the Boston puzzle

This puzzle is made in two parts - the main body of the medal and the upper piece. Enlarge the puzzle on 1/8-inch plywood, using the grid under the diagram below. Mark the holes. The shape and position of the holes is important, but you should have no difficulty if you follow the diagram carefully. Use a drill and a triangular file. Cut out both body pieces and glue them together. Sand the assembled puzzle smooth and oil or varnish it. Use a curtain ring to complete the puzzle. Its size depends on the dimension of the puzzle. Cut a section from the ring the same width as the thickness of one layer of plywood. That's it!

To remove the C from the AB, simply follow the route indicted by the arrows. The route followed to remove the ring from the Boston In-and-Out puzzle is based on the same principles as

that for the A-B-C puzzle. See if you can discover it for yourself.

Far right: The rather beautifully made Boodle Alderman. The important piece - the piece to be removed - has been removed, and unfortunately lost!

The Puzzle Pup was made from sheet metal. The puzzle was to remove the collar from the dog. This was also the puzzle in the Doggie Puzzle sold by mail order in the United States before World War II. This puzzle is illustrated far right. The route followed to solve the puzzle was on a card given with the puzzle.

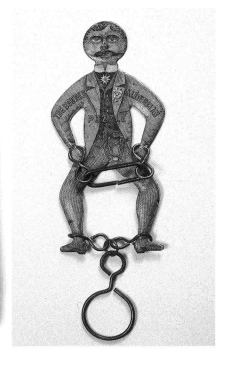

The Puzzle Pup

The Puzzle Pup was a standing dog wearing a collar. The puzzle was to remove it. The same puzzle, except that the dog was sitting rather than standing, appeared in the Johnson Smith catalog of 1939 under the name Doggie Puzzle. Puzzle Pup was sold by Magno's in a box with a forlorn-looking pup on the lid. He's plaintively asking 'Please take my collar off'. Johnson Smith's Doggie Puzzle was made in Japan.

The Boodle Alderman Puzzle

The model of this puzzle shown above is incomplete. The part which had to be taken off is missing - probably because its original owner couldn't get the puzzle together again and lost it! The inspiration for this puzzle came when members of the New York Board of Aldermen were charged with accepting bribes in connection with the granting of a franchise for a street railroad on Broadway. The term 'boodle' came into common use to signify bribery in general.

Several versions of the Interlocking Key Puzzle have been marketed since they were first patented by H.L.Davis in 1892.

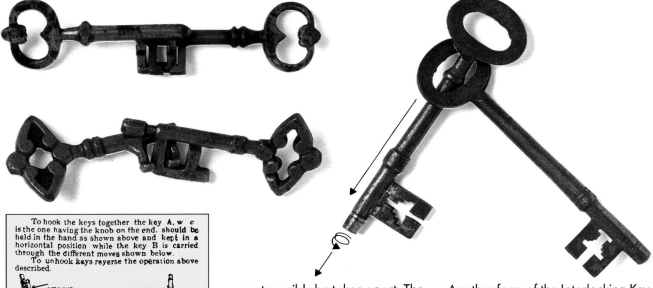

Here is the solution of the version known as Magic Keys. There are four moves needed to unlock the two keys.

To hook the keys together the key A, w c is the one having the knob on the end, should be held in the hand as shown above and kept in a horizontal position while the key B is carried through the different moves shown below.
To unhook keys reverse the operation above described.

1ST MOVE 3D MOVE
2D MOVE 4TH MOVE

Key Puzzles

The two keys seem to be inextricably interlocked and to all appearances cannot possibly be taken apart. The puzzle was patented in 1892 in the United States by H.L.Davis. It was sold in London streets in 1895, when it proved to be enormously popular. Several versions of the puzzle have since been marketed under names such as Puzzle Keys, The Key Puzzle, Magic Keys and the Max and Fritz puzzle. (Solution on the left!)

Another form of the Interlocking Key puzzle is shown above. The head of one key is on the shaft of another. This is obviously impossible to take apart - unless you know the secret. The brass ring and key shown below appeared in Hoffmann's *Puzzles Old & New* in 1893, and is based on exactly the same principle as puzzle above. It was patented in 1894.

Right: The Fire Irons Puzzle, one of a large number of similar disentanglement puzzles which were offered in the mail order catalog of Johnson Smith in 1929.

Center right: Collin's Puzzle, patented in 1898. The secret lies in a small indentation in one arm of the H. This allows the studs on the blades of the propellor to pass.

Hoffman's Brass Key and Ring opens in the same way as the key puzzle at the top of the page.

The Fire Irons Puzzle

The Fire Irons Puzzle was one of several dozen cast metal and wire disentanglement puzzles (none of them costing more than 15 cents) featured in the 1929 mail order catalog of Johnson Smith. The puzzle, which is nickel plated cast iron, consists of a shovel and tong through rings on the ends of arms separated by a poker. The puzzle is to remove the tong.

Collin's Puzzle

This ingenious puzzle from the Hordern Collection was patented by S.J.C. Collins in 1898. One of the parts is a six-bladed propellor, and each blade has a stud embossed on it. The other part is a closed H-shaped slot with an indentation on the upper right inside arm of the H. The studs on the blades can only pass through the H at this point. The puzzle is to pass the propellor through the H.

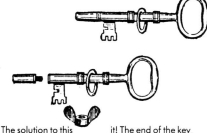

The solution to this Interlocking Key Puzzle is rather devious but obvious once you know it! The end of the key must be unscrewed with a wing (butterfly) nut.

Loop the Loop

This puzzle is sometimes known as The Devil's Keys. To separate them they should be held between thumb- and forefinger-tips. One key is swung through 180°, so that the twisted end can be pushed into the curl of the other key. Now the first key is slid forward and to the side and the keys are free.

The Double Star and Crescent

This puzzle was patented in 1901. Johnson Smith offered a version made in stamped steel for 10 cents in their 1919 catalog. The problem is to hold the puzzle with the crescent down and remove the lower star.

Top left: The Three Snakes Puzzle.
Top right: The Double Star and Crescent.
Lower left: Loop the Loop or the Devil's Key.

This puzzle is known as the Star and Garter or The Star and Snake.

The Snake Puzzle

The puzzle is to separate the three snakes from each other. It was registered in the U.K. in 1914. Another clever snake puzzle, this time linked to a pair of scissors by a thin ring, appeared with the three snakes puzzle in Johnson Smith's mail order catalog.

To solve this puzzle: Fold the 'U' shaped piece down, getting the stars in the position shown in the 2nd diagram.

Next, place one of the points of the star to be removed over the end of the crescent as in the 3rd diagram.

The star can now easily be removed by guiding it down around the crescent in the direction shown.

The Star and Garter Puzzle

There have been many forms of this ingenious puzzle. It was one of the first cast metal puzzles and was shown in Stanyon's 1905 Novelties Catalog. At first sight it seems so simple that it is hardly worth attempting, yet when you try to separate the two pieces you find it is not quite as easy as it seemed. Just when you are about to give up, the pieces fall apart of their own accord. How to get them together? That's another puzzle altogether!

The Four Keys Puzzle

This puzzle appeared in both The Magician's Own Book (1857) and

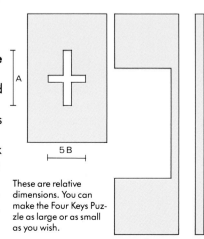

Puzzles Old and New. It consists of a 'lock', which is a piece of wood with a cross cut out of it and four 'keys' which are inserted in the 'lock'.

How to make the Four Keys Puzzle

The diagram on the right gives you the relative dimensions of the lock and key. You can make your puzzle as large or as small as you wish. The keys should be cut from a hardwood such as birch, which is very strong. The lock should be in a contrasting wood, such as mahogany. We cannot tell you how to make your puzzle without giving away its secret. The trick lies in the twin facts that one arm of the cross

must be just a little wider than the others and that the broad portion of one of the keys must be just a little narrower than the others.

A

5 B

A B

These are relative dimensions. You can make the Four Keys Puzzle as large or as small as you wish.

GILBERT NAIL PUZZLE

THE PROBLEM—To separate the nails.
THE SOLUTION—Hold the nails as in Fig. 1, taking hold of A and the points "C" and "O". Press the bend "D" around back on "A" and then down in the course of the dotted line, which will leave the nail as in Fig. 2. Then hold at the bends and pull them apart.

THE A. C. GILBERT COMPANY.   NEW HAVEN, CONN., U. S. A.

Gilbert Tangle Twister Puzzle

DIRECTIONS FOR OPERATING—

To take apart.—Hold puzzle upright as in "Fig. 1" then taking hold of A and rotating loop pointing from you, pass F and of single loop pointing to you through the loop C push ing B and at the same time turning end A around over the cross bars. Loops B and C will then intersect. Holding puzzle with and K perpendicular, slide end F behind cross bar and when end A is to perpendicular exactly as in "Fig. 2," let go of end A. Loop B will thereat interfere of loop C and fall off as Fig. 3.

To put back on.— Proceed A through loop C and end E through loop D, as in "Fig 3" push to gether.

same time turning end F around over end E. Locks C and D will again interlock.

Hold end F with end A in front of end E, as in "Fig. 4."

Push in end F at same time turning end E around under cross bar.

Loop B will again slip onto the cross bar as in "Fig. 1."

Loop B will also come off through loop E by taking hold of end F and passing end A through loop E, etc.

THE A. C. GILBERT COMPANY   NEW HAVEN, CONN., U. S. A.

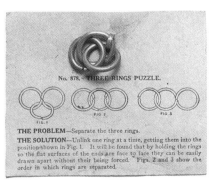

No. 878. THREE RINGS PUZZLE.

THE PROBLEM—Separate the three rings.
THE SOLUTION—Unlink one ring at a time, getting them into the position shown in Fig. 1. It will be found that by holding the rings so the flat surfaces of the ends are face to face they can be easily drawn apart without their being forced. Figs. 2 and 3 show the order in which the rings are separated.

Wire puzzles were considered great family entertainment in the first decades of this century and they were sold in elaborate boxes. Gilbert Puzzle Parties, such as the one shown here, were sold from 1920 on in many different sizes including various combinations of puzzles. Matchstick puzzles were included in the booklet which accompanied the box.

Puzzle Parties

The beginning of the 20th century saw a boom in wire puzzles, then considered suitable family entertainment, and elaborate boxes of them were produced. These boxes were used at puzzle parties, which were in fact more like puzzle contests. Family and friends gathered together to see who could take apart and put together the most puzzles the fastest.

The A.C.Gilbert Company (New Haven, Connecticut) - until 1916 called the Mysto Manufacturing Co. - made many such Puzzle Parties sets. They were available in various sizes and some of them contained not only wire puzzles, but also other types,

such as dexterity puzzles. The Gilbert Puzzle Parties set shown above left was sold starting in 1920 and was accompanied by an instruction booklet, also shown here. In this booklet, instructions are given for no less than 22 different puzzles (see the illustrations above and left on the opposite page).

One of these is the Three Rings Puzzle. For this puzzle, the problem is to separate the three rings. You start by unlinking one ring at a time, getting them into the position shown in fig.1.

You will find that the rings can be easily drawn apart without being forced if they are held in such a way that the flat surfaces of the ends are face to face. Figs. 2 and 3 show the order in which the rings are separated.

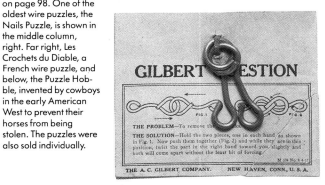

Here you can see several wire puzzles. They were often sold in sets, attractively boxed, like the Puzzle Parties illustrated on the opposite page and the Super Puzzles on page 98. One of the oldest wire puzzles, the Nails Puzzle, is shown in the middle column, right. Far right, Les Crochets du Diable, a French wire puzzle, and below, the Puzzle Hobble, invented by cowboys in the early American West to prevent their horses from being stolen. The puzzles were also sold individually.

The Nails Puzzle

The Nail Puzzle, which has always been one of the most popular wire puzzles, was patented in the United States in 1910 by Walter Jenkins. It is a simple puzzle, with a simple problem: to separate the nails. The basic nail puzzle, called the 'bent nails' puzzle, has been around for a long time and was probably played as long ago as the first half of the 17th century.

A.C.Gilbert packaged the Nail Puzzle (above) and sold it attached to a card showing the solution, either individually or as part of a boxed set with other puzzles (several of which are illustrated on these pages). The Nail Puzzle was often used to advertise products. This was the case with many other puzzles, such as the 'T' and 'H' puzzles (see page 21).

The Puzzle Hobble

In the early days of the American West, the horse was often the only available means of transportation. At night, cowboys had to guard their horses so that Indians or other cowboys couldn't steal them. To make their job easier, they invented the puzzle hobble. They made it very difficult so that so that it was impossible to take apart in the dark. Since the hobble was made of iron, it couldn't be removed except by working the puzzle. The puzzle hobble allowed the horses to move short distances so they could graze, but prevented them from running off . (On the left, the puzzle hobble is shown fitted together.)

Les Crochets du Diable

Les Crochets du Diable is, as the name indicates, a wire puzzle made in France. It was also sold in England and the United States. It dates from around 1900. The problem of this puzzle is, of course, to separate the hooks. This is done, and it is quite simple really, by sliding them through the claws.

This attactively-boxed Super Puzzles set (left), manufactured by Sherms, Bridgeport, Connecticut, contains wire puzzles such as the Pretzel, the Knotted Rings, the Question, the Heart, and the Doggie (with an original problem: how to get the key out of the dog's mouth). The problem of the Old Hinged Metal Puzzle is to free the circular ring from the main component. This is done with some subtle bends and twists and careful manipulation of the four parts (see the solution below).

The puzzle is made of hand-forged metal and dates from the late 18th or early 19th century.

Right: Super Puzzles, a wire puzzle box for the whole family, very similar to the Puzzle Parties on page 96, was manufactured by Sherms, of Bridgeport, Connecticut.

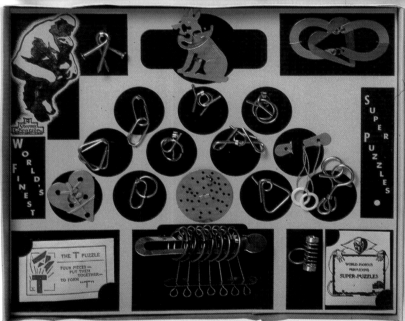

Solution

To free the ring, twist the movable 'handle', carrying the ring, to hang underneath the metal U. Then fold the puzzle over toward the left. Slide the ring over the point between the U and the left handle, as shown in the diagram above. In this way it passes off the right handle and comes to lie around the U and left handle. Now work it around the U and left handle at the same time. Then the ring is released at the joint.

Hand-forged metal was used to make this old 'wire' puzzle from the late 18th or early 19th century, called the Old Hinged Metal Puzzle.

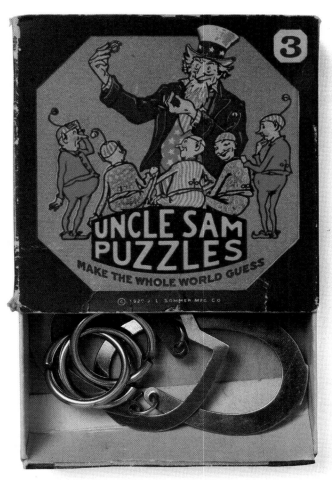

Uncle Sam's Puzzles

The J.L. Sommer Manufacturing Company manufactured many wire puzzle boxes, among which the Uncle Sam's Puzzles (starting in 1920). Like the Puzzle Parties, they were used for family entertainment. A set of four boxes was sold with two wire puzzles in each box. Included were the Three Rings puzzle (see page 96) and the Horseshoe puzzle.

To solve the Horseshoe Puzzle (illustrated above), hold one horseshoe in each thumb and finger parallel with the large ring hanging on the left-hand side. Move this ring towards the center so that it lies with one side on the top side of the right-hand horseshoe and the other side on the bottom side of the left-hand horseshoe. Next push the right-hand horseshoe towards the left keeping the small rings parallel. Now fold the two horseshoes downward till the wide ends come together. The large ring will now fall into both the large ends of the horseshoes and it can be lifted off.

Even though the Ring of the Nibelungs puzzle (above right) is not under a curse like the ring it is named after, many a curse may well pass your lips before you find the solution. It was one of the puzzles in a 1915 German puzzle box (see page 102). It is based on the same principle as the Horseshoe and its solution is to be found in much the same way.

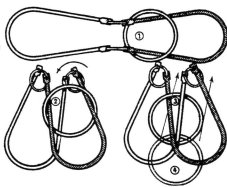

The Fish and the Duck

The Fish and the Duck puzzles are two pretty examples of Ingenious Ring puzzles which we introduced on page 88-89. The problem of the Duck is to remove (or attach) the ring. The Fish puzzle is very similar to the 'B' puzzle on page 88. These puzzles were made by a Chinese man between 1955 and 1957 and sold to a Japan Air Line's pilot on Hong Kong's Nathan Road.

The Duck is another example of an Ingenious Ring puzzle. The problem is to remove (or attach) the ring.

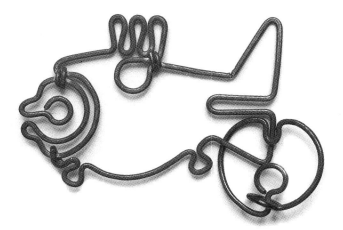

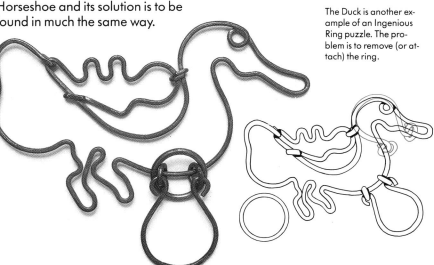

Ingenious Ring Puzzles

All the Ingenious Ring puzzles on these pages were made by Bob Easter, of San Francisco, California, from designs in the Ingenious Ring Puzzle Book, by Ch'ung-En Yü, which was first published in 1958.

Ingenious Ring Puzzles, also known as Wisdom Ring Puzzles, have been popular in China for more than eight hundred years.

Not only are they fascinating puzzles in themselves, but according to Chinese legend they are also conducive to the training of the intelligence. The great scientist, Albert Einstein, discoverer of the Theory of

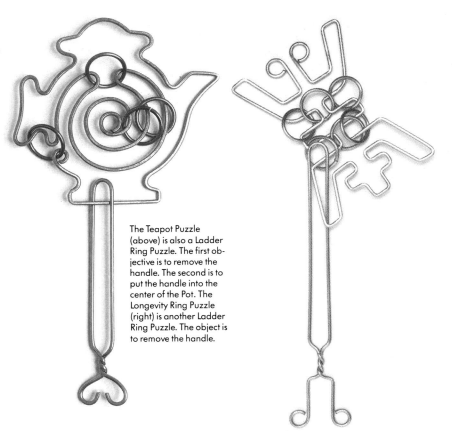

The Teapot Puzzle (above) is also a Ladder Ring Puzzle. The first objective is to remove the handle. The second is to put the handle into the center of the Pot. The Longevity Ring Puzzle (right) is another Ladder Ring Puzzle. The object is to remove the handle.

The Snake and Scissors Puzzle. This is in cast iron and perhaps should belong with the puzzles on pages 92 and 93.

However, the principle of this puzzle is exactly the same as for a Chinese Ring puzzle, even though it is made from a different material. The three components, scissors, body and ring, are equivalent to the cross-handle, the principle frame and a gate-ring.

Relativity, used them to keep his mind supple and sharp.

There are many forms of the Ingenious Ring puzzle and they vary enormously in complexity, but, in general, their basic structures are the same. They consist of three parts: the principle frame, the ring and the handle, all of which seem to be inextricably interlocked. Long ago, in China, some people used wire puzzles as locks, with the frame fixed to the doorpost and the handle fixed to the door. When the handle was inserted in the frame the door was effectively locked. Unlocking the door was a time-consuming business, and the puzzle was soon replaced by regular locks and became a game in itself. The puzzle is to remove the ring or the handle from the frame. The 'principle frame', as its name implies, is the basic framework of the

puzzle and it has various shapes. The names of many Ingenious Ring puzzles are determined by the shape of the principle frame - the Tower Ring Puzzle and the Teapot Ring Puzzle shown on this page are good examples of this. There are two types of principle frame: one kind is fixed and its shapes and positions cannot be altered; the other kind is movable and its shapes and positions can be altered.

The 'ring' refers to each single small ring attached to the principle frame. Some are fixed to the frame and cannot move about; some are put on the frame and are movable. There are five kinds of rings: slip-rings, gate-rings, end-rings, joint-rings and decoration-rings. The slip-rings are the rings for the handle to be put into or to be removed from the principle frame. All the Ingenious Ring puzzles which do not have a handle require the slip-ring(s) to be removed. Some puzzles have only one slip-ring, some have several, but regardless of their number, slip-rings are the main part of this kind of puzzle. The gate-ring is

The Tower Ring Puzzle, designed by Liu-ch'i Juan, an old craftsman in Suchou, China. It is a beautiful example of a Ladder Ring type Ingenious Ring puzzle.

the one at the outside opening of the puzzle. Once the handle removes it, it is detached from the body of the puzzle. The end-ring is fixed at one end of the principle frame. It is usually smaller than the slip-rings. Joint-rings are only found on puzzles with a movable principle frame and are used to join the parts of the frame. They are much smaller than slip-rings. The decoration-ring is simply for decoration and has nothing to do with the solution of the puzzle.

The third part of the puzzle, the handle, is inserted or removed from the frame. Handles are divided into three groups, according to their shape. That most often used is the rectangular handle. It is oblong and the easiest to make. Its important characteristic is that it can pass completely through slip-rings or gate-rings. It is not suitable, however, for puzzles in which it is not necessary to make the whole handle pass through the slip-rings or the gate-rings. The second group of handles are cross-shaped handles. The arms of the cross prevent the handle from passing completely through the slip-rings or the gate-rings. The length that can pass through - the body of the cross up to the arms - is

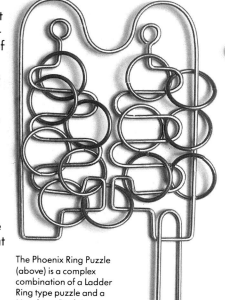

The Phoenix Ring Puzzle (above) is a complex combination of a Ladder Ring type puzzle and a Mandarin-Duck Ring puzzle. The object is to remove the handle. The Dragonfly Ring Puzzle (Right) is another Ladder Ring puzzle, similar to the Longevity Ring Puzzle shown opposite.

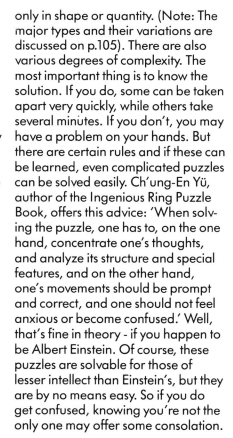

The Butterfly Ring Puzzle is an Interlocked Rings type of puzzle. Again the objective is to remove the handle. The four stages are shown above. If you follow the arrows precisely, you should have no problem solving the puzzle and removing the handle. The third stage may seem strange, but once you actually do the puzzle you'll see the logic of it.

known as the 'effective' length. The shape of this kind of handle can be altered - to make a 'scissors' handle, for example - but the effective length is still that part up to the point where the handle broadens out. The third kind of handle is known as the recessed handle. It is less often used than

the other two kinds of handle, because the effective length is usually very short. In fact, the recessed handle is very similar to the cross handle, the difference being that the effective length is drawn inside.

General Solving Principles

There are many types of Ingenious Ring puzzles, but most of them vary only in shape or quantity. (Note: The major types and their variations are discussed on p.105). There are also various degrees of complexity. The most important thing is to know the solution. If you do, some can be taken apart very quickly, while others take several minutes. If you don't, you may have a problem on your hands. But there are certain rules and if these can be learned, even complicated puzzles can be solved easily. Ch'ung-En Yü, author of the Ingenious Ring Puzzle Book, offers this advice: 'When solving the puzzle, one has to, on the one hand, concentrate one's thoughts, and analyze its structure and special features, and on the other hand, one's movements should be prompt and correct, and one should not feel anxious or become confused.' Well, that's fine in theory - if you happen to be Albert Einstein. Of course, these puzzles are solvable for those of lesser intellect than Einstein's, but they are by no means easy. So if you do get confused, knowing you're not the only one may offer some consolation.

Patience only will do it!

At least according to the German manufacturers of the puzzles shown on this page, it will! Then they spoil it by saying keen observation, manual skill and logical reasoning are also necessary! There were 21 puzzles in the set, all made from strong wire. Instructions for disentanglement were included in each box, although the manufacturers pointed out that solutions other than the one given exist. No force is needed to separate the parts of these clever little puzzles, although the natural elasticity of the wire is exploited in some cases. All the puzzles are 'double' puzzles in the sense that once you have managed to get them apart it is equally puzzling to get them back together again. You can easily make some of these puzzles if you follow the general instructions on page 107.

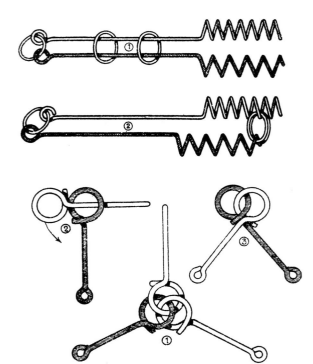

The Naughty Twins. The rings come off the spirals easily enough, but it is a much tougher proposition to get them back on again. When the procedure is reversed, unless correctly done, a strong tension soon arises between the spirals, making it impossible to turn them.

The Witch Trio. This puzzle is similar to the Double Witch Key Puzzle, but it has three elements. One has no eye at the end. Each key must cling round the other two, making this quite a difficult puzzle to entangle.

The Double Witch Key. There are three solutions: union of the large spirals, union of the small spirals, union of a large spiral with a small spiral. The third solution is more difficult than the other two and needs slight pressure when putting the rings together.

The Wedding Ring in the Trap. The diagram shows the first four stages necessary to move the 'trapped' wedding ring. When stage four is reached, the lower loop is removed by putting the small ring aside through it. The wedding ring can then be released through the slit in the large ring.

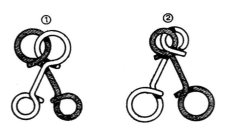

Right: This box of puzzles was made in Germany in around 1915. The instructions were printed in many languages and the puzzles enjoyed a wide sale throughout Europe.

The Caught Heart. This is one of the simpler of these wire puzzles. The heart can be released in two moves. When the pieces are in position two, shift the ring of the bar through the loop of the heart and it is free.

The Lyre Star. The three pieces of the Lyre Star are easy to disentangle. The solution rests on the fact the two pairs of wires, running parallel each other, may be passed alongside, even though the distance between them is smaller than their diameter. (This is the same puzzle as the cast metal Three snakes puzzle shown on p. 95.)

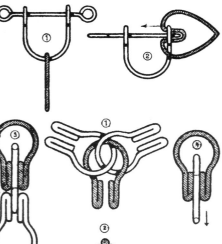

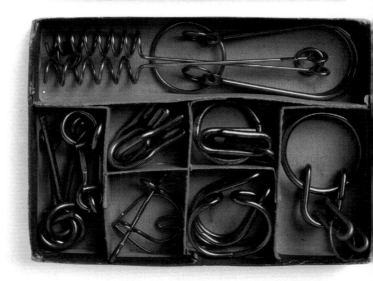

This puzzle is from Ch'ung-En Yü's *Ingenious Ring Puzzle Book*. It is called the Pigeon Ring Puzzle and the object is to free the bird from the other part of the puzzle.

Below: One of the boxed puzzle sets so popular in the 1920's and 1930's. Manufactured in London, it contains a variety of metal and wire puzzles.

Varieties of Wire Puzzles

Wire Puzzles vary from the simple two or three piece wire or cast metal puzzles shown on these pages and on previous pages, to the elegant and complex Ingenious Ring Puzzles which originated in China. The latter, also called Wisdom Ring Puzzles, are particularly interesting. Although every one appears to be different, there are, in fact, only three basic major types and a few minor ones. The first is the Ladder Ring type of puzzle. Its characteristics are:

(a) The principle frame is of a ladder shape, the lower part is broad but the upper part is narrow. However, the 'ladder-distance' of each lattice and the distance between lattices are still equal.

(b) Even-number rings, are on the left, odd-number rings are on the right. These should not be confused, or the puzzle cannot be solved.

(c) The number of ladders and rings can be increased or decreased at will; however, the increase or decrease of ladders and rings should correspond with each other.

The second major type of Ingenious Ring Puzzle is the Chinese Rings type, also called The Interlocked Rings. Several of these are shown on p. 105. Its characteristics are:

(a) The number of rings can be increased at will, but there should not be less than three.

(b) The method of disentanglement of even-number ring puzzles and odd-number ring puzzles is similar, except for the first step. To solve odd-number puzzles the first ring is removed singly. In even-number puzzles, the first and second rings must be removed at the same time. The third type is the Incomplete Ring Puzzle. Its characteristics:

(a) There is no handle.

(b) The principle frame is movable and is made up by connecting several incomplete rings in order. In this type of puzzle, two incomplete rings are joined together with a 'joint-ring', and a complete ring interlocks between them. Incomplete ring puzzles are often used in combination with other types so that they form one part of another puzzle.

There are also three minor types of Ingenious Ring Puzzles; namely, the Gate Ring Puzzle, the Nine-Nine Ring Puzzle and the String Puzzle. These types are easily made and are often combined with major types to form one part of a complicated puzzle. Part of the fascination of Ingenious Ring Puzzles lies in the fact that within the basic structure an almost infinite number of variations can be devised. The most common variation is in the principle frame. This can be in the shape of animals, plants, daily utensils (the Teapot on p. 100, for example), architectural forms such as towers or gates, and written Chinese characters. Some puzzles belong to the same type and have the same solution, but because of the variation in the shape of the principle frame, they appear to be completely different types of puzzle. The rings can also be varied in number and shape.

As long as they match the principle frame and do not affect the solution, round rings can be replaced by triangular, hexagonal or elliptical 'rings'. The size of the rings within the puzzle can also vary. The handle does not offer much scope for variation, although the cross-shaped handle can be made in the form of, for example, a pair of scissors or a human hand. Still further variations are possible when we consider the possibilities of combining different types. This can be done in two basic ways. The first is to combine two different types organically to form another new type.

Ch'ung-En Yü has created many new types of puzzle by this method. One particularly fine example is called the Layer Ring Puzzle and it was created by combining a Gate Ring Puzzle with a Ladder Ring Puzzle. The second way of producing further variations is to simply put together several different types which still remain independent parts in the combined puzzle. Ch'ung-En Yü made a puzzle called the Flying Bird Ring puzzle, in which the head of the bird is a Gate Ring Puzzle and the feet an Incomplete Ring Puzzle, yet both puzzles are worked separately.

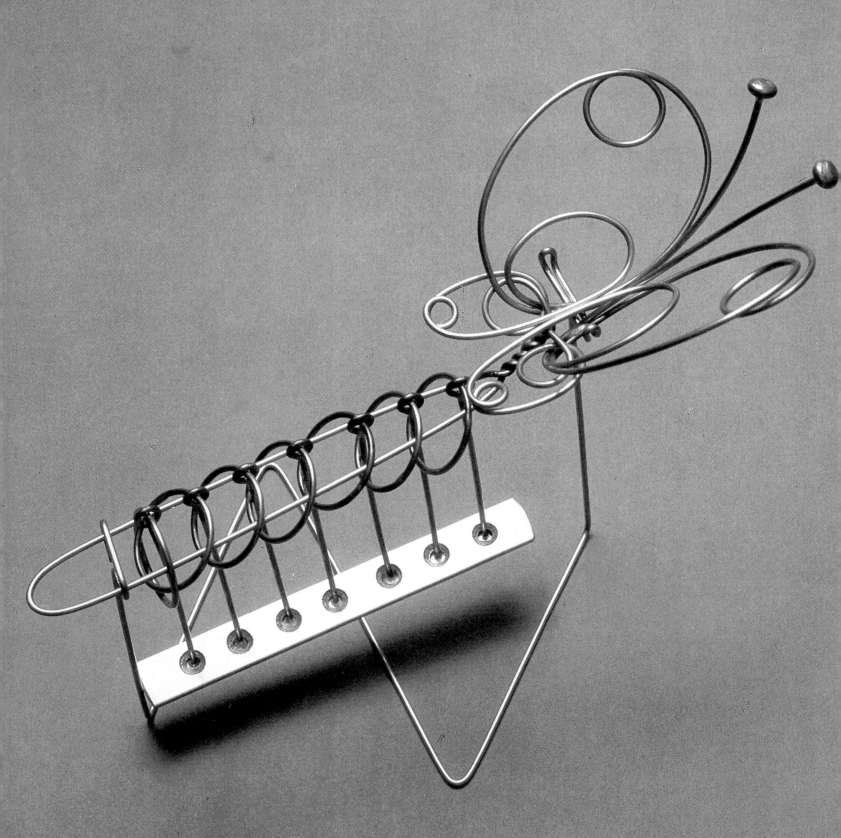

Chinese Rings

The Chinese Rings Puzzle is an example of a puzzle that is not easy to classify. Most often it is categorized as a disentanglement wire puzzle, especially as far as the classic Chinese Rings is concerned. However, the solution of this puzzle involves a sequence of moves which is very similar to that used when solving the Tower of Hanoi - which is a sequential movement puzzle.

There are many stories and legends about the origin of the Chinese Rings puzzle. (Some people even say that the puzzle about the Chinese Rings Puzzle is not so much how to do it, but what it is and where it came from). Stewart Cullin, in his book Games of the Orient, records a story that the Chinese Rings puzzle (Lau Kak Ch' A') was invented by the famous Chinese hero, Hung Ming (A.D.181-234). He apparently gave it to his wife when he went to war so she would have something to keep her busy in his absence. The story relates that she forgot her sorrow while trying to solve the puzzle.

The Ingenious Ring Puzzle Book by Ch'ung-En Yü, published in 1958 in Shanghai, describes a prolific family of puzzles. It includes Chinese Rings and 23 other wire puzzles (fish, labyrinth, butterfly, dragonfly, etc.). Ch'ung-En Yü indicates that the Chinese Ring Puzzle was very popular and known to almost every Chinese family during the Sung Dynasty (960-1279). It was originally used as a lock, but it was found to be too time-consuming for that purpose.

The puzzle was very popular in Scandinavia, where it was also used as a lock. In Norway it has been known as such for centuries. And at the National Museum of Finland it is exhibited as a traditional folk toy, under the name Prisoner's Lock. But the Finns are the first to admit its foreign origin; their claim to the lock is based only on its continued popularity in Finland over the last 150 years. Both children and adults find the lock a perfect pastime during the long, cold winter nights in the Land of the Midnight Sun. It is a most ingenious

Opposite page: At first glance this may strike you as a beautiful piece of jewelry, but it is, in fact, a homemade, highly decorative, Chinese Rings puzzle, made of wire, by Rick Irby of Eureka, California.

Far right: The Chinese Rings puzzle has inspired many people all over the world to make their own version. As can be seen here, an unlimited variety of materials can be used: curtain rings, wood, and ivory, to name only a few.

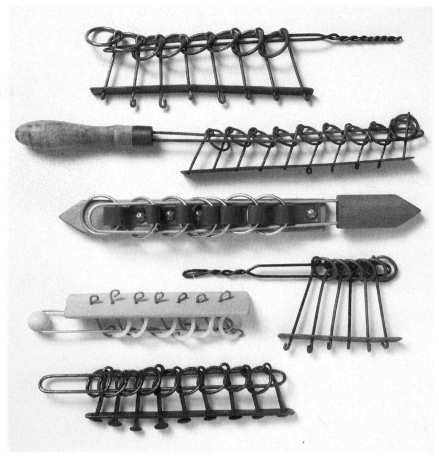

device and can be solved only with a great deal of patience. The story of its origin is a most romantic one. It is said that the Prussian Baron, Frederick Von der Trenck, was in love with the sister of King Frederick the Great. The Prussian King, suspecting the Baron of having only dishonorable intentions, imprisoned him for ten years. It was in prison that the unfortunate Baron is said to have invented the fascinating puzzle.

In France Le Baguenodier - Ring Puzzle - was originally used as an effective device to deter burglars. And in England the lock was known at least as early as the 18th century, under the name Chinese Rings. In Italy, it acquired the name 'Cardans Rings', after the outstanding Italian mathematician Geronimo Cardan, who described it in 1550. In Venice it was called Il Sigillium Salomonis, or Sigillo Salamone, which means the Seal of Salomon. Yet another name for the puzzle was 'The Delay Guest Instrument', given to it in Korea.

However, it was not until L.Gros wrote the Theorie du Baguenodier, in 1872, that the theory of the solution was understood. (If 64 steps in removing the rings can be performed in one minute, 10 rings can be taken off in less than eight minutes. At the same rate it would take 582 10-hour days to remove 25 rings and 55 billion years to take off 60 rings.)

An astonishing number of modern puzzles is based on the Chinese Rings principle. In contemporary Japan there is a great variety of ring puzzles, which are known as chiye no wa, or 'rings of ingenuity'. Other interesting modern variations of the Ring Puzzle include the Brain puzzle (see p. 107).

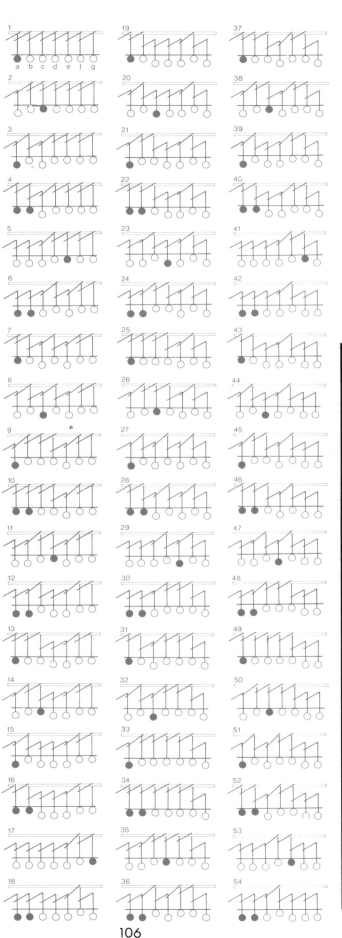

How to solve
The Chinese Rings Puzzle

The object is to remove all seven rings, and the balls and bars, from the hairpin-shaped loop around which they are linked. To take the rings off the loop, the first ring, a, or a and b (see diagrams) together, can be dropped simply, by taking them over the end of the loop and dropping them through the central space. But any other ring can be removed only when it is second from the leading end of the loop. To remove ring c, you must drop ring a, slide b temporarily over the end of the loop, and follow it with ring c which can be dropped through the central space. Then replace b on the loop. To replace the rings, reverse the procedure.

Below: Chinese Rings, made out of ivory, and exquisitely carved. Their box (shown on page 2) is equally beautiful. The puzzle was made in China during the mid-19th century.

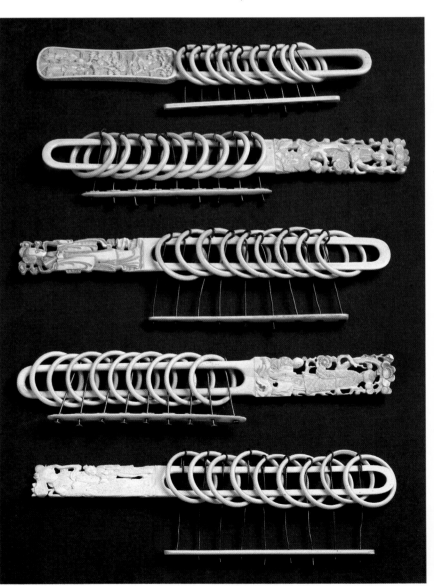

How to make the puzzles

These directions apply to bending acetylene-welding wire of at least 2 mm. thickness. Thinner wire can often simply be bent around a wire-bending form with pliers.

Before starting to bend the wire, first draw up the pattern of the puzzle on a grid, and enlarge this to the required size. This size will be dependent on the thickness of the wire you use; the thicker the wire, the larger the puzzle that can be made. Take care that you have a long enough piece of wire for the entire puzzle, bearing in mind that the thicker the wire, the greater its length should be.

To make large puzzles with thick wire, a bench vise and gas welding torch are essential. To bend, for example, a thick wire into a round shape with an inner diameter of an inch, you will need a steel tube with an outer diameter of an inch, clamped in the vise. After heating the wire, hold it firmly against the steel pipe, using pliers, and bend the free end around it. Remember that the wire can only be bent when it is red hot. Before starting to make any specific wire shape with the thick wire, it is a good idea to make it first in thin wire, bending it only with pliers. By doing this you can find out how the puzzle works and where the difficulties will arise. (For more detailed information see page 110.)

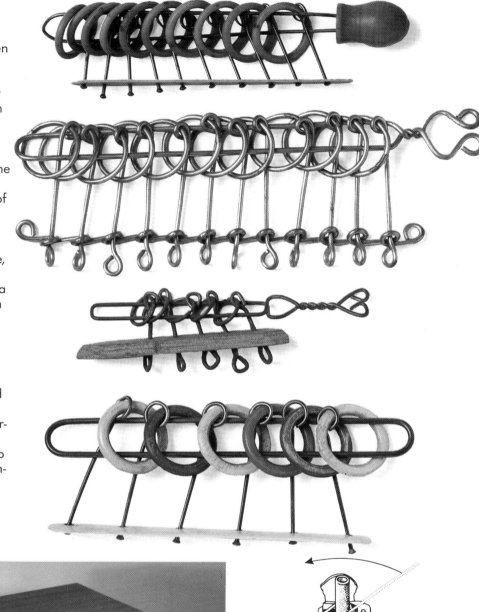

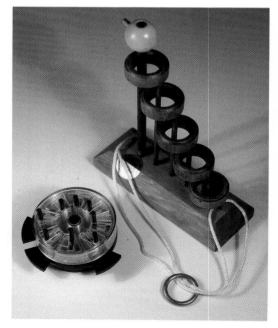

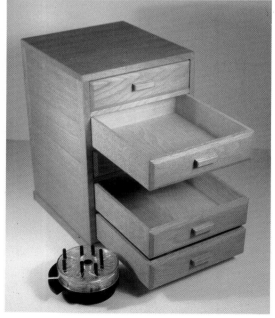

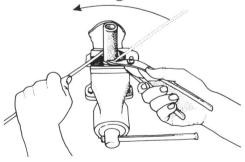

Above: The heated end of the wire must be clamped to the underside of the pipe.

Below: Having wound the wire around a steel pipe in a spiral, clamp it lengthwise in the vise.

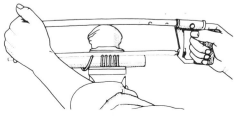

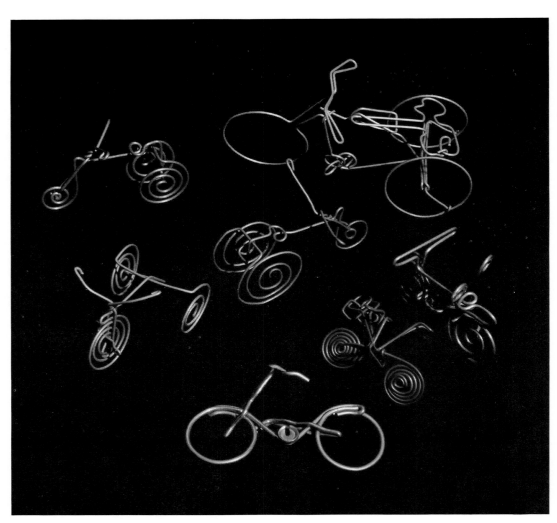

The Pentangle Story

Pentangle was formed in 1971 by James Dalgety and Ron Cook with the purpose of producing 'Fun Things' of high quality. These fun things were designed primarily to appeal to adults with an enquiring mind, who after all, are really only grown-up children. Pentangle was one of the first companies set up expressly to produce puzzles - previously puzzles were produced almost as a sideline by companies whose primary product was something else. The Pentangle range includes several topological wire puzzles, some of which are illustrated below. They all require patience and logical thought, and none of them are easy. In fact, they could almost be described as 'tremendously trying and totally terrible topological teasers'!

Pentangle does not include solutions with the puzzles because they believe that 'a true puzzlist does not wish to have hours of pleasure reduced to a few minutes by looking at the solution'. The company is based in a small village in Hampshire in the south of England but their puzzles are sold in stores all over the world and by mail order.

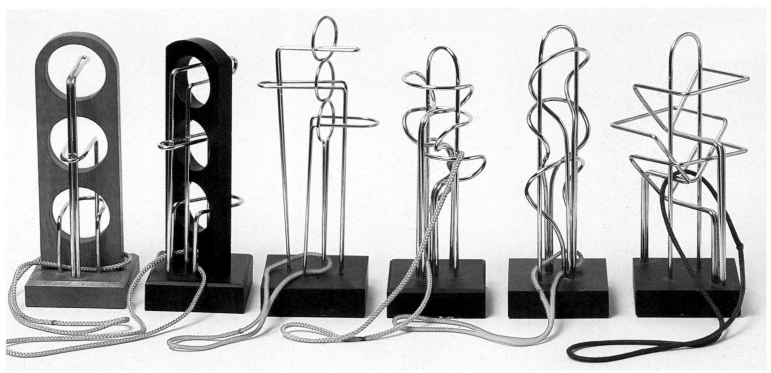

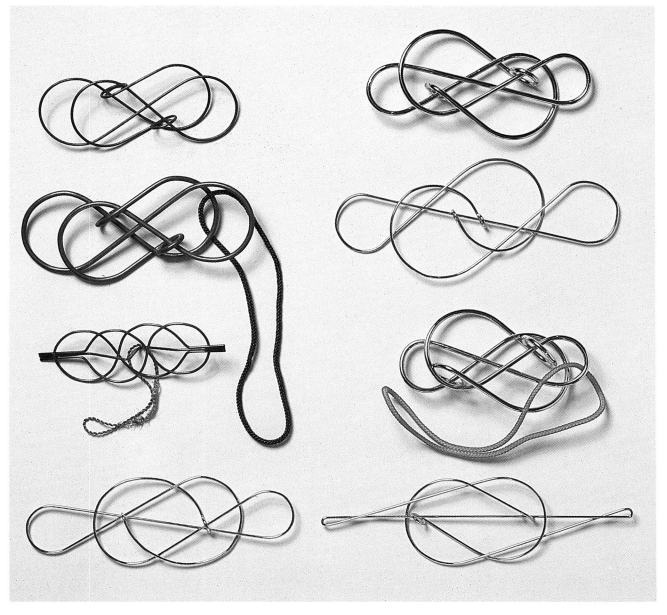

James Dalgety, who founded Pentangle with Ron Cook, is now Project Director of The Exploratory in Bristol in the West of England. This is Britain's first Hands-on-Science Center, where young and old alike can learn by *doing* rather than by looking and reading.

Left: These wire puzzle bicycles and tricycles were sold in England during the 1920's. They are disentanglement puzzles, the object usually being to remove the front wheel and handlebars.

Right: This shows the development of a puzzle during the various design stages. The initial model is top left and the final model, in the form of a treble clef, is at bottom right.

Left: Six of the topological puzzles in the Pentangle range. Second from the left is Traffic Lights, designed by John Snow in 1977. Fourth from the left you can see Tangleweed, designed by Geoff Wyvill, also in 1977. According to Pentangle, Traffic Lights 'stops you when you want to go', while Tangleweed is a 'cruelly convoluted convolvulous'.

Invention or Design?

How are good puzzles invented? There really is no one answer to this question. Some puzzles are invented by accident, some by adapting another puzzle and some when looking for the solution to an unrelated problem. And occasionally an inventor just has a moment of inspiration. What is certain is that the *design* of a puzzle begins the moment it is invented. The series of illustrations above demonstrate this clearly. James Dalgety had an idea for a string and wire puzzle based on topological principles (topology is the study of geometrical properties and spatial

relations unaffected by continuous change of shape or size). His first model is the one top left. The other models show how he slowly developed the design of his puzzle until finally he achieved the form he wanted. That is the treble clef which is shown bottom right. This is an excellent and tricky puzzle because the string is double looped around the center pin.

People have been inventing puzzles for many centuries. The Ancient Greeks built mazes and labyrinths and Archimedes invented a dissection puzzle. Everybody has heard the story of the Gordian knot which so frustrated Alexander the Great that

he sliced it in two with his sword. Wire ring puzzles and dissection puzzles were known centuries ago in China and Japan. However, it wasn't until the 19th century that puzzle inventors began to take out patents. Most of the puzzles which appear in this book are patented.

If you want to invent a puzzle of your own, start by studying some of the examples shown. Ask yourself if they could be improved or changed in some way. Or if they could be made in different materials. Who knows, you may invent a new puzzle which will be as popular as Sam Loyd's 14-15 Puzzle or Rubik's Cube.

109

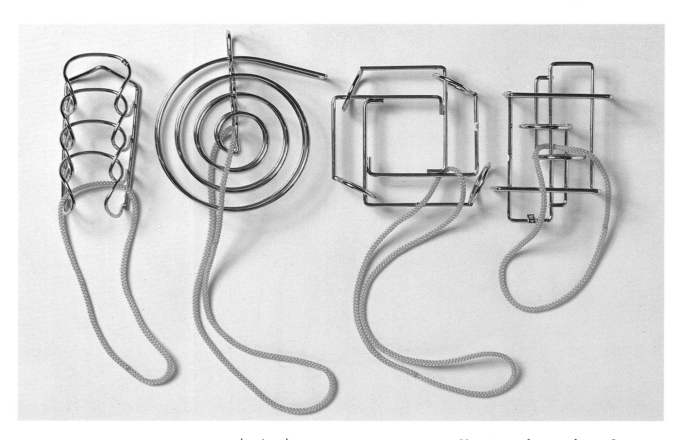

The Ball and Chain Puzzle

The problem is: How do you get the closed ring free when its diameter is less than that of the wooden ball? This puzzle was invented and made by Pentangle. It is a very difficult puzzle. With the Pentangle one, a solution is enclosed which details the pitfalls lying before the solver. If you start with

With the cord coiled as shown in the diagram, follow the direction arrows to release the ring. Finally pass the ring through the metal loop at the base of the puzzle again, and you should be able to solve this one without tying yourself in knots.

the ring the wrong way up or move clockwise instead of anti-clockwise, it goes on twice. After telling you why you got it wrong, the solution ends on an optimistic note - 'Alternatively you will have got into a terrible tangle in which case we cannot help you until you untangle it.' The brass Triangle, Loop and Chain Puzzle dating from around 1900 is very similar but allows an alternate, much easier, solution.

The Tenyo Computer Puzzles

This modern set of four Computer Puzzles is made by Tenyo Company, of Tokyo, Japan. The puzzles are based on the binary system - which explains the name given to them by the makers. Each puzzle consists of a metal frame and a loop of cord. The object is to separate the two. These are difficult puzzles which will test even the most experienced puzzler. Fortunately, the manufacturers enclose simple step by step solutions with the puzzles so you at least have a lifeline to rescue you from total frustration. See how long you stand it before giving up the ghost and looking at them!

How to make puzzle no. 3

The third puzzle is made from four identical pieces. Each piece consists of a ring welded on the end of an arm. The arms are then welded to each other to form the puzzle. You should use fairly heavy gauge wire. To make the rings bend lengths of wire round a metal pipe of 1'' diameter using a pair of heavy pliers. Nip off any excess wire. To make the arms clamp 5'' lengths of wire in a vise and use a hammer to make the 90° corners. The ratio of the three parts of the arm should be close to ½'' (for welding the arms together), 2½'' and 2''. To assemble the frame, first weld the rings to the ends of the arms. It is neater to weld at the point where the slight gap in the rings falls. Now weld the arms to each other to form the finished square frame. If you do not have welding equipment, you can solder the arms together, but the finished puzzle will not be as strong.

You could chrome-plate the puzzle, but this is probably better left to a professional. All you need now is a 15'' length of brightly-colored cord and the puzzle is ready.

Opposite page: A modern set of four Computer Puzzles, made by Tenyo Company, Tokyo, Japan. The puzzles are based on the binary system, hence the name Computer Puzzles. Also on the opposite page are the instructions for how to make puzzle number 3 and on this page (right) the solution for this puzzle.

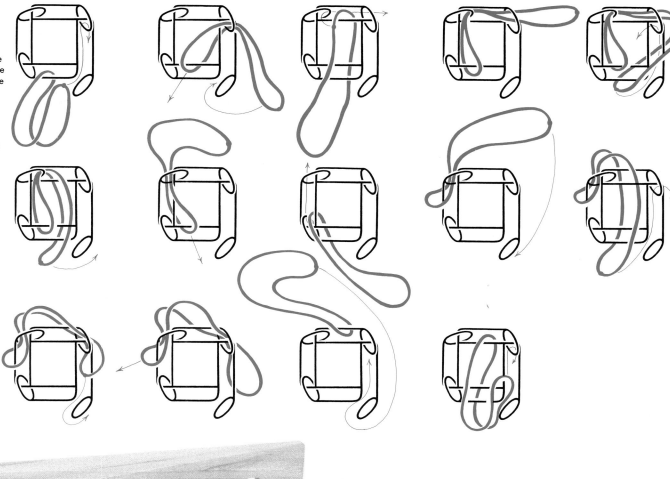

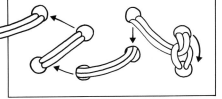

Above: The Swiss Cheese Puzzle. The problem is to untie the mouse from the cheese.

The diagram on the right shows you the position of the cord in the Swiss cheese. Use the grid under the diagram to draw the mouse onto a piece of thin plywood.

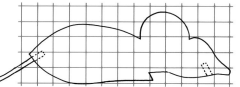

How to make the Swiss Cheese Puzzle

To make the cheese all you need is a wedge-shaped piece of wood (mahogany of birch) about 8'' x 4'' and tapering from about 2'' to 1''. Drill eight holes as marked in the diagram. They should be about five times the diameter of the cord you intend to use. Their exact position isn't important as long as they are not too close together. Draw the mouse on a piece of thin plywood using the grid under the diagram. Cut it out. Drill a hole about 1½ times the thickness of the cord as the 'mouth ' and a hole to seat the cord tail in. Glue in the tail. Sand both mouse and cheese smooth and oil or varnish them. Loop the cord through the mouse's mouth.

To thread the mouse: Mark the holes 1 to 8, starting with the top hole nearest the thinner end, then moving down, up, down and so on. Hole 8 is the lower hole at the thicker end. You need around 40'' of cord. First pass the cord through hole 8, then pass it back through hole 7, through hole 3, back through hole 1, through hole 2, back through hole 4, through hole 6, back through hole 5, through hole 7, back through hole 8, and then around the mouse.

This is one puzzle of a complete line of beautifully made clever topological puzzles designed and made by Charlie Maiorana who lives in Washington, D.C.

Un Coeur En Peine is a French wood and string disentanglement puzzle dating from the second decade of this century. It consists of a heart fastened by a cord to a wooden sphere. The puzzle is to free the heart from the cord that binds it.

The Red Goose Puzzle dates from the 1920's and is really quite easy to solve. A cord fastened to a ring is threaded through four holes. The puzzle is to free it.

Your grid can use squares of any size, but remember that the bigger your puzzle, the longer the length of cord you will need. You can easily work this out by trial and error. Thread your puzzle using the same principle described earlier for the Swiss Cheese Puzzle.

Un Coeur En Peine

This French disentanglement puzzle dates from between 1915 and 1920. It consists of a wooden heart through which passes a cord fixed to a wooden sphere. The puzzle is to remove the cord from the heart. Un Coeur En Peine is based on the same principle as the Swiss Cheese Puzzle shown on the previous page. The Red Goose Puzzle is a much easier puzzle because it only has four holes. It dates from the 1920's and was used as an advertisement by a shoe company.

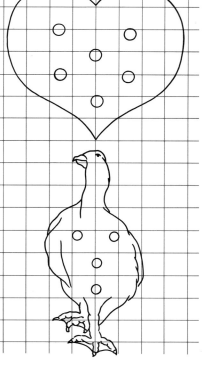

How to make these puzzles

These wood and string puzzles are easy to make and would be perfect as gifts. Draw a grid on a piece of birch plywood - your puzzle can be any size you like, so you can use ½'', 1'', or even 1½'' squares. Draw the heart or the goose using the diagram below to guide you. Cut the shapes out with a scroll saw. Mark the positions of the holes and drill them out. They should be around four times the diameter of the cord. Sand the pieces smooth and finish them off by painting them in bright colors. Or perhaps you can decorate the heart with the name of a loved one. To thread the puzzle? We don't want to make it too easy for you. If you follow the principle described for the Swiss Cheese Puzzle, but using only six holes you will soon find the solution! Once you have found it, threading the Goose should be quite easy.

The Lumberjack Puzzles are simply labelled with a letter of the alphabet. The three shown here are, from left to right: Type 'L', Type 'F' and Type 'A'.

Lumberjack String Puzzles

Rikk Kvitek, who designed these puzzles, started making puzzles for the children while working as a teacher. Because the kids loved them so much, a friend suggested he try and sell them. The first day, at an open-air flea market near San Francisco, he managed to sell only three and decided to forget the idea. However, he was soon asked to supply a local shop and within a short time his puzzles were selling well. The Lumberjack Puzzles are beautifully made of hardwoods, rope, and brass and they are all based on topology, the study of forms and surfaces.

The Sword Puzzle

The Sword Puzzle is the same as the third Lumberjack Puzzle, except the string passes only once round the center slot instead of twice, which makes it much easier to solve. If you are really clever you might be able to make a Sword Puzzle without any further instructions. The sword is shown in its original position and in its disentangled position.

The Sword Puzzle was patented in the United States in 1968 by Robert Boomhower. The example illustrated was made in Japan. There are no 'How to make' instructions for the sword, but the step-by-step solution should help you.
(1) Turn the sword so it is blade down.
(2) Pull down one string.
(3) Pull the metal ring up to the top of the slot and hold it.
(4) Pass disc A through the slit.
(5) Lower the metal ring to the end of the sword.
(6) Take the ring out through the slot.

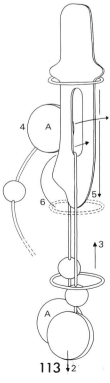

The Jolly Nigger Puzzle

This is a version of a puzzle which has been played in Europe and North America for centuries. According to legend, African tribes used a similar, but - obviously - differently looking and differently named puzzle.

The diagrams below show a step-by-step solution. Both balls must be on the same side. The second puzzle is to remove the ball bearing.

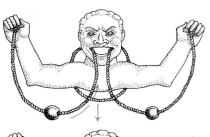

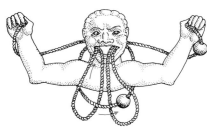

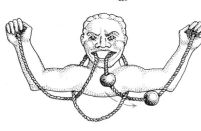

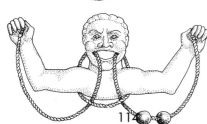

The Buttonhole Puzzle

This amusing puzzle was invented by Sam Loyd, who we have met before in this book. It was made for the President of the New York Life Insurance Company and designed to help insurance agent's sell life insurance. Loyd relates an amusing story. He showed the puzzle to the President, John McCall, who was not impressed. Loyd fixed it to McCall's buttonhole and bet him a hundred dollars to one that he couldn't get it off in half an hour without cutting the string. McCall couldn't and lost his dollar. Loyd then said 'I'll take it off for you if you'll agree to take out a ten thousand dollar policy on your life!' The puzzle became famous and Loyd said it was one of his most successful. The insurance agents must have used it with success - 'to buttonhole' became an expression meaning to grab somebody's attention.

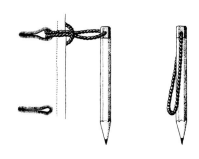

How to make the Buttonhole Puzzle

Fold an 8'' piece of cord in half, and thread the loop through your buttonhole. Thread the cut ends of the cord through the loop and pull them taut. Thread and tie the cord through a hole made in a 6'' pencil. Now try to remove the pencil from the buttonhole without cutting the cord. The loop is too short for the pencil to pass through, so you must bunch up the cloth around the buttonhole and pass this upward through the loop. Then push the pencil up through the hole.

The Sheaves and Reaping Hook Puzzle. This is one of the many advertising puzzles which have appeared over the years. It was made for the Binding Mower Manufacturing Company of Chicago and is based on a very old puzzle which was published as long ago as 1735. It uses the same principle as the puzzle shown on the left. The puzzle is to get both sheaves on the same side.

This puzzles us! Maybe you can help. We think it is a puzzle with one or more parts missing.

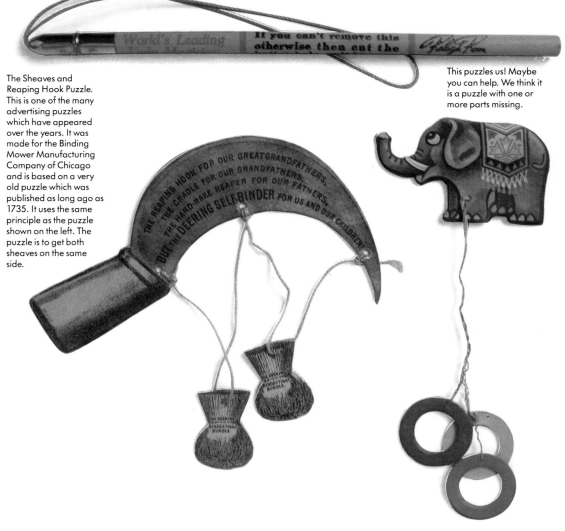

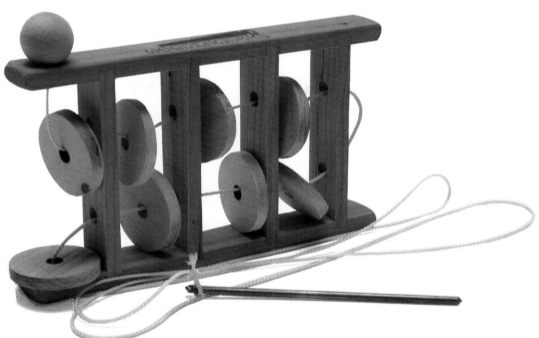

The Chinese Ladder

This puzzle is one of many to come out of China. It consists of eight disks lying on the steps of a small ladder, held in place by a long cord that passes through them and through the slats of the ladder. The aim is to take the disks off the ladder but to keep them on the cord like a string of beads, attached to the ladder only at the left hand knot.

How to make the Chinese Ladder

The illustration shows you how the Chinese Ladder is made, so you don't need detailed instructions. Drill the four slats clamped together before you make the ladder to make sure the holes are aligned. Use checkers for the pieces. Thread the pieces as indicated using a thick darning needle. Finally knot the free end of the cord.

The Love - Can You Make It? Puzzle

This puzzle was patented by John Trumbull in 1890 and produced soon after by Milton Bradley. The blocks are to be placed in such a manner that when they are laid upon the table before you with the ball-end of the cord at the left hand, the letters will be properly faced, that is none being upside down owing to a reversed block. The problem is to place the blocks upon the cord at random, then make in succession the words LOVE, GAME, CASH and TIME without removing the blocks from the cord, having words composed of letters of the same style. The puzzle is very easily solved if you know how to do it, taking only around 30 seconds for a word. But if you don't know, it can take hours.

Wind the cord once around the top of the right-hand upright. Thread the cord down through the right-hand disks and the holes in the slats, and up through the disks and slats on the left-hand side. Wind the cord around the top of the left-hand upright. Thread the cord back the opposite way but pass it only through the disks. Between the disks run the cord around the front of each slat. Slip the loops off the uprights, pull the cord and work the disks free.

L	O	V	E
C	A	S	H
M	E	G	A
E	M	T	I

How to make the Love Puzzle

All you need to make this puzzle are four wooden building blocks, a 30'' length of cord with and a wooden bead. Seal one end of the cord with a thin metal sleeve and tie a knot in the other end. Drill a small hole in the head and thread the cord through. Drill fairly large holes in the blocks and bevel the edges. The diagram shows how to letter your blocks. Use a different color for each set of letters.

How to solve the Love Puzzle

The blocks are held in a perpendicular position, the cord is passed through them all, leaving a loop at the top in which the fore-finger of the left hand is inserted. The end of the cord is run in succession through the blocks according to their order in the word, the cord always being inserted from the under side. Take the word 'love' as an example. The cord is doubled at A and passed through all the blocks, doubled again at B and passed through the L block, entering at C and coming out at D. It next enters the O block at E and comes out and turns at F. Block V is then entered at G and emerged from at H and the last block, E, is picked up by entering at I and leaving J. Now take the end K in one hand and the ball in the other. Pull the cord straight and the blocks will assume their proper positions. The process is now repeated to produce the other words in succession. The letters of the word must be of the same color - the E's cannot be exchanged.

John Trumbull's puzzle. The problem is to place the blocks upon the cord at random, then make different words without removing the blocks from the cord.

Solitaire

J.W.S. & S.
BAVARIA

SEQUENTIAL MOVEMENT PUZZLES

Solitaire
Left: A solitaire puzzle made by J.W.S.&S. Bavaria, Germany, and sold by Spear's Games. This particular set was sold in 1913 by Gamages, London. The 33-peg version was also included in Bestelmeier's Toy Catalogue of 1803.

Sequential movement puzzles require a series of steps or moves, following a set of rules, to reach a predetermined goal. Puzzles in this category include solitaire puzzles, sliding block puzzles, counter puzzles (hop-over), rotating cube puzzles, and maze and route puzzles. The first known written reference to solitaire was found in a paper written for the Berlin Academy in 1710 by Gottfried Leibnitz. Peg solitaire is shown in an engraving dated 1697 by Claude-Auguste Berey, entitled *Madame la princesse de Soubize jouant au jeu de Solitaire*, and also in an engraving of 1698 by Trouvain. The game was obviously already popular in France at that time. The earliest sliding block puzzle known is the Puzzle of Fifteen, which consisted of 15 square blocks in a 4 x 4 square box and included a piece numbered 16 to allow the 4 x 4 magic square to be made. In the early 1870's, puzzle inventor and author Sam Loyd discovered that half of the possible starting arrangements in the Puzzle of Fifteen made it impossible to solve. Loyd came out

with his own version called the 14-15 or Boss puzzle, in which all the pieces were in the correct order, except the 14 and 15 pieces, which were in the reverse order. These had to be put back in their correct order - which was impossible! The Fifteen Puzzle has been one of the most successful of all puzzles.

In 1957, the American Larry Nichols thought of a way to improve and extend the concept of the Fifteen Puzzle in a 3-dimensional (cube) puzzle. He envisioned a 2 x 2 arrangement of eight cubes, with each of the six faces of the composite cube a diferent color, and considered magnets or a double tongue and grove arrangement to hold the cubes together.

In April 1972, he was issued a patent for the cube puzzle, along with several variations. The Hungarian Erno Rubik, independently of Nickols, reinvented the Cube puzzle in 1974 as a teaching aid. Rubik's patent included a very clever mechanism to hold together the pieces of a 3 x 3 x 3 cube.

Right: Another version of Solitaire. ''The Well-Known Game'', as the cover of the box says. Date and manufacturer of this puzzle are unknown.

Solitaire

The origins of peg solitaire, often called simply solitaire, are not known with certainty. John Beasley's recent book 'The Ins and Outs of Peg Solitaire' is by far the best work on the subject and contains the following comments on the origin of peg solitaire: 'The earliest clear evidence known to me is an engraving by Claude-Auguste Berey, dated 1697. The earliest description of the game known to me was written by Leibnitz for the Berlin Academy in 1710. Nevertheless, I doubt if this is the whole truth; the rules are so simple that I believe that games which we would recognise as Solitaire were indeed played, even if not recorded, in very early times. John Matltby, who has looked as deeply as anyone into the early history of the game, concurs with this opinion.' In the most widely known solitaire puzzle the 33-cell 'English' board is used. The method of making moves is always the same. All cells are filled, except the one in the center. The object of the game is - by successive jumps - to remove all the pegs from the board except one, which should be left in the center hole. However, many other puzzles can be devised, as you can see on these and the following pages.

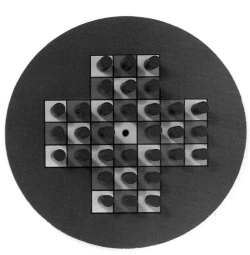

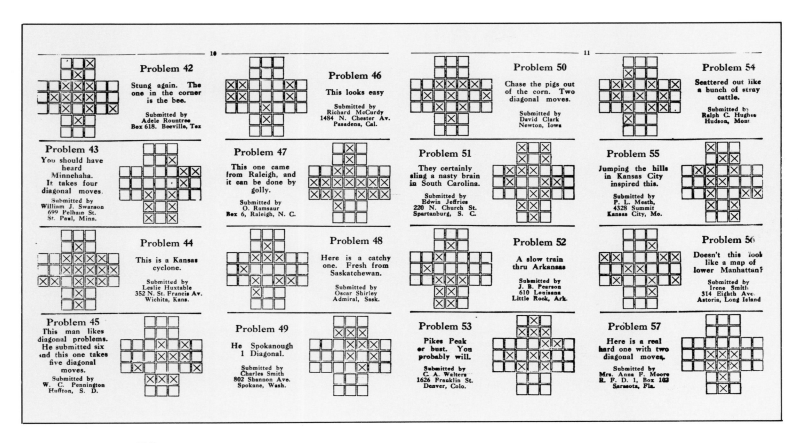

Jump for Solitaire

This version of the solitaire puzzle is called JUMP and was made by the Selchow & Richter Co. of New York. The jumps have to be made diagonally.

In this solitaire game, the jumps are made diagonally, forward or backward. There are two stages of the game. For the first stage, place the 24 men on the 24 stars. The object of the first stage is to make as many jumps at possible. When all possible jumps have been made, count the number of men left on the board. For the second stage, again place the 24 men on the 24 stars. The object now is to have the greatest number of men on the board after all possible jumps have been made.

The number of men left on the board after the first stage is subtracted from the number of men left on the board after the second stage, and the resulting figure is the Net Score. The object of the game is to have the highest possible Net Score. A net score of 15 is Fair, 16 is Good, 17 is excellent.

How to make solitaire board

Mark the grid shown in the diagram below on a 6 x 6 inch square of larch, mahogany, or other attractive wood, ¾ to 1 inch thick. The grid squares have sides of ¾''.

To make the cells, drill 3/8'' holes at the points marking the cell positions. Make the holes of equal depth, which should be about half the thickness of the board.

To make the pegs, cut 3 foot of wooden dowel, 5/16'' thick, into 36 pieces, each 1 inch long. Varnish the wood and the pegs or apply primer and enamel paint. Paint the pegs in a color contrasting with that of the board.

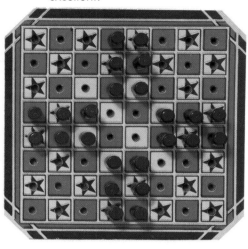

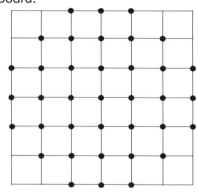

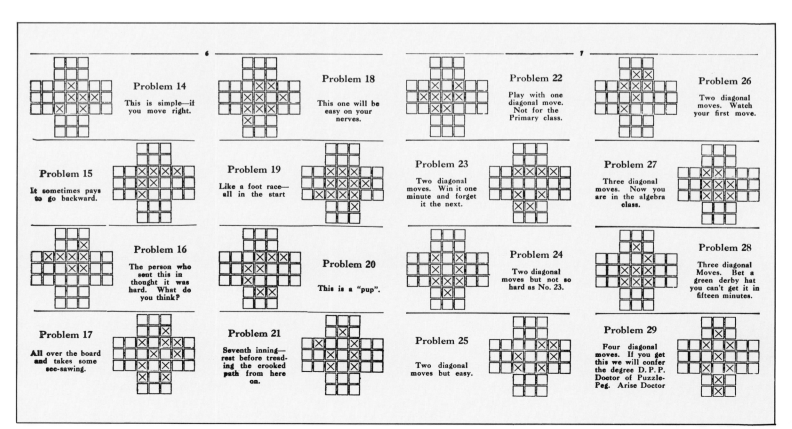

Problem 14
This is simple—if you move right.

Problem 15
It sometimes pays to go backward.

Problem 16
The person who sent this in thought it was hard. What do you think?

Problem 17
All over the board and takes some see-sawing.

Problem 18
This one will be easy on your nerves.

Problem 19
Like a foot race— all in the start

Problem 20
This is a "pup".

Problem 21
Seventh inning— rest before treading the crooked path from here on.

Problem 22
Play with one diagonal move. Not for the Primary class.

Problem 23
Two diagonal moves. Win it one minute and forget it the next.

Problem 24
Two diagonal moves but not so hard as No. 23.

Problem 25
Two diagonal moves but easy.

Problem 26
Two diagonal moves. Watch your first move.

Problem 27
Three diagonal moves. Now you are in the algebra class.

Problem 28
Three diagonal Moves. Bet a green derby hat you can't get it in fifteen minutes.

Problem 29
Four diagonal moves. If you get this we will confer the degree D. P. P. Doctor of Puzzle-Peg. Arise Doctor

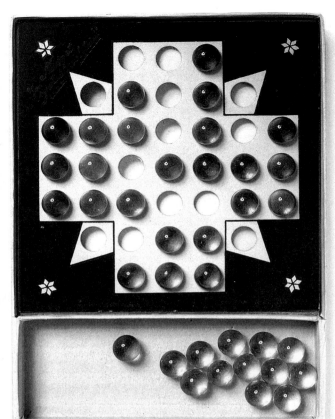

Above: The Crystal Solitaire, first made by S.A. Derwik of Yonkers, New York, in 1935, has a 37-hole board and uses marbles for pegs.

Many different puzzles have been devised for the solitaire board and some of them are shown on these pages.

The Midget Crystal Solitaire was first produced in 1935. It has a 37-hole board (which can also serve as a 33-hole board) and marbles are used instead of pegs.

The Double Diamond Puzzler is a gem of a solitaire puzzle from the 1960's. To start, you place the pegs in the upper left square, with three golden pegs in the circled holes. The object is to move all the pegs to the lower right square, again with the three golden pegs in the circled holes, using straight line jumps only. It is not that easy to solve, but very rewarding. The object of the 3 Square Puzzler is to have the 9 gold pegs, placed in the upper left square, exchange places with the 9 silver pegs, placed in the lower right square. This is a puzzle that has tested the skill - and patience! - of many an experienced puzzler.

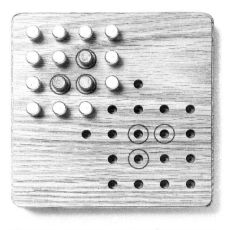

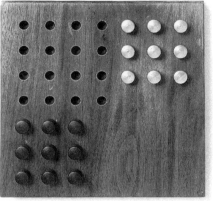

Above: Two solitaire puzzles produced in the 1960's by the Setko company of Bartlett, Illinois: the Double Diamond and the 3 Square puzzle.

Triangle Solitaire

Triangle Solitaire is an interesting and difficult puzzle. It differs from other solitaire games in that it uses a different shape of board and, more importantly, in that the board does not have a center hole.

Twenty pegs are placed in the solitaire board, leaving one hole vacant. A peg may be jumped over an adjacent peg into the hole immediately beyond, provided it is vacant. The jumped peg is then removed from the board. The object of the puzzle is to reduce the board to a single peg by a series of such moves, with the last peg in the hole from which you started. You have every reason to be proud of yourself if you manage to end up with only one peg - whatever hole it is in - because it means you have done very well indeed. Having two or three pegs left is no reason for shame - on the contrary, it is considered a very good result.

Gary Foshee published a very interesting analysis of the puzzle in 1977, in which he creates five solutions. We give you one of these in the back of the book.

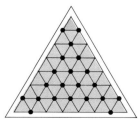

Above: The diagram of the Triangle Solitaire board consists of equalateral triangles.

Right: This difficult solitaire puzzle is called Triangle Solitaire. The model shown dates from 1915/1920 and is made from inlaid wood. This puzzle is relatively unknown. Gary Foshee published an analysis of it and created five solutions.

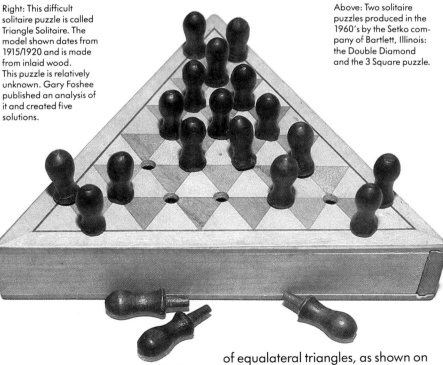

How to make a Triangle Solitaire

For the construction of the board, follow the instructions for the making of the solitaire board on page 119. However, instead of using the cross diagram you use a diagram consisting of equalateral triangles, as shown on the left bottom of this page.

You can make the pegs from dowels or ornamental pegs (marbles can also be used). Make your Triangle Solitaire more attractive by painting or varnishing the board and pegs.

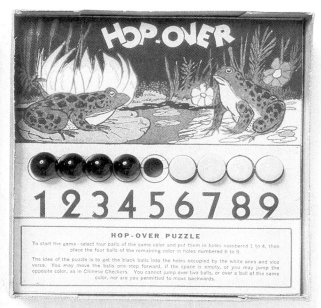

The Hop-Over Puzzle

The names of the puzzles illustrated on this page, Hop-Over and Jumping Frog (Jeu des Grenouilles), could well be used for all the puzzles of this type, as they describe the move that is the basis of the puzzle.

Your own hop-over puzzle is very easy to make. Rule on cardboard a rectangular figure consisting of seven equal spaces, each one inch square. You need six counters or checkers: three red ones and three white ones, for example. (If you use coins, three quarters and three pennies would fit the bill.) Place the three red counters in the spaces to the left and the three white ones in the spaces to the right, leaving the space in the middle unoc-cupied. The aim is to move the red counters to the right and the white ones to the left. The counters may only be moved in a forward direction (i.e. red to the right, white to the left) and only one space at a time. If a counter is divided from a vacant space by a single counter only, it may pass over it into that vacant space.

The Hop-Over puzzle and the Jeu des Grenouilles date from around the turn of the century. For the Hop-Over, you start with four black balls in holes 1-4 and four white balls in holes 6-9. You can move one space or jump over a ball of the opposite color, with the object of reversing the balls - black to white, white to black.

The Jeu des Grenouilles was made in France, by Watilliaux of Paris. Three black frogs are placed on the left and three white ones on the right. The object of the game is to end up with the black frogs on the right and the white ones on the left with a minimum number of moves. This puzzle and its solution were described by Edouard Lucas in 1883 and by Professor Hoffmann in 1893. More examples of puzzles based on the hop-over principle are described and illustrated on page 125.

The Siege of London Puzzle

This puzzle from the Hordern collection is one of several variations of the 8-point star puzzle. The basic puzzle of this type was included in the Bestelmeier Toy Catalog of 1803, described by Lucas and in Hoffmann's Puzzles Old & New, published in 1893. Hoffman's instructions for this puzzle read as follows: 'Given, an eight-pointed star and seven counters. You are required to place the counters on seven of the points of the star (...) Each counter is to be drawn from a vacant point along the corresponding line to another vacant point, and there left. You then start from another vacant point, and proceed in like manner till the seven points are covered.'

The Siege of London puzzle has a map of England with the 8-point star diagram drawn on it. There are seven white counters, each representing a part of the invading army, and one red counter, representing the commander-in-chief. The different groups of soldiers have to get from an open port to one of the opposite unoccupied ports on the same line, without passing through London, and remain stationed there until each port is occupied, except one, from which the commander-in-chief can march on London.

An example: you place a white counter on Newport (the one in Pembrokeshire), march it across the country along the line to Flamborough Head, then on to another port, say Harwich, to Newport, and so on. When all seven counters are 'stationed', and provided all the moves are executed in the right way, there will be one port left open, from which the red counter can move on to London. Why not make your own Siege puzzle? A map of your city or area, a felt-tipped pen and ...away you go!

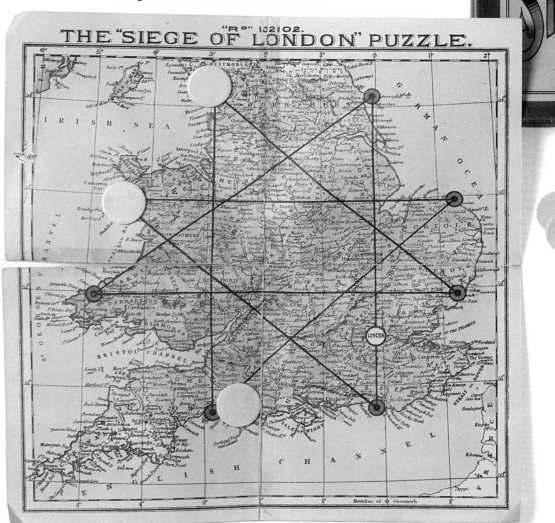

The siege of London (from the Hordern collection) is one of several variations of the 8-point star puzzle. It has a map of England with the 8-point star diagram drawn on it.

Le Moulin Rouge dates from around 1890. It was invented by M. Fleury and made by Mauclair Dacier of Paris. The object of the puzzle is to place the letters in such a way that they form the words 'Le Moulin'.

Le Moulin Rouge

In spite of the picture of the windmill on the box, this is not a Dutch puzzle. The Le Moulin Rouge puzzle was actually named after a famous nightclub in Paris. It was invented by a Frenchman, M. Fleury, and made by Mauclair Dacier, of Paris, around 1890.

First you place the eight letters at random on eight of the nine points. The object of the game is to restore them to their places so that they compose the word Le Moulin. Any letter can be pushed along one of the lines to a vacant place, and those on the mill sails can be moved to or from the central spot. There is no fixed limit to the number of moves, but the idea is to have the broken and disordered word restored to its proper reading around the mill in as few moves as possible.

Question du Jour

The French puzzle Question du Jour (translated: Problem of the day) dates from around 1900. The object of the puzzle is similar to that of Le Moulin Rouge: to get the counters in the corresponding circle (in other words, the circle with the same letter and of the same color) so that the letters end up forming a name, in this case Question du Jour.

You start by placing the blue discs on the red circles, and the red discs on the blue circles, again, of course, in no fixed order. As you can see, two circles remain empty. The discs can be moved forward or backward, but you are not allowed to jump your disc over another disc or to move in between two circles which are not connected by a line. There are many different ways to arrive at the solution. Try and limit your moves to as few as possible.

Far right: The French puzzle Question du Jour was made around 1900. The 14 discs with letters have to be moved in such a way that they end up in their corresponding circles to compose the name Question du Jour.

The So Easy Puzzle

Another example of a sequential movement puzzle. This one, as the name tells you, should be easy for you to solve. It probably dates from

around the 1920's or 1930's and consists of a cardboard box with dyed ivory counters. There are four counters: one blue, one yellow, one red, and one green. You place the counters on the corresponding letters (B=blue, Y=yellow, R=red, G=green). The object of the puzzle is to move the counters to their respective colors without jumping over a counter. Note the immovable partitions and the fact that the counters can move any distance. The solution can be reached in seven moves.

If you want a moment of relaxing with a puzzle that is not too taxing, the So Easy puzzle should come in handy. It consists of an attractive cardboard box and dyed ivory counters.

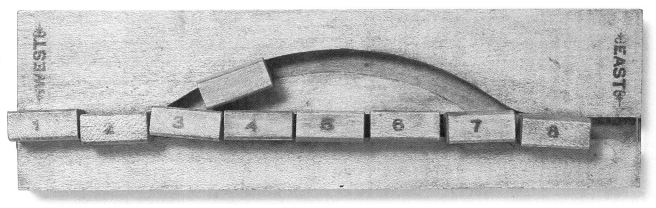

An example of the Shunting Problems, the Switchback Puzzle. In Ball's Mathematical Recreations and Essays, it was called Chifu-Chemulpo Puzzle.

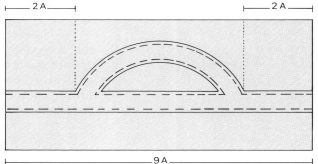

Three layers of wood are required for the making of a shunting puzzle. The diagram on the right is copied on two of them.

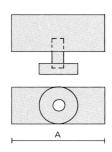

How to make a shunting puzzle

You need three layers of wood measuring 9 x 4 inches. Copy the outline (left) onto two of the three pieces of wood, on one in dotted lines and on the other in straight lines. With a scrollsaw, saw the diagram out along the lines. You can make the puzzle any size you want, but see to it that the dimensions are correct (the diagram indicates the proportions. A = one inch). Glue the three layers on top of each other, the one with the dotted lines on top of the one with the straight lines and both on top of the unmarked one.

The railroad cars you make from 9 small pieces of wood with the dimensions A x ½ A. Drill holes of approximately 1/8'' in the pieces of wood and insert dowels 1/8'' x 3/8''. For the bottom part you can use wooden buttons or small pieces cut out of a dowel. The thickness must always be less than the thickness of one layer of wood. Drill holes in the buttons (or dowel pieces) and glue them onto the dowels inserted in the cars. This construction is used to slide the cars through the layers, as you can see on the photo above and on the diagram. Number the cars 1 to 8. The unmarked piece will be the locomotive.

Shunting Problems

In the old days of railroading, there were few double tracks, turntables, or sidings and the business of marshaling cars and locomotives to assemble a train was far more complex than it is now. The puzzles on this page concern the problems connected with this - hence the name shunting puzzles. The Switchback Puzzle (illustrated above) is probably the best known of these shunting puzzles. In Ball's Mathematical Recreations and Essays it was called the Chifu-Chemulpo Puzzle and it was sold under that name in 1905. Dudeney published this puzzle in 1919 in his book 'Canterbury Puzzles'.

On the track and loop of the Switchback Puzzle are eight railroad cars, (from west to east numbered successively 1 to 8) and one locomotive. The object is to reverse the order of the cars on the track so that (from west to east) they will be numbered successively 8 to 1. There should be as few transferences of the cars or the locomotive to or from the loop as is possible. There is more than one solution and 26 moves are required.

The decorative shunting puzzle illustrated below is British in origin. It consists of metal pieces on a metal board with a turntable, a number of railroad cars and a locomotive. When you start playing, the two arrows on the platform must point toward you. The cars must be in the order 1 to 6 (from west to east). The goal is to reverse the train, leaving it in the same order, in as few moves as possible. It can be done in 19 moves.

A very decorative shunting puzzle from the Hordern collection.

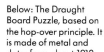

Ten Little Nigger Boys

This sequential movement puzzle, made by the Tin Plate Decorating Co. (U.K.), dates back to 1893. You place 'the boys' in any position at random in the outer circle. The object is to slide them to their corresponding position and finish as shown, without lifting the counters and without two passing each other in the inner circle.

Above: The Ten Little Nigger Boys puzzle A similar puzzle was invented in 1898 by F.H.Donaldson (U.S.).

Below: The Draught Board Puzzle, based on the hop-over principle. It is made of metal and dates from about 1912.

Draught Board Puzzle

This decorative puzzle made of metal is very similar to the Frog puzzle described on page 121 and the Four and Four puzzle described by Hoffmann in Puzzles Old and New. The Draught Board puzzle dates from around 1912 and was designed by Sydenham and McAustra (U.K.). The problem is also very similar to that of the two puzzles mentioned above: to reverse the position of the black and the silver balls, without going over two men at one time.

Far right: The Presidential Muddle Puzzle is, of course, of American origin and dates from 1894. There are 45 possible starting positions.

The Presidential Muddle Puzzle

This sequential movement puzzle dates from 1894. It is very similar to Tait's Counter Puzzle (Hoffmann's Four & Four), which was published by Tait in 1884 and by Nakane in 1743. The puzzle is accompanied by an amusing text, part of which reads: 'I am of American construction, the accident of a train conductor and the genius of success. My best friends to day are those whom I have earned with hardest effort. Those who love me most are those who study me deepest. I have often wished I could smile at the many helpless endeavors to solve me. The more intimately I discerned the inability of men, women and children 'to make me out' the stronger and greater became the proof of their determination not to let me go. I am neither Democrat or Republican, but I am of the opinion that when both parties get tangled up, as is shown in my several combinations, they ought to be separated.'

Don't let this discourage you! The Presidential Muddle may be a bit difficult but impossible it is not.

You start playing by arranging the checkers in any of the 45 possible starting combinations (there are eight on the board), leaving two vacant spaces at one end. The object is to end up with four black checkers on the left and four white ones on the right, or vice versa, and two empty spaces at one end.

How to make the puzzle

The Presidential Muddle Puzzle is made with a piece of plyboard measuring about 12 x 4 inches, a piece of dowel of about 9'', and 16 checkers, 8 black and 8 white. Draw the outline of the slot on the wood following the diagram at the bottom of this page. Drill a small hole through the wood in the area that is going to be removed so that you can pass the fretsaw blade through it. Saw out the slot, and sandpaper its edges. Varnish or paint the frame.

Cut the dowel into eight 1'' sections. Drill a hole ¼ inch wide and ¼ inch deep in the center of each of the checkers. Take four of the black checkers and four of the white ones, and glue one end of a piece of dowel into each. When the glue has set firmly, mount each of these checkers with its attached dowel in the frame and glue a like-colored checker to the free end of the dowel. You can now attempt the puzzle as described.

Sliding Block Puzzles

Sam Loyd, the Prince of Puzzle-Makers, as he was once described. Many puzzle experts still rate Loyd as the best ever and many of his puzzles are as popular today as they were at the time he invented them.

Below: Two pages from Sam Loyd's Cyclopedia of Puzzles together with the puzzle box lid and an early 14-15 puzzle.

No-one seems to know when the first sliding block puzzle was invented or made. What is certain is that in the 1870's, America's greatest puzzle expert, Sam Loyd, "drove the entire world crazy" (as he himself put it) with his newly invented 14-15 puzzle. He offered a $1000 reward to anyone who found the solution and his puzzle created a world-wide interest not seen again until the Rubik's Cube craze swept the world more than 100 years later. The most incredible stories were told of shopkeepers neglecting to open their stores; of a well-known clergyman standing under a street lamp through a frosty winter's night trying to solve the puzzle; of a famous Baltimore editor who went for lunch and was discovered by his staff long past midnight pushing pieces of pie around his plate in a futile attempt to find the solution. Futile because no solution to the puzzle existed. It was impossible! What Loyd had done was to apply a remarkable twist to the Puzzle of Fifteen which at that time was being manufactured and sold by the Embossing Company of New York. This puzzle consisted of 15 numbered blocks placed in a square box. The object was to slide the blocks about, one at a time, until all the blocks were in serial order with the empty space in the lower right hand corner. Loyd realized that half the possible starting positions do not allow the solving of the puzzle because rearrangement of the blocks by sliding them can give rise only to an even number of exchanges. Loyd's idea was as simple as it was brilliant. He changed the positions of the 14 and 15 and challenged the puzzler to get them back in the correct order. Since this would have been equivalent to only a single (and therefore uneven) exchange of blocks, it was therefore impossible. And, of course, Loyd's $1000 was safe! In fact, there are over 600 billion arrangements of the blocks which can be made from the original position and there are an equal number that cannot be made,

including the one Loyd used. Years later both Larry Nichols and Erno Rubik credited the 14-15 puzzle with helping to stimulate their designs of Cube puzzles. The story of Loyd's invention has an amusing sequel, a tale Loyd himself often told. In those days it was necessary to file a working model of a device with an application for a patent. When Loyd applied for a patent he was asked if the positions of the 14 and 15 could be changed. He replied that it was mathematically impossible. The Commissioner, with impeccable logic, retorted "Then you can't have a patent. If the thing won't work, how can you file a working model of it?"

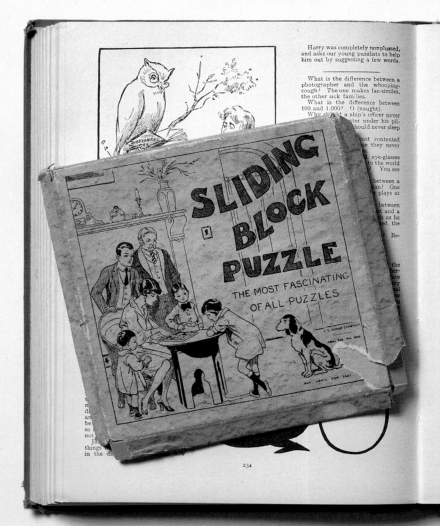

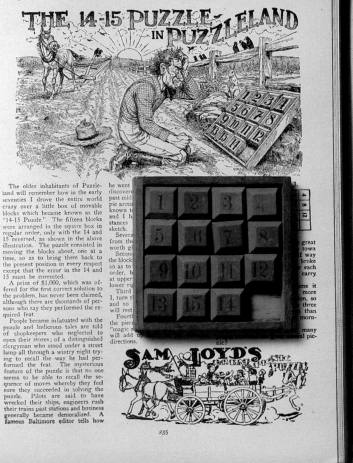

Right: The Get My Goat puzzle, first patented in 1914 in America. The object is to move the goat into the pen. Some later versions copied the design but did not realise that the top right piece must be rectangular. They substituted it with two square pieces, which effectively ruined the idea. For this puzzle to work, pieces 2 and 6 must be identical. There is a solution in 36 moves.

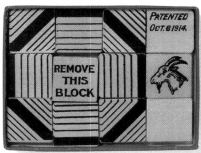

There is a peculiar fascination in pushing pieces of wood or plastic around a board to reach a particular position or achieve a certain objective. Once they have picked them up most people find these kind of puzzles hard to put down. But what exactly are 'sliding block' puzzles?

Edward Hordern, an expert on sliding block puzzles, whose book entitled Sliding Piece Puzzles will be published by Oxford University Press in 1986, defines a sliding block puzzle as a group of pieces of any shape(s) enclosed within a confined area, in which the purpose is to rearrange the pieces either into a certain order or to get a particular piece to a specified position. This is accomplished by sliding the pieces or 'blocks', usually one at a time, into areas not occupied by other pieces. The lifting of pieces is never allowed, nor must they hop or jump over other pieces. Finally, rotation of individual pieces is only allowed if specifically stated. Some puzzles contain obstacles or immovable barriers. Others introduce restrictions: for example, pieces may have to follow specific routes or there may be a requirement that certain pieces do not touch certain other pieces. Sometimes a piece may not be allowed to move at all.

Since Sam Loyd's famous 14-15 puzzle, literally hundreds, perhaps thousands of sliding block puzzles have come on the market. A great many of them have been puzzles which have no set start position. It is usually required only to muddle up the pieces to 'set' the puzzle. Most of these, when solved, form some kind of picture or design. Using rectangular pieces among square ones was an idea which originated around 1909. These puzzles are usually much more difficult than puzzles consisting only of square pieces. Neither have they been mathematically analyzed. Short of trial and error, no-one knows how to determine if a given state is obtainable from another given state, and if it is, no-one knows how to find the minimum chain of moves for achieving the desired state. This is still a challenge for the computer programmers.

This rather neat puzzle is based on Sam Loyd's 14-15 puzzle which was produced in the 1870's. In place of 14-15, we see that the last two letters of the word PAL have been exchanged to read PLA. The puzzle is to change them back again. According to Loyd exchanging two blocks is a mathematical impossibility. But there is a way of doing the puzzle (without ripping the pieces out!). We won't spoil your fun by telling you the secret. But we will give you a clue. One exchange (LA) is impossible. But two are not. Think about it!

Right: The Puzzle of Fifteen dated October 1865, is the earliest known sliding block puzzle and predates Sam Loyd's 14-15 Puzzle by at least 8 years. The object was to scramble the numbers and then rearrange them in serial order so that the bottom right square was empty. Sam Loyd adapted this puzzle to invent his famous puzzle which "drove the entire world crazy". The Popular 15 Puzzle was manufactured by the International Card Co., London, U.K.

More sliding block puzzles

Loyd drove the entire world crazy because no-one realised for some time that his puzzle was imposssible to solve. Mathematicians wanted to find out why. Further they wanted to know the principle that governed possible and impossible positions. To find the number of arrangements of the pieces is easy enough. That is the result you arrive at by multiplying 15 x 14 x 13...x 2 x 1. We'll leave you to work it out. But it's an awful lot. It turned out that exactly half of all possible arrangements (to be reached from a given start position) were possible and half were not. There is a very easy way of finding if any position can be reached from another. This is what mathematicians call a parity check. Exchange any two pieces (by lifting them); repeat as often as it is necessary to transform any given arrangement to the desired one; count the number of exchanges.

If the number is odd, it is impossible, if it is even, it is possible. This check works for all puzzles with identical size pieces in a square or rectangular arrangement. Sometimes it can be extended to puzzles with some rectangular pieces. The parity principle has been used to advantage in the design of several puzzles to make them more difficult. The RATE YOUR MIND PLA puzzle is a good example. By including two pieces with the same letter the puzzle can be made impossible to solve unless the positions of the two identical pieces are exchanged (by sliding). Once this has been done, it is then possible to reverse the positions of the L and A, so making RATE YOUR MIND PAL. Darn it! Now we've gone and given the secret away and spoiled your fun. Or maybe you were intrigued enough to figure it out before you turned over to this page.

On these pages you can see a few of the sliding block puzzles which have

Right: The Boss Puzzle is the name generally given to Sam Loyd's 14-15 puzzle. The one shown here is from the Hordern Collection. It consists of ceramic pieces in a metal box with a leather insert on top of the lid. It was made in Germany. The Fifteen Puzzle gave rise to a popular song of the day - *The Wonderful Puzzle Fifteen* which was part of a burlesque drama *The Forty Thieves*. In the song, the singer's lady friend promises her 'heart and hand' if he manages to get the pieces in the right order. Of course, he always gets stuck!

been on the market over the years. Opposite page: 16 and 34 dates from 1950 and was made by Plas-Trix Co., Brooklyn, NY. It is a variation of the 15 puzzle. The number 16 is pressed in the box at each piece location so the vacant space always reads '16'. The 34 puzzle requires forming a magic square so that the total of the numbers in each row, column, and diagonal adds to 34.

Opposite page below: The Boss Puzzle is the name usually given to Loyd's 14-15 puzzle.

Top left: L'iL Abner was one of a set of Picto Puzzles produced by Plas-Trix Co., Brooklyn, NY. The object is to disarrange by making 15 moves and then rearrange. 30 minutes was reckoned par for the course.

Bottom left: Solvit dates from 1906 and was made by E.Y. Horder, Chicago, Ill. The picture of a baseball game appears when you slide the pieces.

Center below: The Spirit of St Louis dates from 1927 and was designed by Edward H. Anshelm. The name of Lindbergh's history-making plane is spelled out when the puzzle is solved.

Below right center: These are two more modern sliding block puzzles. The Da Vinci Puzzle and Wonder Woman Puzzle are made by the American Publishing Corp., Watertown, Mass.

Bottom right: The Crossword Addict is made by in England by Dodo Design. There are clues on the back and when you have solved those you have to rearrange the letters to make the answers. Strikes us as diabolical.

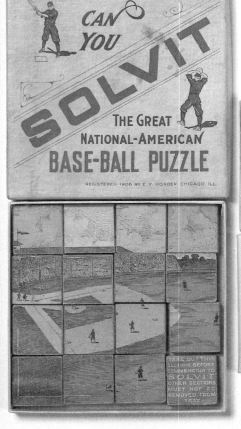

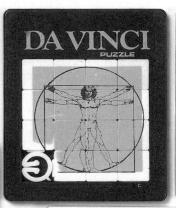

On these pages, a number of variations on the basic 14-15 Puzzle.

THE CROSSWORD ADDICT PUZZLE

Solve this CROSSWORD by rearranging the tiles. Clues to help you are on the back.

Dad's Puzzle first appeared in 1909 and may have been the first to use rectangular pieces. Since its introduction it has become one of the most commercialized of all sliding block puzzles.

Here are 12 versions which have appeared over the years.

Top row, left to right:
(1) The "Teaser" E&S (Copyright) England. (2) Dad's Puzzler. Advertising for Independent Oil, by Valley Oil Co., Conn. (3) Eskimo Pie Puzzle. Advertisement for ice cream by Eskimo Pie Corp., Louisville, KY.

2nd row, left to right:
(4) The Moving Puzzle. Advertising for Bekins Van & Storage Co. (5) Dad's Puzzler. Made by The Standard Trailer Co., Cambridge Springs, PA. Copyright J.W.Hayward, 1926. 6) Dad's Puzzler. Inside it advertises Ma's Puzzle and Flying Puzzle.

3rd row, left to right:
(7) The Moving Puzzle. Advertising for Argonne Van and Storage Co., Los Angeles, California. Copyright F.E.Aaron, 1927.
(8) The Moving Puzzle (lid of box on the left) says Can You Solve Our Moving Puzzle? We Can Solve Yours.
(9) The Humdinger Puzzle. Made by Wood Products Sales Co., York, PA.

4th row, left to right:
(10) The Moving Puzzle. Advertisement for Argonne Fireproof Storage Co. Copyright F.E.Aaron, 1927.
(11) It Can Be Done (inside box) Copyright 1926, J.W.Hayward. Advertising food for Merritt, Critchley & Co., New York.
(12) The Moving Puzzle. Advertisement for Bekins Van & Storage Co. Copyright F.E.Aaron, 1927.

The Tit-Bits Teaser No. 4

This is one of a whole series of Traffic Jam Puzzles which introduce L-shaped pieces. This significantly increases the difficulty. The puzzler is asked to imagine that he is sitting in his car, A, and has to reach his home in the bottom right-hand corner. As always the puzzle is 'What is the smallest number of moves necessary?' This puzzle was patented in America in 1928 by F.L.Babcock. In 1931, it was used in Britain as a competition puzzle by the makers of Van Houten's Cocoa in conjunction with Geo.Newnes Ltd., the proprietors of the very popular magazine, Tit-Bits. A total of £850 in prizes was offered, with a first prize of £100 - a great deal of money in Britain in 1931. We have no record of the lucky winner, or of how close he or she came to the correct solution. But the lowest number of moves anyone has been able to do it in so far is 132. A similar puzzle begins with car A almost home yet needing 263 moves!

The Flying Puzzle

This puzzle for armchair aviators first appeared in 1928 and was inspired by Charles Lindbergh's great transatlantic flight of the previous year. The puzzle player was invited to imagine himself facing the dangers of rain, fog and wind without having to leave the comfort of his own chair. The square block representing the airplane starts in the left-hand top corner, marked New York, and must be moved to the bottom right-hand corner, marked Paris. Since the vacant space is only half as big as the block representing the airplane, the plane can only be advanced by half its own width or height at a time. In this puzzle, a simultaneous move by two pieces counts as a single move; as do two consecutive moves by one piece. The Flying Puzzle can be solved in 31 moves. If we take Hordern's definition of a move as being the shifting of one piece only in any direction or combination of directions, then 55 moves are needed.

How to make a Sliding Block Puzzle

Making sliding block puzzles is easy, especially after you have tackled some of the wood interlocking puzzles described earlier. The simplest material to use is paper. The pieces can be cut out in seconds and they can be confined to the required area simply by drawing a 'box' on another piece of paper. Thin colored card is better and just as quick to cut. Best of all is to use birch plywood, or a hardwood such as mahogany. The pieces are marked and cut using the grid shown below. Sand the edges and round off the corners with a rasp. This allows the pieces to slide freely without the corners catching each other. Now make a wooden tray just bigger than the assembled pieces, again to allow freedom of movement. As a rough guide, Edward Hordern suggests leaving an extra margin of one quarter of the dimension of the smallest piece. A rectangle of plywood forms the base and thin strips are glued on to form the sides.

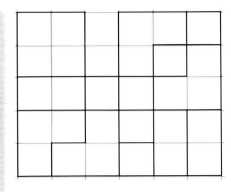

To add the finishing touch oil or varnish your pieces. If you base your pieces on a particular dimensional unit you should be able to work out a system where one box can be used for several puzzles. You could also make pieces from different colored plastics. Plastic isn't the easiest material to work with, especially when it comes to rounding off the corners. But it will give you a colorful and durable puzzle. Why not try your hand at designing your own sliding block puzzle? Make a simple one to begin with and later a more complex one.

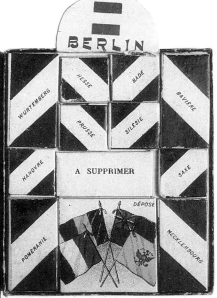

Ma's Puzzle was first marketed in 1927. It is noteworthy in that it has two L-shaped pieces and a vacant space that can be divided into two parts. As you might guess, the object is to bring Ma and My Boy together in spite of the tribulations shown on the other blocks. The L-shaped pieces are united to form a rectangle in the top right-corner.

Both World Wars produced a crop of puzzles designed to whip up patriotic fervor. During World II, for example, sliding block puzzles with names like A Yank Thru the Lines and Bombing Tokyo enjoyed great popularity. The two puzzles illustrated on this page date from World War I, however, and come from opposite sides of the Atlantic. The one shown above, Eureka, is French in origin. The box lid shows flags of the Allied nations and poses 'the most passionate question of the day':

How shall the Allies enter Berlin? In the instructions it says that a little patience and reflection is needed before this can be achieved! The Preparedness Puzzle, shown below, comes from the other side of the Atlantic. It was made by the L&S Novelty Company, of Lancaster, PA. It is not dated, but appears to be prior to World War I, which the United States entered in April, 1917. Preparedness was a national issue from 1915 onwards. The puzzle is the same as Dad's Puzzler but under each block's starting position lies a stirring motto such as 'Patience is a virtue. Be patient.' It was intended to demonstrate that things that appear easiest often prove to be the most difficult, and thus to warn against the complacency which leads us to confront difficulties without adequate preparation.

The other two puzzles shown on this page are similar to the ones already described. The one shown above is the daddy of so many commercial puzzles, Dad's Puzzler. This one was made by Henry Ettinger, a Repair Department craftsman for Tiffany & Company, of New York. The other is Japanese in origin. Again it is an extension of Dad's Puzzler. If two of the two-by-one rectangles in that puzzle are cut in half to make four unit squares, the resulting eleven pieces provide the sliding blocks for an even more difficult puzzle. The object is to move the large square piece to the bottom center so that it can be slid out of the box.

Right: The Preparedness Puzzle is one of the many puzzles with a patriotic theme which were produced during both World Wars. It shows a determined looking Uncle Sam and carries several patriotic slogans.

Far right: The Japanese puzzle is one of a group of puzzles similar to a 1932 patent by J.H. Fleming, although it may have originated earlier in France, under the title ''L'Ane Rouge''.

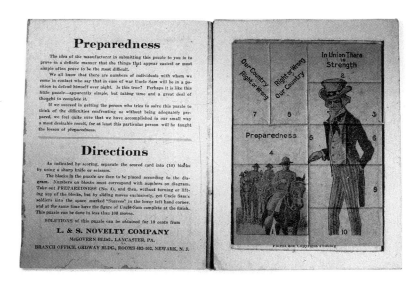

The Century of Progress Puzzle is also based on Dad's Puzzler. It was produced in 1933 to mark Chicago's 100th anniversary.

Line up the Quinties was produced a year later, in 1934. This pretty puzzle marked the birth of the Dionne quintuplets. the world's first surviving fivesome.

Below: Les Bourgeois Punis Puzzle is a sequential counting puzzle in which the object is to get the townsmen to settle the bill after an evening's drinking.

Century of Progress Puzzle

In 1933 Chicago marked its 100-year anniversary with the Century of Progress Exposition. This exposition emphasized science and industry and it was an outstanding success. The Century of Progress Puzzle was produced to commemorate the event. Its original pieces were East, West, airplanes, automobiles, world wonders, machinery, inventions, progress, century, Chicago, you and see. The puzzle was to move either East or West to the bottom left-hand corner. This could be done in 37 and 42 moves respectively.

Les Bourgeois Punis

The manufacturer of Les Bourgeois Punis, which dates from around 1900, is unknown. In this puzzle it is supposed that eight students and two townsmen are enjoying a convivial evening together. When the time comes to pay the tab, the students suggest sitting around the table and counting so that every nth person leaves. The two remaining at the end pay the bill. Of course, being students they were quite intelligent and they quickly devised a method of ensuring that the two unfortunate townsmen were left holding the baby - and the bill! This sliding block puzzle is related to a problem that dates back to Roman times. According to the story, a certain Josephus and forty Jews took refuge in a cave after their city had been captured. All the Jews, ex-

cept Josephus and one other man, resolved to kill themselves. Josephus pretended to agree and suggested that they stand in a circle. Every third person should be killed until there was only one left, who would then commit suicide. It is said that he placed himself and the other man in the 31st and 16th positions, thus saving both their lives. Many problems have been based on this principle and it is not difficult to see that in such a method there must be one or more 'safe' positions, no matter which number is used to count place. In fact, the students reversed the procedure and made sure that the two townsmen were in the so-called safe positions, which turned out to be not quite so safe after all!

Line Up The Quinties

This puzzle was created in 1934 by Richard W. Fatiguant to celebrate the birth of the world's first surviving quintuplets, the Dionnes. The object is to line up the quints along the center row and move the flowers to the top and bottom rows as shown. The vacant squares lie in opposite corners. The puzzle was made by The Embossing Company, Albany, New York.

River Crossing Problems

Puzzlers have long been fascinated by problems involving the crossing of rivers. As long ago as the 8th century, Alcuin, a great scholar and cleric, proposed puzzles similar to that of ferrying the goat, wolf and cabbages which appears below. A thousand years later the citizens of Königsberg asked themselves whether it would be possible to walk across all the bridges of the city without retracing their steps. The great mathematician, Euler, analysed the problem and proved the proposed tour was impossible, so founding a new branch of math called topology. Of the two river crossing problems proposed here, one is very easy and one is quite difficult. Let's begin with the easy one. Suppose a farmer has to cross a river in a boat big enough to carry only him and either his goat, the wolf or the cabbages. The cabbages will be eaten if they are left with the goat and the goat will be eaten if it is left with the wolf. How does the farmer manage it?

The Capital and Labor puzzle was made in 1910 by the Arbiter Co., Philadelphia. The solution is as follows: First number the men from 1 - 6, starting with the Capitalists. The sequence is then: 1 takes over 2 and brings the boat back.
1 takes over 3 and brings the boat back.
4 and 5 go over and 4 brings back 2.
4 takes over 1 and brings back 3.
4 and 6 go over and 1 brings the boat back.
1 takes over 2 and brings the boat back.
1 takes over 3.
The only complaint we had was that poor old 1, a soft-handed Capitalist, finished up with blisters. 4 did a lot of rowing too, but being a horny-handed Laborer, it didn't bother him one little bit!

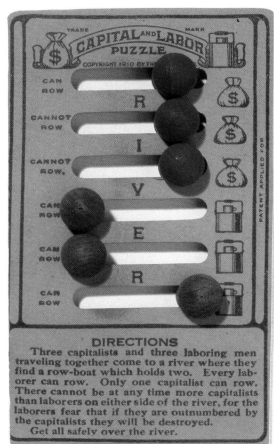

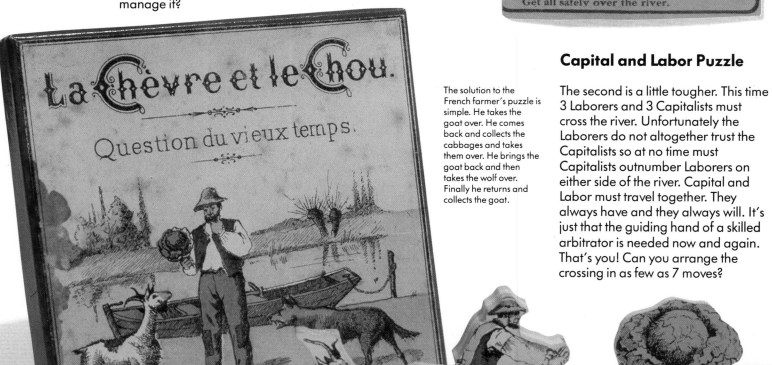

The solution to the French farmer's puzzle is simple. He takes the goat over. He comes back and collects the cabbages and takes them over. He brings the goat back and then takes the wolf over. Finally he returns and collects the goat.

Capital and Labor Puzzle

The second is a little tougher. This time 3 Laborers and 3 Capitalists must cross the river. Unfortunately the Laborers do not altogether trust the Capitalists so at no time must Capitalists outnumber Laborers on either side of the river. Capital and Labor must travel together. They always have and they always will. It's just that the guiding hand of a skilled arbitrator is needed now and again. That's you! Can you arrange the crossing in as few as 7 moves?

The Tower of Hanoi

In the great temple of Benares, so legend has it, are 64 golden disks, all of different sizes and mounted on three diamond pegs. At the time of Creation, the god Brahma placed all the disks on one peg, in order of size with the largest at the bottom. The task of the temple priests is to transfer the disks unceasingly from peg to peg, one at a time, never placing a larger disk on a smaller one. When all the disks have been transferred the universe will end. But there's no need to worry just yet. If the priests transfer one disc a second, day and night, it will still take them many thousands of millions of years to complete their task.

The Tower of Brahma, or the Tower of Hanoi, as it is sometimes called, was the invention of Edouard Lucas and was sold as a toy in France in 1883. The legend of the temple of Benares is also his invention. The puzzle is reduced to more manageable proportions if we consider fewer disks than the 64 in the legend. It is easy to prove that the number of moves required for a given number of disks is $2^N - 1$, where n is the number of discs. Thus, eight disks could be transferred from one peg to the second in only 255 moves. If you move the disks at the same speed as the legendary priests, the job will be finished in $4\frac{1}{4}$ minutes flat! Considerably before the end of the universe - or at least let's hope so!

The Pyladisk Puzzle made by The Embossing Company, New York. This is an eight disk Tower of Hanoi.

The Eight Puzzle was copyrighted in 1887 by Edward A. Filene. It is an advertising version of the Tower of Hanoi. A variety of products were advertised in the eight disks which made up the puzzle.

The Brain, made by Mag-Nif, is another form of the Tower with eight rings. The black pins, when moved from the inner to the outer position, are equivalent to removing a ring.

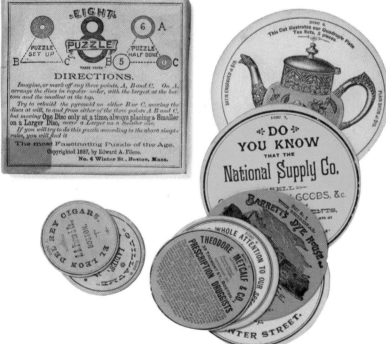

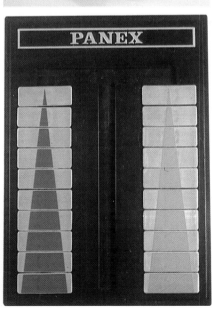

The fiendishly difficult Panex Puzzle is manufactured in Japan. Its solution is so difficult that no-one knows the minimum number of moves necessary to solve it.

The Panex Puzzle

A few years ago a Japanese Magic Company produced a fiendish elaboration of the Tower of Hanoi puzzle. The company called it the Panex Puzzle and it is so difficult that the smallest number of moves needed to solve it remains unknown. Several top mathematicians at the Bell Laboratories have been working on the theory behind the Panex Puzzle, but so far the best they have managed to do is to prove a lower (27,564) and an upper (31,537) bound to the number of moves needed.

The puzzle looks deceptively simple. It consists of a flat plastic panel with three vertical grooves joined at the top by a horizontal groove. Lying in the left-hand groove are ten rectangular plastic pieces. Ten pieces of a different color lie in the right-hand groove. The trick is to change the two columns of pieces over by using the middle groove. Sounds easy. The secret lies in the mechanism which prevents some of the pieces sliding where you want them too!

Pike's Peak or Bust, a sequential movement puzzle made around 1895 by Parker Brothers (Salem, Mass.). The goal is to reach the top of the mountain with the help of the metal 'traveler'.

Maze and Route Puzzles

A famous sequential movement puzzle, Pike's Peak or Bust was patented by Judson M. Fuller around 1894 and made by Parker Brothers of Salem, Massachusets.
The cardboard box of the puzzle contains a wooden board with the drawing of the mountain glued on it. The metal hook with the string are hooked on the nails protruding from the board. It goes without saying that the aim is to get to the top of Pike's Peak. This is done with the metal 'traveler'. Encircle the pin at the base with one end of the traveler, then with the other end encircle any pin it will exactly reach. Continue spanning from pin to pin and proceed until the highest point is reached by one end of the traveler. The traveler spans easily to any pin it is intended to reach. Don't try to twist or stretch it because you think it is inaccurate.
On the box of Pike's Peak or Bust, these encouraging words: 'It can be done. It's lots of fun. You'll say so when you've begun.'

Africa Puzzle

At the bottom left of this page, the original and decorative Africa puzzle. It is made of tin and consists of a layout of the African continent and a lion. The aim is to 'get the lion out of Africa'. The animal is placed with his feet in a maze, from which he has to be extricated. This is done by moving him through the slots - or the gaps at both ends of the slots - in the maze. Since the lion is always spanning two slots (front legs in one, hind legs in another), the distance between his feet determines which way he can move.

The Eclipse

The puzzle game The Eclipse was copyrighted in 1936 by Myart Mfg. Co. of New York, N.Y. It features a golden disk and, as the name tells us, a sky with a moon. You start playing by placing the disk on the starting point 'S'. Without lifting the disk from the board, move it through the various nails until the moon 'F' is covered, thus completing the eclipse. The disk must not be forced through the nails.

Below left: The Africa puzzle, made of tin, features a lion to be extricated from a maze.

Below right: The aim of the puzzle game The Eclipse, dating from 1936, is to cover the moon with the golden disk.

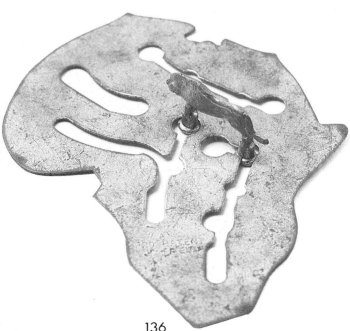

136

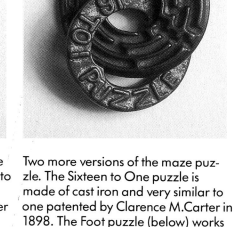

Above: Ring for Mistress was made by Loncraine Broxton & partners of Stamford, England, and dates from 1883.
The object of the puzzle is to move the ring from the large hole until it reaches the ring finger.

The Maze Medal

This maze puzzle dates from 1888 and is made of brass. It was described in Puzzles Old & New by Professor Hoffmann and is somewhat more complicated than most maze puzzles. The ring which has to be moved through the maze is detached from

the medal when you start solving the problem and the puzzle is to get it into the hole marked 'home'.
We're giving you a break, or, in other words, the solution:
Insert the ring at point A and slide the open portion along into the space marked 1. Now turn the ring around till the opening comes outside the

Two more versions of the maze puzzle. The Sixteen to One puzzle is made of cast iron and very similar to one patented by Clarence M.Carter in 1898. The Foot puzzle (below) works on the same principle as the Ring for Mistress.

The attractive Bolt Maze Puzzle was patented in 1972 by the American Marvin I. Glass, and is 12 inches high. It is beyond doubt an extremely ingenious maze puzzle. Here the maze is in the screw thread and the problem is to unscrew the nut from the bolt via the series of spaced-apart annular grooves that form the maze.

medal; pass it in again at point B and slide it along till the opening reaches the hole 2. Turn the opening back to 1, and from there slide it into the hole marked 3. Turn the opening back to 2, then slide the ring into hole 4. Continue this way until you are back at A, at the outside of the medal. Then work the opening back to 6 and pass it, along the dotted line, into the final hole - HOME. To extricate the ring, proceed in precisely the reverse order.

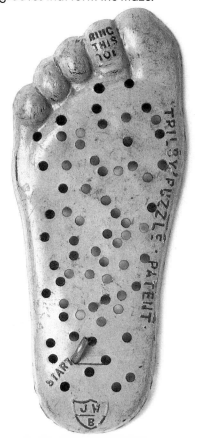

Rubik's (or Nichols'*) Cube

Rubik's cube or not Rubik's cube?* That is the question! Erno Rubik's patent for the cube puzzle was issued in Hungary in 1976 and was the basis for the licensed puzzle which Ideal Toy Company sold worldwide. However, a Massachusetts chemist named Larry Nichols came up with a 2 x 2 x 2 cube puzzle in 1957 and his patent for cube puzzles was issued in 1972. In 1984 he won a federal patent infringement suit against Ideal Toy Corp., which sold millions of the cubes in the early 1980's. The court ruled that Nichols' patent was valid and infringed by Ideal Toy's sale of Rubik's cubes. So there we are. In the U.S., at least, Rubik's cube is now officially Nichols' cube.

The Cube gave birth to a thriving industry, spawning dozens of variations and new sequential movement puzzles of all shapes and sizes, books and even a hit record. It is possibly the only puzzle that has ever appeared on a postage stamp.

Cubitis magikia (Rubikmania), n. A severe mental disorder accompanied by an itching of the fingertips that can be relieved only by prolonged contact with a multicolored cube originating in Hungary. Symptoms last for months. Highly contagious.

The Rubikmania 'disease' reached epidemic proportions in the early 1980's. In offices, in bars, in parks, in the subway, no matter where one went, it seemed that everybody in the world was twiddling the cube. The former mayor of an English city was operated on for tenditis of the thumb after a long cube twiddling session. A German woman sued for divorce after giving her husband a cube as a gift and then finding he was so obsessed with it he had no time for her. A postal engineer wrote that cube playing had reduced the efficiency of his office to zero, but that 'being a government department, no one noticed'. If the cube had been around in his day, Nero would doubtlessly have twiddled while Rome burned. At the height of its popularity the cube had become a minor industry, spawning dozens of variations and solution manuals by the score. At one point three of the top five books on the New York Times Bestseller list were solution books for the cube. The craze hit the height of absurdity when 'Mr Rubik', recorded by the Baron Knights, became a hit. Naturally enough, all this hype provoked a backlash. A Californian company produced what they called 'the ultimate solution': the Cube Smasher, a plastic paddle guaranteed to smash the puzzle to bits. Books with titles such as Not another Cube Book and 101 Uses for a Dead Cube began to appear. Slowly but surely the world returned to normal.

Büvös Kocka (the Magic Cube) took the puzzle world, the mathematics world and the computing world by storm soon after it appeared in the late 70's. Rarely has a puzzle fired the imagination of so many people, perhaps not since Sam Loyd's famous 14-15 Puzzle, which is supposed to have driven hundreds of people mad when it first came out.

The cube is certainly one of the best and most elegant puzzles ever made. It is self contained, colorful, a simple shape and it is obvious what the puzzle is. The twisting motion is natural and satisfying. The cube puzzle is rich in metaphors as is shown by its use in describing events in such diverse worlds as politics and particle physics. In fact, the 14-15 Puzzle and the cube are very similar puzzles, the one being a two-dimensional problem of restoring the scrambled numbered pieces of a 4 x 4 square to their proper positions and the other being a three-dimensional problem of restoring the scrambled colored pieces of a 3 x 3 x 3 cube to their proper positions. The Hungarian cube was developed in 1974 by Erno Rubik, a Hungarian professor of architecture, to give his students greater experience in dealing with three-dimensional objects. It has six sides, each of a different color. Each side is divided into three rows, each row into three smaller cubes. Each row can be made to rotate 360° so that one can twiddle the cube from top to bottom and from side to side. The aim is to scramble the colors by rotating at random (that's the easy bit) and then manipulate them back the way they were (that's the bit that drives you crazy). In fact, if you twiddle at random, you could spend the rest of your life playing about before you find the solution. Potential color patterns number

43,252,003,274,489,856,000, and it would take the most modern computer 1.4 million years to figure out all the possible combinations. But take heart, it can be done!

It is known that the cube can certainly be solved in fewer than 50 twists and some people think that it could be done in as few as 20. Approaching the problem from another direction, many cube addicts concentrated on speed, some even taking their cubes apart and 'tuning' them by lubricating the moving parts. Some whizz kids can unscramble the cube in less than 30 seconds. There are dozens of books on the market, all of them offering sequential move solutions. So if you can't do it, we advise you to buy one.

Puzzle Vessels

When we began to research the origin and history of puzzles for this book, we found to our surprise that the ancient Phoenicians and Greeks made puzzle vessels of several types. This makes them one of the oldest known forms of the mechanical puzzle. Among Phoenician pottery found in Cyprus in the 1870's were several vases which filled from small holes in the bottom. Several of these are included in the 'Treasure of Curium', which form part of the Cesnola Collection in the Metropolitan Museum of Art in New York. Puzzle drinking vessels made in Greece in the 5th century B.C. worked in much the same way as the earlier pieces found in Cyprus. During the 1st century A.D., Hero of Alexandria and Philo made several puzzle or trick pitchers for wine or water. The development of these vessels reached a remarkable peak in Turkey during the 9th century. This is well documented in The Book of Ingenious Devices which describes almost one hundred very sophisticated pneumatic and mechanically-operated puzzle and trick vessels, designed primarily by Ahmad Musa Bin Shakar of Bagdad. One of the principles used in the puzzle pottery made by the Phoenecians and Greeks, filling through a hole and tube in the bottom, is found much later in Chinese wine pots of the early 18th century and in Cadogan teapots wich were first made at the Rockingham pottery in England in 1806.

1 2 3 4 5 6

Right: A John Lowndes puzzle jug from 1859 which has the figure of a man in the center hole. The handle has been broken and repaired and it doesn't work any more.

Below, left to right:
(7) A Snake Pottery jug from 1974. An amusing inscription says that the pot's contents may be fit for a parson but trying to drink them will try the patience of a saint.
(8) An Austrian-made English souvenir. It is a copy of a puzzle jug in a London museum.
(9) Pentangle jug, in stoneware, made in 1972 by the St. Mary Bourne pottery.
(10) A set of fuddling cups from the Snake Pottery. The idea is to fill all three and then drink one without spilling the liquid in the other two. As all three are interlinked this is difficult - but it can be done!
(11) This jug was made in Ashbourne, England, and dates from 1861. It once belonged to William Lees.

The trick in drinking from puzzle jugs or glasses is not to spill the contents. These vessels have a lattice or a series of holes around the top and the liquid spills if you try to drink in the conventional manner. The trick is to discover a hidden or disguised tube which is then used like a straw to suck the liquid out. The remaining holes are covered with the fingers. Jugs using this syphon principle were made in the wine-growing region of Bordeaux, in France, as long ago as the 13th century. They were sometimes sent to England with wine shipments. Similar jugs were made in England, the Netherlands and Germany during the 16th, 17th and 18th centuries. One of the techniques used in the Greek amphorae of the 4th century B.C. and in those made by Hero of Alexandria in the 1st century is that of concealing a 'control hole' in the handle. This technique has been used in puzzle pitchers made in England in the 18th and 19th centuries. When the vessel is filled, the contents will not drain out of a hole in the bottom unless the vessel is tilted back toward the handle. The liquid will then continue to drain, even though the vessel is tilted in other directions, until a 'controle hole' hidden on the inside of the handle is covered by the pourer's finger. Presumably these vessels were used to play a trick on some unsuspecting friend.

7   8   9   10   11

Dexterity Puzzles

Dexterity puzzles have been popular for centuries in many different cultures and civilizations. Although they are often called games, they are puzzles since they are solved by only one person and are based on the use of manual dexterity. Many different types of puzzles are based on the use of manual dexterity for a solution. These types include Throw and Catch, Mazes with Balls, Glass Topped Rolling Ball Puzzles and many more. Long ago, dexterity puzzles often required skill related to survival and may have been used to teach eye-hand coordination and other hunting skills to children. In the pre-Columbian Americas, one of the most popular of them was Pommawonga (Spear The Fish). Its variations were endless; its name changed as the toy was altered and its construction was modified depending upon the natural materials at hand. The Indians had many versions of the toss-and-catch dexterity puzzle and Eskimos in Alaska used walrus ivory to make a skill puzzle called Gazinta, which consisted of a spike and washers. Today the Cup-and-Ball is thought of as a traditional folk toy of Mexico, but its original home probably lies in the

East. The Flip-Ball played in ancient China is believed to be the forerunner of the Cup-and-Ball toy of the Western world. Other reports trace the game back to ancient Greece and Italy. The puzzle is known to have been very popular in France - where it was called Bilboquet - in the 16th, 17th, and 18th centuries. It was probably one of the first puzzle crazes. In the United States, in February 1889, Charles Crandall started producing a rolling ball puzzle called Pigs in Clover. This dexterity puzzle took the country and the world by storm almost instantly. Crandall may have gotten his idea for Pigs in Clover from a British wooden puzzle of a very similar design. An example made of turned elm is described in Edward H.Pinto's book 'Treen and Other Wooden Bygones'. Pinto dates the puzzle around 1840.

On these pages, many versions of the dexterity puzzle are illustrated, a large number dating from around 1900.

Above: Bilboquet was the rage in 16th century France. Many were the victims of the Cup-and-Ball passion. In this print (owned by Radio Times Hulton Picture Library), the normal business of the day has been forgotten as the citizens play the game that obsessed even Henry III of France.

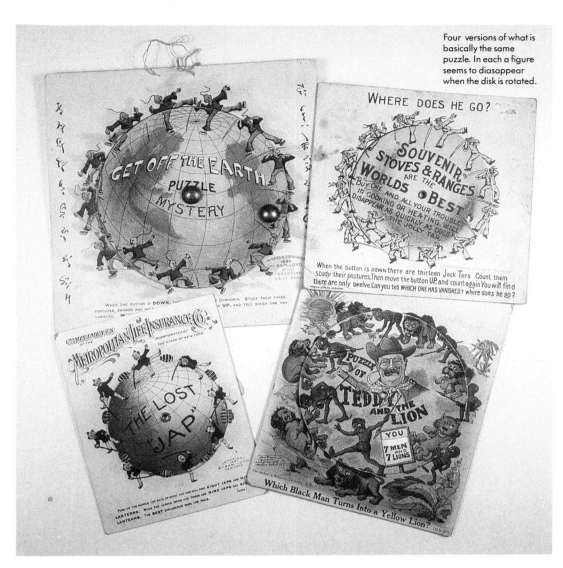

Four versions of what is basically the same puzzle. In each a figure seems to diasappear when the disk is rotated.

paradox try a 'line vanishing' version yourself. Draw ten parallel lines on a piece of paper. Join the bottom of the first line to the top of the last by a dotted line. Cut along this diagonal and slide the lower part downward and to the left by one position. Now you have only nine lines! This increase is so small that you do not see it. In 1880, Wemple and Company of New York used a similar principle in the Magic Egg Puzzle. An illustration of a hen and nine eggs was cut into four pieces. These pieces could be rearranged to show 6, 7, 8, 10, 11 or 12 eggs. This puzzle may well inspired Sam Loyd to produce what many think was his greatest achievement, his Get off the Earth Puzzle. It appeared in 1896 and was enormously popular. It consisted of a brightly colored miniature world revolving on a central pin. Thirteen figures of Chinamen could be clearly seen. When the world was rotated, one figure mysteriously vanished, leaving only twelve. This baffling puzzle has a simple explanation. The men, as they cross the circumference of the circle, spiral towards its center. Each man sends forward a larger section of his anatomy than he receives from his neighbor, thus producing the accumulated figure at the end of the line.

Vanishing Puzzles

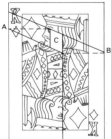

The Magic Playing Card. Mark the playing card exactly as shown and cut it. Piece C can be thrown away. The remaining four pieces can be rearranged to make a complete card! Do this with the face of the card downwards. Then turn it over and show it face up, with the piece missing!

There are many geometric paradoxes which involve the dissection and rearranging of parts of a figure. When the rearrangement is completed, a portion of the original figure (either part of its area or one of a series of pictures drawn on the figure) has apparently vanished without a trace! When the pieces are further rearranged to their original form, the missing area or picture mysteriously appears again. Magic? No, just a fascinating type of puzzle.

The elementary paardox of an apparently disappearing area is very old. William Hooper, in his book Rational Recreations, published in 1794, described the paradox as 'The Geometric Money'.

As an aid to understanding the

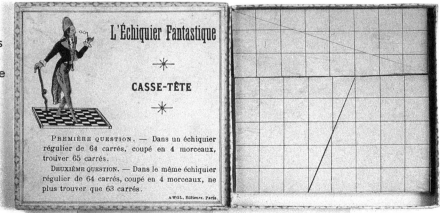

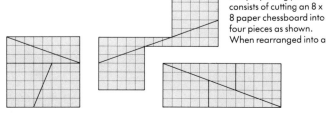

This perplexing puzzle consists of cutting an 8 x 8 paper chessboard into four pieces as shown. When rearranged into a rectangle, the 64 small squares seem to have increased to 65! When rearranged into the figure shown in the center, there seem to be only 63!
L'Echiquier Fantastique made by A WGL, Paris, around 1900, is a wood version of this puzzle.

Impossible Object Puzzles

The puzzle for all the impossible objects on this page is to explain how they were made. They are not intended to come apart, although some puzzlers have taken them apart into many pieces by extreme force in extreme frustration. One fact is given to eliminate the only obvious and easy solution - no glue or adhesive was used to make the impossible objects.

Gary Foshee, the maker of this impossible puzzle. According to him, the design of original puzzles is limited only by your imagination.

To make this puzzle, you really do need a wooden arrow and a bottle with a hole drilled through it. There absolutely is a way to insert the arrow in the bottle. The only trouble is, the authors of this book haven't let us writers in on the secret. So we know just about as much as you do! Maybe less!

This puzzle can also be made out of objects other than bottles. Anything can be used. The picture bottom left shows an arrow through the neck of a bottle, and bottom right a picture of an arrow through a Japanese coin. We've even seen an arrow through a book!

The arrow through the bottle problem

First look at the photograph below. You don't believe it? Well, neither do we. And we've got the thing on the desk right in front of us. The puzzle is to insert the arrow in the bottle. The question is - how?
Let's start with the easy bit. The arrow. If you study the one shown in the photograph, you shouldn't have any difficulty in drawing it. Trace it on a piece of plywood measuring ¼'' x 1'' x 6'' and cut it with a handsaw. The next step is to drill the hole in a bottle. This must be done with a diamond-tipped drill, which you can buy at your hobby shop. Glass gets hot and cracks when it is drilled - therefore it must be cooled.The best thing is to drill it in water.
Supposing you have got this far. You now have an arrow and a bottle with a hole in it. How to get them together? That's the problem!

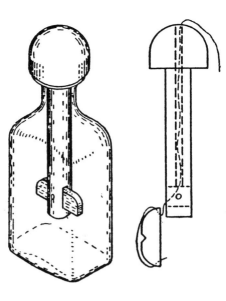

Most people know the secret of how to get a sailing ship into a bottle. But how do you get a screw or a wooden peg into one? Very easily, as it happens. The screw in the bottle puzzle was patented by W.W. Brown in 1891. There is a hole drilled down a central rod. This intersects with a hole drilled through the rod. The screw is put into the bottle which is then shaken about until the screw drops into the hole. It can then be pushed right in by pressing the head against the side of the bottle. It is secured by pushing a thin dowel down the centerhole and screwing on the top piece. The puzzle shown here was made by Gary Foshee, using a slightly different principle. He wound a very thin copper wire arround the threads of the screw and led the wire up through the central hole in the rod. He then pulled the screw into the cross hole. As he pulled the wire the screw turned itself into the wood.

The puzzle on the right uses the same principle and it appeared in Wyatt's *Puzzles in Wood*, first published in 1928. It is easy to make. A hole is drilled down the middle of a thick length of dowel. A mortise is cut through the rod to meet the drilled hole. The peg is shaped with a sharp hobby knife so that it fits the mortise loosely. A notch is cut in the center of the peg and a

little split is made at each end. A strong thread is passed down the rod and drawn through the splits. With patience the peg can be manoeuvred into the hole. When it is in position, fix it with a long needle or hat pin while you withdraw the thread. A slender pencil of wood, which fits the hole, is then pushed in until it seats in the top notch of the peg, thus securing it. The assembled rod is now fitted with a 'cork' and the puzzle is complete.

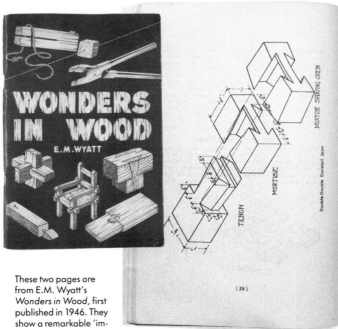

These two pages are from E.M. Wyatt's *Wonders in Wood*, first published in 1946. They show a remarkable 'impossible' joint - a double-double dovetail.

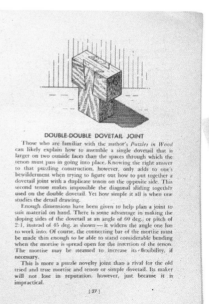

Figuring out how an ordinary double dovetail can possibly slide together is difficult enough, but if we add a duplicate tenon on the opposite side, the problem is even more complex. The double dovetail fits by diagonally sliding the parts together, but the extra tenon makes this impossible.

How is it done? The diagram in Wyatt's book shows you how simple it really is when you know the secret. The mortise is cut so that the cross piece is very thin. This allows sufficient flexibility for it to be sprung open and forced round the tenon. When the joint is closed it is impossible to see how thin the cross piece really is.

The little giant, on the left, was being sold in 1896. It has a clever lock using a pin and magnet. These prevent its opening unless it is tapped hard to dislodge the pin. The Up and Down Double Dovetail on the right was made by Allan Boardman in 1984.

How to make a puzzle joint

The apparently impossible joint shown in the photograph bottom left is not quite as impossible as it looks. But it is a challenge to all except the skilled craftsman. It is made from two woods of strongly contrasting colors. Mahogany and birch or sycamore are easy to work with but any two contrasting woods will do just as well. The blocks should be 3″ in length and 1″ x 1″ in cross-section. They must be planed so that they are perfectly square. The ends which are to be joined must also be perfectly square with the sides. The edges must be sharp and well defined. Such precise planing is quite difficult, but if it isn't done well, the difficulty of marking and cutting will be increased and the joint will not fit together properly. One solution might be to buy the pieces machine planed. Then they should be perfect. Each piece is marked identically for cutting and this is shown in the diagram. Mark each piece halfway along its length. The marks on the end are parallel and equidistant. The easiest way to draw them is to mark both diagonals and divide one into eight equal lengths. The other six lines can then be drawn at right angles to the marked diagonal. Mark the lines on the sides to form the dovetails. The exact angle is not important, but it is important that all four sides of both pieces are marked indentically. Now shade the waste areas on each piece. On one they are the two corner sections and the center. On the other they are the two in-between sections. Now comes the tricky part. Saw carefully along the lines on the waste side with a fine-toothed saw, following the marked lines exactly. Cut away the waste with a chisel. If great care is taken, the two pieces should fit exactly when you slide them together diagonally. They should now be glued, rubbed down with sandpaper and varnished. If you succeed in making this puzzle joint you will have accomplished a woodworking feat of which you can feel justly proud. Then perhaps you might like to try the double-double dovetail shown on the opposite page. The exploded diagram isn't easy to decipher but, after all, by now you're an expert!

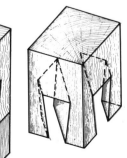

Above: A Double Dovetail, with pointed ends, which was given to co-author Jerry Slocum in 1979 by Helge Helme of Copenhagen. The earliest known reference to this type of joint was in the May 1902 edition of *The Woodworker*.

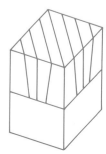

This diagram shows how to mark out the pieces for cutting. When cut, the pieces should look like the two in the center. Slide together diagonally to produce the finished joint.

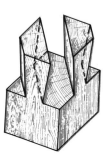

If you work with care you can produce a model as elegant as this one, which was made by Allan Boardman.

Folding puzzles

'The easiest way to refold a road map is differently', according to Jones' Rules of the Road. Anyone who has experienced the problem of refolding a road map - a common folding problem - will certainly agree. A map is precreased along vertical and horizontal lines to form a matrix of identical rectangles. The folds are confined to the creases, and the final result must be a packet with any rectangle on top and the others under it.

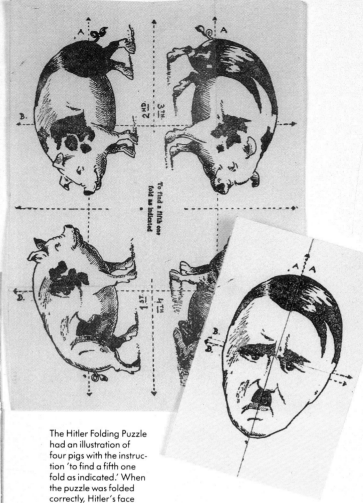

The Palace Puzzle was produced as a souvenir of the Royal Wedding in 1981 of Lady Diana Spencer and His Royal Highness, the Prince of Wales. The problem is to fold the puzzle to correctly make the Royal couple. This is known mathematically as a tetra-tetraflexagon, and it is no easy matter to fold it so that the two figures appear correctly.

The Hitler Folding Puzzle had an illustration of four pigs with the instruction 'to find a fifth one fold as indicated.' When the puzzle was folded correctly, Hitler's face appeared.

Sounds simple enough. Yet one of the most unusual and frustrating unsolved problems in modern combinatorial theory is the problem of determining the number of different ways of folding such a rectangular map. You don't have to be a mathematician to figure out that there are a great number of ways of doing so - any driver who has used a road map knows it only too well.

The Mobius Puzzle was produced by Japan Mobius Planning of Hiroshima. It is comprised of 16 square paper panels. Each panel has a quarter section of a full-size picture on both front and back sides. By folding and turning, eight full-size pictures can be made.

148

This puzzle was made by Copr. R. Lichter, Mt. Vernon, New York, in 1942. The puzzle is to fold so that two of the three 'boss gangsters' - Hitler, Mussolini and Tojo - are behind bars. The fold is not difficult but it does require a final 'tuck'.

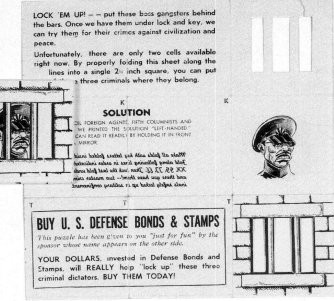

The 'Pick the Pickaninnies' Puzzle was patented in 1907 and made by the Ullman Mfg. Co., New York. Although it is totally tasteless by today's standards, it doubtlessly provided a good deal of amusement at the time. It is a folding puzzle of a different type than the others shown here. There are six flaps, each of which has one or more heads of black and/or white children and one or more holes. The puzzle is to overlap the flaps in such a way as to end up with eleven black heads. As the lady on the puzzle says 'I don't want to see no white trash'.

How to make a hexaflexagon

Hexaflexagons are flexible six-sided figures with remarkable properties. They were discovered in 1939 by A.H. Stone, while he was a Princeton University graduate student. As so often happens in the puzzle world, Stone discovered the mathematical principle of hexaflexagons when he was working on an entirely different problem. He went on to penetrate the mysterious world of the 'hex' and in so doing left us a fascinating puzzle. To make one, all you need is a strip of thin cardboard 20'' long and about 2'' wide. Mark 2'' lengths along one side of the strip. Use a pair of compasses, set to a width of 2'', to draw arcs to indicate the apexes of a series of 19 equilateral triangles as shown in the diagram. Complete the triangles and score them gently with a sharp hobby knife, being very careful not to cut too deep. (This is to make the folding operation easier). Draw a line connecting the apexes and cut off the surplus strip of cardboard. Turn the strip over and draw and score a similar series of triangles on the other side. On our hexaflexagon we decided to use numbers of dots as decoration, but as long as you follow the order of the dots carefully you can use any pattern you wish. The primary colors, red, yellow and blue together with the secondary colors, green, orange and violet are a very suitable alternative. You will notice that a triangle has been left blank at one end of each side. These are the flaps for gluing the model together. Now comes the tricky part - folding the strip to form the finished model.

The Camel Puzzle (also called the Good Cheer Puzzle) was patented in 1943 by Harold Edborg. The puzzle is to fold along the dotted lines until three triangles make a complete picture of a camel.

The strip is first folded to produce the shorter strip shown in the bottom diagram. This is done by twisting in the same direction and creasing every third fold. The result will be a shorter strip (see bottom diagram). The dotted lines and arrows indicate the final two folds.

Now slide the flap in and glue the blank faces together. The model is ready to 'flex'. By pinching and flexing and then opening out flat again, the hidden colors or patterns appear. Some are remarkably difficult to find, but they are there, so don't give up.

SOLUTIONS TO THE PUZZLES

For each of the solutions given on the following pages, the page number where the puzzle can be found is also indicated. In several of the puzzles the given solution is not necessarily the only one and readers are invited to submit any further solutions they may find to the authors.

Furthermore, in some of the puzzles no solution is given. Sometimes this is because the puzzle is so simple that we do not feel it necessary to give a solution and prefer to use the space to include other puzzles. Sometimes it is because we want to leave you something to puzzle over without the temptation of peeking at the solution. And just occasionally it is because we don't know!

Page 14
Checkerboard
Here is one of the four possible solutions to this problem. Can you find the other three?

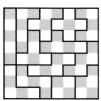

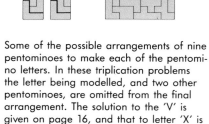

Page 16
Pentominoes
Here are some of the possible solutions to the pentomino puzzles. There are 2170 ways of making squares with corners missing; 1010 ways of making 5 x 12 rectangles, and so on. There are only two possible solutions to the 3 x 20 rectangle, but the 6 x 10 rectangle has no fewer than 2339 solutions. The number of cross and bridge solutions is not known.

Some of the possible arrangements of nine pentominoes to make each of the pentomino letters. In these triplication problems the letter being modelled, and two other pentominoes, are omitted from the final arrangement. The solution to the 'V' is given on page 16, and that to letter 'X' is something for you to discover for yourself.

Page 22
The Loculus of Archimedes

Page 19
The Egyptian Puzzle

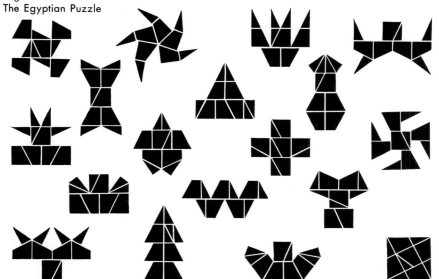

Page 22
Sei Shonagon Chie No-Ita

Page 29
The Egg of Columbus

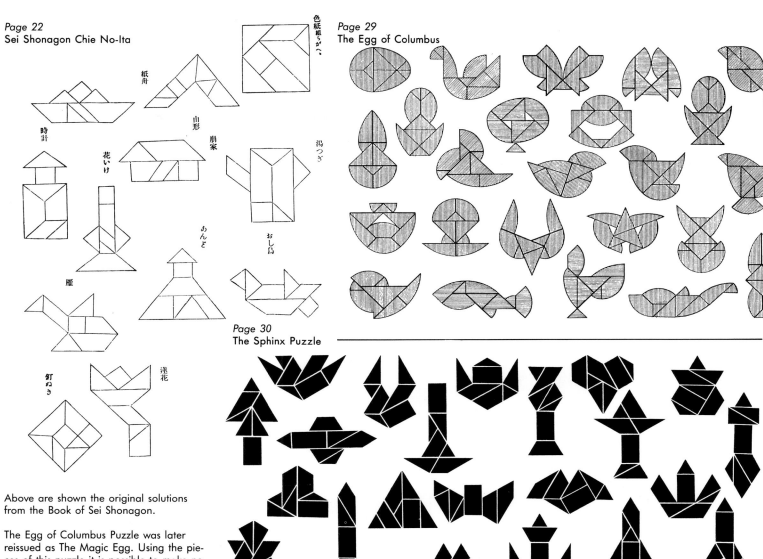

Above are shown the original solutions from the Book of Sei Shonagon.

The Egg of Columbus Puzzle was later reissued as The Magic Egg. Using the pieces of this puzzle it is possible to make no fewer than 106 different birds. See how many you can find.

Page 30
The Sphinx Puzzle

Page 31
The Zornbrecher Puzzle

Page 32
The Circular Puzzle
These are only a small selection of the shapes which you can make with the pieces of the Circular Puzzle. Try to find new and interesting shapes yourself.

Page 34
The Cowboy and Bull Puzzle
This is our deliberate mistake! The puzzle as shown is impossible to solve. However, there is a way of finding the solution.
HINT: Make the pieces of the puzzle from very thin paper.

Page 35
Question du Lapin
The bluebell is positioned incorrectly. If you turn it to its correct position, the rabbit will appear.

Page 37
The Problem of the Eight Queens
On the right you see the twelve solutions to this classic problem.

Page 38
Instant Insanity
Below is shown the solution to the Katzenjammer Puzzle.

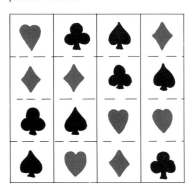

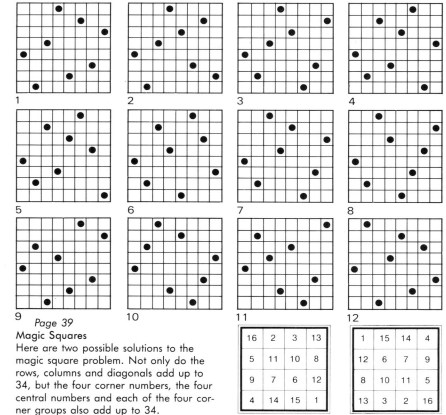

1   2   3   4

5   6   7   8

9   10   11   12

Page 39
Magic Squares
Here are two possible solutions to the magic square problem. Not only do the rows, columns and diagonals add up to 34, but the four corner numbers, the four central numbers and each of the four corner groups also add up to 34.

16	2	3	13
5	11	10	8
9	7	6	12
4	14	15	1

1	15	14	4
12	6	7	9
8	10	11	5
13	3	2	16

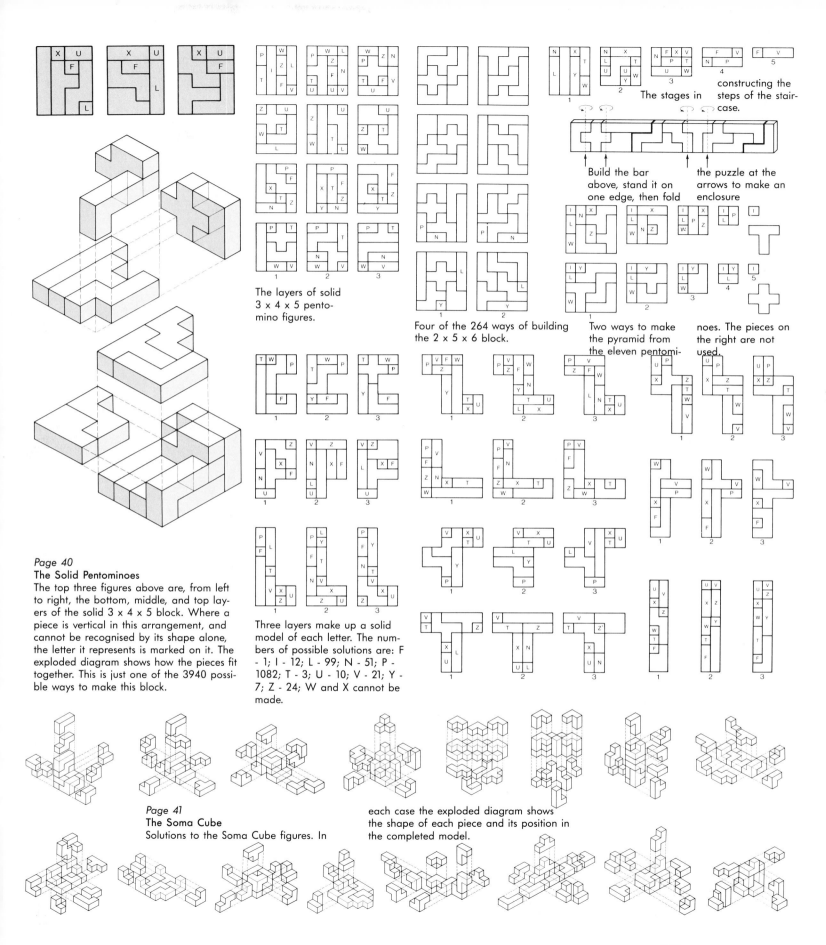

The stages in constructing the steps of the staircase.

Build the bar above, stand it on one edge, then fold the puzzle at the arrows to make an enclosure

The layers of solid 3 x 4 x 5 pentomino figures.

Four of the 264 ways of building the 2 x 5 x 6 block.

Two ways to make the pyramid from the eleven pentominoes. The pieces on the right are not used.

Three layers make up a solid model of each letter. The numbers of possible solutions are: F - 1; I - 12; L - 99; N - 51; P - 1082; T - 3; U - 10; V - 21; Y - 7; Z - 24; W and X cannot be made.

Page 40
The Solid Pentominoes
The top three figures above are, from left to right, the bottom, middle, and top layers of the solid 3 x 4 x 5 block. Where a piece is vertical in this arrangement, and cannot be recognised by its shape alone, the letter it represents is marked on it. The exploded diagram shows how the pieces fit together. This is just one of the 3940 possible ways to make this block.

Page 41
The Soma Cube
Solutions to the Soma Cube figures. In each case the exploded diagram shows the shape of each piece and its position in the completed model.

153

Page 42
The Vanishing Space
The series of four drawings on the left show how to pack all the balls into the box. The series of drawings on the right show how to fill the box with only 13 balls.

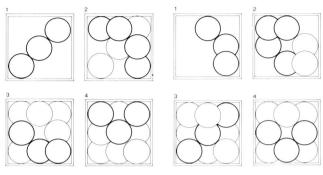

Page 68
Bill Cutler's Set of Burr Pieces
Solutions 1 to 158 are made using an uncut key piece.

Page 82
The Block Puzzle
As Stewart Coffin remarked in his book Puzzle Craft : 'Making this puzzle assembled spoils the fun'. We'd hate to spoil your fun, so we aren't giving you the solution.

Page 83
The Fearsome Four
No solution is given but we assure you that each puzzle has one. If you make these puzzles and try to solve them, you will know why we call them the 'Fearsome Four'! (After all, we did give the 314 solutions using Bill Cutler's Set of Burr Pieces)

Page 118
Puzzle Peg
Try to find the solutions to these simple problems yourself.

Page 120
Triangular Solitaire
The vacant starting hole is hole 4.
The sequential moves are: 2 - 4, 8 - 3, 1 - 5, 6 - 3, 3 - 8, 8 - 6, 18 - 8, 16 - 18, 21 - 12, 8 - 18, 19 - 17, 17 - 7, 14 - 16, 6 - 14, 13 - 15, 16 - 14, 20 - 9, 9 - 11, 11 - 4. *(Thank you, Gary Foshee!)*

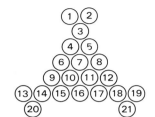

1	AI-QN-YY	46	AW-XR-YG	91	AX-XL-WU	136	AJ-WT-YI	181	DU-VF-OX	226	BR-QT-OY	271	CB-MY-YY
2	AI-QO-XY	47	AW-XV-JG	92	AY-XF-WU	137	AY-WT-QI	182	BG-YO-IX	227	DR-NT-OY	272	BB-QU-YY
3	AI-UR-YY	48	AJ-NN-YY	93	AY-XO-IU	138	AX-WU-YD	183	DG-VO-IX	228	BT-QW-DY	273	DB-RQ-YY
4	AI-UT-YW	49	AY-NN-UY	94	AI-XU-WJ	139	AY-WT-YD	184	BU-YO-DX	229	DT-NW-DY	274	DB-RY-YJ
5	AH-YQ-JY	50	AJ-RR-YY	95	AW-XT-OJ	140	AI-YM-WX	185	DU-VO-DX	230	BD-QT-YW	275	DB-NU-YY
6	AH-YM-YY	51	AY-RR-YQ	96	AJ-XR-WJ	141	AW-YK-OX	186	BQ-YF-WT	231	BT-QR-OY	276	DB-NY-JY
7	AE-YM-YY	52	AI-VM-YY	97	AY-XR-OJ	142	AW-YQ-DX	187	DQ-VF-WT	232	BR-QY-DY	277	BB-MY-YY
8	AI-YF-YY	53	AI-VQ-JY	98	AJ-XW-IJ	143	AG-YM-WX	188	BM-YM-WT	233	DR-NY-DY	278	BD-MV-YY
9	AI-YN-JY	54	AW-VK-QY	99	AY-XW-DJ	144	AQ-YM-OX	189	DM-VM-WT	234	BO-YF-YT	279	BB-YQ-JY
10	AH-YU-YJ	55	AW-VP-GY	100	AX-XS-WG	145	AJ-YF-WX	190	BP-YL-WT	235	DO-VF-YT	280	DB-VQ-JY
11	AH-YY-JJ	56	AG-VM-YY	101	AY-XR-WG	146	AY-YF-OX	191	DP-VL-WT	236	BN-YO-JT	281	CD-MV-YY
12	AI-YR-YJ	57	AQ-VM-QY	102	AY-XW-IG	147	AJ-YO-IX	192	BQ-YO-IT	237	DN-VO-JT	282	DD-FV-YY
13	AI-YV-JJ	58	AJ-VF-YY	103	AV-QO-YT	148	AY-YO-DX	193	DQ-VO-IT	238	BL-YM-YT	283	DD-VN-JY
14	AX-ON-UY	59	AJ-VN-JY	104	AW-QN-YT	149	AU-YM-WT	194	BG-YT-WI	239	DL-VM-YT	284	BB-YU-YJ
15	AX-SR-QY	60	AY-VF-QY	105	AW-QO-XT	150	AX-YL-WT	195	DG-VT-WI	240	BN-YL-YT	285	BB-YY-JJ
16	AV-WK-QY	61	AY-VN-GY	106	AS-YM-YT	151	AY-YF-WT	196	BU-YT-OI	241	DN-VL-YT	286	DB-VU-YJ
17	AV-WP-GY	62	AU-VM-YU	107	AV-YL-YT	152	AY-YO-IT	197	DU-VT-OI	242	BO-YN-JT	287	DB-VY-JJ
18	AP-WM-QY	63	AX-VL-YU	108	AV-YO-JT	153	AJ-YT-WI	198	BG-YY-II	243	DO-VN-JT	288	DD-VR-YJ
19	AX-WF-QY	64	AX-VO-JU	109	AW-YF-YT	154	AY-YT-OI	199	DG-VY-II	244	BN-YU-YD	289	DD-VV-JJ
20	AX-WN-GY	65	AY-VF-YU	110	AW-YN-JT	155	AJ-YY-II	200	BU-YY-DI	245	DN-VU-YD	290	DR-XK-OW
21	AV-WT-QJ	66	AY-VN-JU	111	AV-YU-YD	156	AX-YU-WD	201	DU-VY-DI	246	BO-YT-YD	291	DT-XF-OW
22	AX-WR-QJ	67	AI-VU-YJ	112	AV-YY-JD	157	AY-YT-WD	202	BP-YU-WD	247	DO-VT-YD	292	DR-XQ-DW
23	AV-WG-QJ	68	AW-VT-QJ	113	AW-YT-YD	158	AY-YY-ID	203	DP-VU-WD	248	BR-YK-OY	293	DK-XM-OW
24	AV-UT-OY	69	AJ-VR-YJ	114	AW-YX-JD	159	BD-MY-XW	204	BQ-YT-WD	249	DR-VK-OY	294	DT-XO-DW
25	AX-UR-OY	70	AJ-VV-JJ	115	AJ-ON-YX	160	CD-MY-XW	205	DQ-VT-WD	250	BR-YQ-DY	295	ND-LW-XT
26	AX-UT-OW	71	AY-VR-QJ	116	AY-ON-UX	161	DD-FY-XW	206	BQ-YY-ID	251	DR-VQ-DY	296	OD-FW-XT
27	AV-YK-OY	72	AX-VS-YG	117	AJ-OO-XX	162	BO-UO-XT	207	DQ-VY-ID	252	BN-YY-JD	297	ND-UW-XD
28	AV-YQ-DY	73	AY-VR-YG	118	AX-OO-YT	163	BO-UY-XD	208	BD-MW-XY	253	DN-VY-JD	298	LD-MW-XT
29	AP-YM-OY	74	AY-VV-JG	119	AY-ON-YT	164	DO-RY-XD	209	BD-MX-YW	254	BO-YX-JD	299	OD-TW-XD
30	AX-YF-OY	75	AJ-TR-WY	120	AY-OO-TX	165	BT-QT-OW	210	CD-MW-XY	255	DO-VX-JD	300	NT-OR-OT
31	AX-YO-OJ	76	AY-TR-OY	121	AI-WM-YX	166	BT-QY-DW	211	CD-MX-XY	256	BK-YM-OY	301	OR-NT-OT
32	AX-YT-OJ	77	AX-TS-WQ	122	AI-WQ-JX	167	DT-NY-DW	212	DD-FW-XY	257	DK-VM-OY	302	OR-NY-DT
33	AX-YR-OJ	78	AY-TR-WQ	123	AW-WK-QX	168	BE-YM-WX	213	DD-FX-YW	258	BT-YF-OY	303	OT-NW-DT
34	AX-YW-DJ	79	AJ-TT-WW	124	AW-WP-GX	169	DE-VM-WX	214	BD-UW-XJ	259	DT-VF-OY	304	NT-YR-OD
35	AW-PN-YU	80	AY-TT-WO	125	AG-WM-YX	170	BS-YK-OX	215	DD-RW-XJ	260	BT-YO-DY	305	OT-XR-OD
36	AW-OP-UX	81	AI-XM-WY	126	AQ-WM-QX	171	DS-VK-OX	216	BN-UO-YT	261	DT-VO-DY	306	NT-OW-DT
37	AW-TR-YQ	82	AW-XK-OY	127	AJ-WF-YX	172	BS-YQ-DX	217	DN-RO-YT	262	BR-YT-OJ	307	OR-XT-OD
38	AW-TT-OY	83	AW-XQ-DY	128	AJ-WN-JX	173	DS-VQ-DX	218	BO-UN-YT	263	DR-VT-OJ	308	NR-OY-DT
39	AS-XM-YU	84	AG-XM-WY	129	AY-WF-QX	174	BM-YM-OX	219	DO-RX-YD	264	BR-YY-DJ	309	NR-YT-OD
40	AV-XL-YU	85	AQ-XM-OY	130	AY-WN-GX	175	DM-VM-OX	220	BO-UX-YD	265	DR-VY-DJ	310	NT-YW-DD
41	AV-XO-JU	86	AJ-XF-WY	131	AU-WM-YT	176	BF-VM-WX	221	DN-RY-YD	266	BT-YR-OJ	311	OR-XY-DD
42	AV-XF-YU	87	AY-XF-OY	132	AX-WL-YT	177	DF-VM-WX	222	BN-UY-YD	267	DT-VR-OJ	312	NR-YY-DD
43	AW-XN-JU	88	AJ-XO-IY	133	AX-WO-JT	178	BG-YF-WX	223	BD-UO-XY	268	BT-YW-DJ	313	NR-OT-OT
44	AV-XS-YG	89	AY-XO-DY	134	AY-WF-YT	179	DG-VF-WX	224	BD-QX-JW	269	DT-VW-DJ	314	OT-XW-DD
45	AV-XW-JG	90	AU-XM-WU	135	AY-WN-JT	180	BU-YF-OX	225	DD-NX-JW	270	DB-FY-YY		

Page 121
The Hop-Over Puzzle
4 to 5, 6 to 4, 7 to 6, 5 to 7, 3 to 5, 2 to 3, 4 to 2, 6 to 4, 8 to 6, 9 to 8, 7 to 9, 5 to 7, 3 to 5, 1 to 3, 2 to 1, 4 to 2, 6 to 4, 8 to 6, 7 to 8, 5 to 7, 3 to 5, 4 to 3, 6 to 4, and 5 to 6.

Page 121
Jeu Des Grenouilles
Numbered from left to right, 1 to 7.
3 to 4, 5 to 3, 6 to 5, 4 to 6, 2 to 4, 1 to 2, 3 to 1, 5 to 3, 7 to 5, 6 to 7, 4 to 6, 2 to 4, 3 to 2, 5 to 3, and 4 to 5.

Page 122
The Siege of London Puzzle
The secret lies in working backwards throughout, each time covering the point from which you last started. Thus, placing a counter on A, draw it along the line AD, and leave it on D. A is now the next point to be covered, and there is only one vacant line, FA, which leads to it. Place, therefore, your second counter on F, draw it along FA and leave it on A. The third counter must be placed on C, drawn along CF, and left on F. The next placed on H, and left on C. The fifth is placed on E, and left on H. The sixth is placed on B, and left on E; and the seventh placed on G and left on B. You now have the whole seven counters duly placed, and only one point, G, left uncovered.

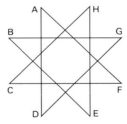

Page 123
Le Moulin Rouge and Question du Jour need no solution.

Page 123
The So-Easy Puzzle
B = blue, Y = yellow, R = red and G = green. The solution is: G - right; Y - down, left; B - up, right; G - left, up, left; R - down, left, up; Y - left; R - down, left.

Page 124
The Chifu-Chemulpo Puzzle
The fewest possible moves are 26.

$$\frac{E\ 5678}{1234} = 10$$

$$\frac{E\ 56}{123\quad 87\quad 4} = 2$$

$$\frac{56}{E312\quad 87\quad 4} = 5$$

$$\frac{E}{87654321} = 9$$

Page 124
The Train and Turntable Puzzle
No solution is given for this problem.

Page 125
Ten Little Niggers
No solution is needed because the starting position is always different.

Page 125
The Draught Board Puzzle
This puzzle has the same solution as Jeu des Grenouilles.

Page 125
Presidential Muddle Puzzle
Start with the pieces positioned from left to right alternately white, black, white, etc. The slots are numbered from 1 to 10. The solution is: 2 and 3 to 9 and 10, 5 and 6 to 2 and 3, 8 and 9 to 5 and 6, 1 and 2 to 8 and 9.

For the following solutions, there are two possible definitions of what constitutes a 'move': (1) Move one piece only in any direction or combination of directions (Under this definition a piece can move round a corner) (2) Move one piece only in any one direction. When necessary move (1) or (2) will be stipulated with the solution.
(Thank you, Edward Hordern!)

Page 126
Sam Loyd's 14-15 Puzzle
No solution to this puzzle is possible.

Page 127
The Get My Goat Puzzle
3 2 1 G 9 3 2 4 5 2 7 6 2 5 4 7 6 8 9 3 1 G 3 1 6 7 G 3 1 9 8 7 G 3 6 9. It is essential that pieces 2 and 6 are identical.

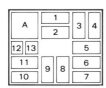

Page 127
Rate Your Mind Pal
When mixing up the pieces slide the R from YOUR into the top left corner. The puzzle is impossible to solve with this R in that position.

For the next solutions : __ means one 'move'.

Page 131
The Flying Puzzle
55 moves
8 9 10 11 13 9 8 5 6 4 3 1 2 A 12 13 9 5
6 4 3 1 2 A 13 8 9 6 5 A 13 12 8 9 6 5 A
13 1 2 3 4 A 13 12 1 2 3 4 A 13 10 7 A

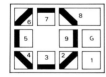

129 moves
8 9 10 11 13 9 8 5 6 4 3 1 2 A 12 13 9 8
5 6 4 3 2 1 A 13 8 9 11 10 6 5 A 13 12 8
9 11 5 A 12 13 1 2 13 12 1 2 13 3 4 12
13 3 4 12 13 A 5 11 9 8 1 2 3 4 13 12 A
5 11 9 8 1 2 3 4 12 A 7 6 10 8 9 11 3 4
2 1 11 8 9 10 6 7 A 12 13 2 3 4 5 6 10 8
9 5 3 4 11 5 8 9 10 7 A 12 13 2 1 3 4
6 7 10 8 9 6

Page 130
Dad's Puzzler.
8 7 A 1 2 7 A 6 5 4 3 8 7 A 6 5 3 7 8 4
3 7 8 4 3 7 5 6 8 7 5 6 + 8 7 5 3 4 A 7
8 1 2 + 7 8 1 6 5 A 8 7 1 2 6 5 A 7 4 3
A
59 moves. + = move only half way.

Page 131
The Tit-Bits Teaser no. 4
Position 1.
A 8 9 10 A 8 9 10 11 5 6 7 13 12 A 11
10 5 6 7 12 A 11 8 1 2 3 4 13 12 A 8 3 4
12 A 8 11 3 4 12 13 A
43 moves

Position 2.
13 7 6 5 A 8 9 10 13 7 6 5 11 A 8 9 10
13 7 6 5 11 12 A 13 10 7 6 5 12 A 13 8 1
2 3 4 11 12 A 8 3 4 12 A 8 13 3 4 12 11
A
52 moves

Position 3.
13 12 7 6 5 10 11 3 4 13 12 7 6 5 11 3 4
13 2 1 8 9 A 10 11 3 4 9 8 A 11 3 4 8 A
11 10 3 4 3 9 A 11 1 2 13 A 11 10 1 2 13
12 A 11 6 7 A
58 moves

Position 4.
12 6 5 11 10 6 13 5 7 4 3 11 10 6 9 8 2
1 A 11 10 3 4 5 7 9 8 2 1 A 10 3 4 7 5 6
A 10 11 3 4 6 A 10 1 2 8 A 10 11 1 2 8
13 A 10 5 9 12 A
60 moves

Position 5. (Move definition 1.)
7 6 5 8 9 12 5 6 7 A 8 9 6 5 + 13 10 7
A 8 9 6 12 5 7 10 + 13 7 A 9 6 12 5 11 7
10 A 9 8 1 2 3 4 13 10 A 8 3 4 10 A 8 9
3 4 10 13 A
57 moves. + = move only half way.

Position 6.
11 10 5 6 7 13 12 3 4 11 10 5 6 7 12 3 4
10 5 6 7 12 13 3 4 10 11 5 6 7 9 8 A 13
12 3 4 8 9 7 2 1 A 12 3 4 8 11 5 6 10 9
7 A 12 13 3 4 7 A 12 1 2 9 A 12 13 1 2
9 10 A 12 5 6 A
76 moves

Position 7.
13 12 11 1 2 7 6 5 A 8 9 1 2 5 A 9 1 2 5
7 6 A 9 8 1 2 11 12 3 4 6 7 5 12 11 10
13 3 4 5 11 10 13 3 4 5 6 7 11 A 8 9 12
13 5 6 7 11 10 A 13 12 5 6 7 10 A 12 9 5
6 7 10 11 A
75 moves

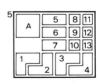

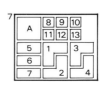

155

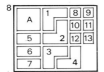

Position 8. (Move definition 1.)
13 12 10 2 1 8 9 11 10 2 1 8 9 11 1 2 12
13 4 3 8 9 11 1 2 11 5 6 7 8 3 4 13 11
5 6 7 9 3 4 11 5 6 7 9 8 3 4 11 13 5 6
12 10 2 1 A 8 9 3 4 11 6 10 12 2 1 A 9 3
4 11 13 6 7 A 9 8 3 4 7 A 9 1 2 12 A 9
8 1 2 12 10 A 9 6 5 A
99 moves

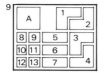

Position 9. (Move definition 1.)
A 8 9 5 6 11 13 12 7 13 12 10 5 6 11 3 4
13 12 7 5 6 11 10 3 4 13 12 7 5 6 10 3 4
12 7 5 6 10 11 3 4 12 5 12 13 2 1 A 9 1 2 13
A 9 8 1 2 10 11 6 5 7 12 13 A 9 1 2 13
A 9 8 1 2 13 12 A 9 5 7 A
80 moves

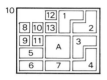

Position 10. (Move definition 1.)
8 9 11 5 6 7 A 13 3 10 11 5 10 13 A 7 6 13
A 3 4 7 6 13 10 A 11 12 8 9 5 A 10 13 6
7 3 4 11 13 10 6 7 13 11 3 4 11 13 7 6 10
12 3 4 11 13 7 6 10 12 A 5 9 8 1 2 11 13
4 3 A 10 12 6 7 4 3 A 10 5 8 1 2 13 3 4
7 6 10 12 5 8 9 1 2 13 11 3 4 7 6 A 13
11 3 4 11 13 A 6 7 13 A 8 9 5 10 12 6 7
13 11 A 8 7 13 11 A
128 moves

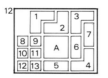

Position 11. (Move definition 1.)
3 11 10 4 9 12 13 6 12 13 8 5 1 2 6 13 8
5 6 13 8 5 9 4 11 10 9 4 7 12 8 5 4 10 9
3 6 9 13 5 8 12 7 10 4 13 5 3 + 13 5 9 6
3 4 5 13 12 7 5 8 9 6 8 9 6 2 1 8 9 5 10
11 4 3 A 8 9 5 10 13 12 6 13 12 11 4 3 A
9 5 10 11 A 9 8 5 10 11 1 2 12 A 9 3 4 6
7 13 12 A 9 11 10 5 8 10 3 4 7 6 12 A 2
1 5 10 3 4 7 6 13 A
132 moves. + = move only half way.

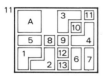

Position 12. (Move definition 1.)
1 2 3 6 7 4 5 13 11 9 A 13 11 5 4 6 7 3
2 1 8 10 A 13 12 1 10 A 13 11 2 11 10 8 A
13 12 9 5 2 1 8 A 12 13 11 1 2 5 9 11 1
2 8 10 A 13 1 2 13 A 9 12 11 2 1 13 A 10 8 5
11 2 1 13 12 A 8 5 13 12 1 2 12 13 5 10
3 6 7 4 9 12 13 2 1 5 10 8 3 6 10 11 13
12 9 4 10 6 11 6 12 13 6 11 7 10 11 12
7 + 10 11 12 4 9 13 6 7 12 4 13 6 7 12
10 11 4 13 9 6 13 12 8 5 1 2 7 12 8 5 7
12 8 5 9 4 11 10 9 4 6 13 8 5 4 10 9 3 7
9 12 5 8 13 6 10 4 12 5 8 + 12 5 9 7 3 4
5 12 13 6 5 8 9 7 8 9 7 2 1 8 9 5 10 11
4 3 A 8 9 5 10 12 13 7 12 13 11 4 3 A 9
5 10 11 A 9 8 5 10 11 1 2 13 A 9 3 4 7 6
12 13 A 9 11 10 5 8 10 3 4 6 7 13 A 2 1
5 10 3 4 6 7 12 A
263 moves. + = move only half way.

Page 132

Eureka and Preparedness type puzzles

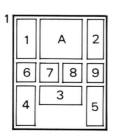

Position 1. (Move definition 1.)
3 7 6 4 3 7 6 4 1 A 8 7 6 7 5 9 2 8 6 A 1
4 7 A 8 6 2 9 5 7 A 8 1 4 A 9 5 7 9 A 4
1 6 8 2 5 A 8 6 1 4 8 3 9 7 A 6 8 3 7 A
60 moves

Position 1. Solution 2. (Move definition 2.)
3 8 7 6 4 3 8 7 4 1 A 6 7 8 5 9 2 6 7 A
1 4 8 A 6 7 2 9 5 8 A 6 1 4 A 9 5 8 9 A
4 1 6 7 2 5 A 6 7 1 4 6 3 9 8 A 7 6 3 3
A
67 moves

Position 2.
3 7 5 2 7 A 1 4 8 3 5 6 8 4 1 A 2 6 8 7 A
1 A 7 8 6 2 7 8 A 1 4 6 A 7 8 2 9 5 6 A
7 1 4 A 9 5 6 9 A 4 1 7 8 2 5 A 7 8 1 4
7 3 9 6 A 8 7 3 6 A
70 moves

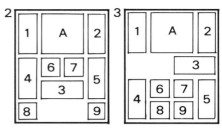

Position 3.
6 8 4 6 8 3 7 9 4 8 3 9 7 4 5 8 6 3 7 4
5 2 A 1 9 7 4 1 A 2 5 6 8 3 1 4 6 A 9 7
6 4 1 8 A 9 2 5 A 9 7 + 6 4 1 8 9 A 5 2
6 7 4 1 A 7 6 2 5 7 3 9 8 A 6 7 3 8 A
78 moves. + = move only half way.

Position 4.
9 + 5 3 6 4 8 + 6 4 3 7 9 4 8 3 9 7 4 5
8 6 3 7 4 5 2 A 1 9 7 4 1 A 2 5 6 8 3 1
4 6 A 9 7 6 4 1 8 A 9 2 5 A 9 7 + 6 4 1
8 9 A 5 2 6 7 4 1 A 7 6 1 5 7 3 9 8 A 6
7 3 8 A
81 moves. + = move only half way.

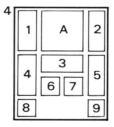

Page 133

Line up the Quinties
9 8 2 4 7 5 1 3 6 8 2 5 1 3 6 2 9 2 8 2 9
8 5 8 3 1 7 1 8 5 2
30 moves

Page 133

Century of Progress Puzzle
11 10 9 A 1 2 9 10 11 3 4 2 9 10 A 8 7 5
6 B 4 3 11 B 6 5 A 10 11 B 6 5 A 10 8 7
A
37 moves

Solution 2
11 10 9 7 8 6 5 9 10 11 B 5 9 11 B 4 3 1
2 10 11 B 4 3 1 2 10 11 A 8 7 B 11 10 A
8 7 B 11 9 6 B
42 moves

E	B	E'	E''
E		B	
E	E	E	

E	E	E''	E
E		B	
E	E'	E	B

Page 133

Les Bourgeois Punis

1. Students remain in place
As shown in the diagram, place the two townsmen (B) each between two students. Count clockwise beginning with E' so that number 3 falls on a townsman. No. 7 then falls on a student (E) who leaves (is removed) and escapes paying the check. Begin counting again with the next piece. Thus all the students escape paying and the two townsmen are left to pay the check.

The same result is obtained by beginning with piece E'' and counting counter-clockwise.

2. Each man on whom number 7 falls leaves the table.
In this case, see diagram, place the two B's next to each other, as shown. Start counting with the second student after the two townsmen (E') and moving clockwise (or start with E'' and go counter-clock-wise). Each man on whom number 7 falls is removed. Continue starting with the next piece (naturally omitting those which have been removed). Only the two townsmen will be left to pay the check.

Page 135

The tower of Hanoi
Solution for a tower with six disks.
Let the peg on which the disks start be called A, and the other two pegs be called B and C respectively. Number the disks from one through six, in order of increased size. The transfer of disk 1 to peg B can be represented by 1B, and so on. Transfer all six disks as follows:
1B, 2C, 1C, 3B, 1A, 2B, 1B, 4C, 1C, 2A, 1A, 3C, 1B, 2C, 1C, 5B, 1A, 2B, 1B, 3A, 1C, 2A, 1A, 4B, 1B, 2C, 1C, 3B, 1A, 2B, 1B, 6C, 1C, 2A, 1A, 3C, 1B, 2C, 1C, 4A, 1A, 2B, 1B, 3A, 1C, 2A, 1A, 5C, 1B, 2C, 1C, 3B, 1A, 2B, 1B, 4C, 1C, 2A, 1A, 3C, 1B, 2C, 1C.

ACKNOWLEDGEMENTS

Some of the remarkable people involved in designing, making, solving and collecting puzzles are mentioned in the book. They, and many other people, have contributed generously to the making of this book. We would especially like to thank Martin Gardner, Edward Hordern, Eileen Scott and Nob Yoshigahara.

We also thank, for contributions of puzzles, for historical information and for furnishing solutions: Kenichi Aoki, Eduard Bakalar, Pat Baker, Joan Benedetti, Allan Boardman, Laurie Brokenshire, Stewart Coffin, Bill Cutler, James Dalgety, Uri Dario Philippe Dubois, Bob Easter, John Ergatoudis, Dan Feldman, Gary Foshee, Kurt Gellner, Len Gordon, Xavier Grandvaux, John Harris, Julia Heard, Dick Hess, Ellen Ireland, Stan Isaacs, Ricky Jay, Akio Kamei, Matti Linkola, Charlie Maiorana, Jim Martin, Dale Overy, Julius Pavlovic, Tom Ransom, Will Shortz, David Singmaster, Will Strijbos, Stanislav Tvrdik, Oskar Van Deventer and Marty Weihrauch. Further we wish to thank Edith Wyle, Patrick Ela, Sharon Emanuelli, Ellen Ireland, Joan Benedetti, and the staff and volunteers of the Craft and Folk Art Museum, Los Angeles, California.

PUZZLES OF THE WORLD

A travelling exhibition organized by the Craft & Folk Art Museum, Los Angeles, to begin in November, 1986

Curatorial Team:

Sharon K. Emanuelli, organizing curator
Jerry Slocum, research curator
Jack Botermans, design curator
Benjamin Kilborne, anthropologist
Martin Gardner, consultant
Joan Benedetti, researcher
Ellen Ireland, curatorial assistant

Exhibition Funding:

Board of Trustees, Craft & Folk Art Museum
California Council on the Arts
California Council on the Humanities

SELECTED BIBLIOGRAPHY - MECHANICAL PUZZLE BOOKS

Adams, Morley (ed.). THE BOY'S OWN BOOK OF INDOOR GAMES AND RECREATIONS. The Boy's Own Paper Office, London, nd., 439pp., hb.

[Arnold, George.] THE BOOK OF 500 CURIOUS PUZZLES: Containing a large collection of entertaining paradoxes, perplexing deceptions in numbers, and amusing tricks in geometry. Dick & Fitzgerald, N.Y., 1859, 116pp., hb.

[Arnold, George.] MAGICIAN'S OWN BOOK, or, The Whole Art of Conjuring. Dick & Fitzgerald, N.Y., 1857, 362pp., hb.

[Arnold, George.] THE SOCIABLE; or, One Thousand and One Home Amusements. Dick & Fitzgerald, N.Y., 1858, 375pp., hb.

Ashley, Clifford W. THE ASHLEY BOOK OF KNOTS. Doubleday & Company, Inc., Garden City, N.Y., 1944, 620pp., hb.

Bakalar, Eduard. I DOSPELI SI MOHOU HRAT. Press Foto, Nakladatelstvi Ctk, Praha, 1976, 194pp., hb., (Czech.)

Beasley, John D. THE INS & OUTS OF PEG SOLITAIRE. Oxford University Press, Oxford, 1985, 275pp., hb.

Benson, J.K. THE BOOK OF INDOOR GAMES FOR YOUNG PEOPLE OF ALL AGES. C.A. Pearson, Ltd., London, 1904, 354pp., hb.

Benson, J.K. (ed.). THE PEARSON PUZZLE BOOK. C. Arthur Pearson, London, n.d., 114 pp., hb.

Botermans, Jack and Pieter Van Delft. SPELLETJES - Spelletjes En Puzzels Om Zelf Te Maken. H.J.W. Becht, Amsterdam, 1980, 96pp., pb. (Dutch).

Canovi, Luisa, G. Ravesi, U. Dario. IL LIBRO DEI ROMPICAPO. Sansoni Editore, Firenze, 1984, 178pp., hb., (Italian).

[Clarke, William.] THE BOY'S OWN BOOK; A Complete Encyclopedia of All The Diversions, Athletic, Scientific, and Recreative, of Boyhood and Youth. Vizetelly, Branston & Co., London, 1828, 448 pp., h.b.

Cmolik, Otto. 333 A JESTE NEKOLIK HER A ZABAV PRO PIONYRY. Mlada Fronta, Praha, 1957, 310pp., hb., (Czech.)

Coffin, Stewart T. PUZZLE CRAFT. Stewart T. Coffin, Lincoln, Mass., 1985, 98pp., pb.

Collins, A. Frederick. THE BOOK OF PUZZLES. D. Appleton & Co., N.Y., 1927, 190pp., hb.

Cross, Charles Arthur. THE CHINESE CROSS PUZZLE. Pentangle, Over Wallop, England, 1979, 41pp., ph.

Dalton, Henry. THE BOOK OF DRAWING-ROOM PLAYS AND EVENING AMUSEMENTS. Cassell, Petter, and Galpin, London, 1868.

Ducret, Etienne. LES PASSE-TEMPS INTELLECTUELS. Chez Tous Les Libraires, Paris, c1910, 386pp., pb. (French.)

Dudeney, Henry E. AMUSEMENTS IN MATHEMATICS. Thomas Nelson & Sons, London, 1917, 258pp., hb.

Dudeney, Henry Ernest. THE CANTERBURY PUZZLES AND OTHER CURIOUS PROBLEMS. E.P. Dutton & Co., N.Y., 1908, 195pp., hb.

Elffers, Joost and Michael Schuyt. DUMONT'S NEUES TANGRAM. Dumont Buchverlag, Koln, 1977, 239pp., pb. (German).

Elffers, Joost. TANGRAM - THE ANCIENT CHINESE PUZZLE. Harry N. Abrams, N.Y., (1973) 1979., 169pp., pb.

Fairham, William. WOODWORK JOINTS. J.B. Lippincott Co., Philadelphia, n.d., 205pp., hb.

Farhi, Sivy. PENTACUBES. Pentacube Puzzles Ltd., Auckland, N.Z., (4th ed.), 1979, 71pp., ph.

Farhi, Sivy. PENTOMINOES. Pentacube Puzzles, Ltd., Auckland, N.Z., (6th ed.), 1981, 50pp., ph.

Farhi, Sivy. SOMACUBES. Pentacubes, Auckland, N.Z., 1979, (4th ed.), 15pp., ph.

Filipiak, Anthony S. 100 PUZZLES, HOW TO MAKE AND HOW TO SOLVE THEM. A.S. Barnes & Co., N.Y., 1942, 120pp., hb. (Reprinted as MATHEMATICAL PUZZLES AND OTHER BRAIN TEASERS by Bell Pub. Co., N.Y.)

Fischer, Ottokar. ILLUSTRATED MAGIC. The MacMillan Co., N.Y., 1942, 206pp., hb.

Fulves, Karl. PUNCH-OUT PUZZLE KIT. Dover Pub., N.Y., 1982, 24pp., ph.

Ganreiken. SEISHONAGON CHIENO ITA (Seishonagon's Plates of Wisdom). Kyoto Shobo, 1742, Revised by S. Takagi, 1975, 32pp., ph. (Japanese).

Gibson, Walter B. FELL'S GUIDE TO PAPERCRAFT TRICKS, GAMES AND PUZZLES. Frederick Fell, Inc., N.Y., 1963, 125pp., hb.

Golomb, Solomon W. POLYOMINOES. C. Scribner, N.Y., 1965, 182pp., hb.

Grumette, Murray. GEOMETRICKS. Edu-K-Toy Institute, N.Y., 1939, pb.

Grunfeld, Frederic V. GAMES OF THE WORLD. Holt, Reinhart & Winston, N.Y., 1975, 280pp., hb.

Hanasaki, Kazuo. CHIENOITA, OHIRA-BUNKO 15. Ohira-Shoten, Tokyo, Japan, 1984, 55pp., ph. (Japanese).

Harbin, Robert. PARTY LINES. Oldbourne, London, 1963, 154pp., hb.

Hoffmann, Prof. Louis (Angelo Lewis). MECHANICAL PUZZLES. Frederick Warne & Co., London, n.d., 144 pp., pb.

Hoffmann, Professor Lewis (Angelo Lewis). PUZZLES OLD AND NEW. Frederick Warne & Co., London, 1893, 394pp., hb.

Hordern, Edward. SLIDING PIECE PUZZLES. Oxford University Press, London, 1986.

Horth, Arthur C., 101 GAMES TO MAKE AND PLAY. B.T. Batsford Ltd., London, 1943, 124pp., hb.

Houdini (Ehrich Weiss). HOUDINI'S PAPER MAGIC. E.P. Dutton & Co., N.Y., 1922, 206pp., hb.

Jackson, John. RATIONAL AMUSEMENT FOR WINTER EVENINGS, or A Collection of Above 200 Curious and Interesting Puzzles and Paradoxes Relating to Arithmetic, Geometry, Geography, etc. Longman, Hurst, London, 1821.

Johnson, Donovan A. MATHMAGIC WITH FLEXAGONS. Activity Resources Co., Inc., Hayward, Ca., 1974, 43pp., ph.

Johnson, Susan. THE FUN WITH TANGRAMS KIT. Dover, N.Y., 1977, 32pp., ph.

Johnson, Susan. TANGRAMS ABC KIT. Dover, N.Y., 1979, 32pp., ph.

Jones, Madeline. THE MYSTERIOUS FLEXAGONS. Crown Publishers, N.Y., 1966, 48pp., hb.

Kenneway, Eric. PUZZLES TO MAKE. Reeves-Oryad Press, Northgates, England, 1974, 20pp., ph.

Kettlekamp, Larry. PUZZLE PATTERNS. Wm. Morrow, N.Y., 1963, 48pp., hb.

Landells, Ebenezer. THE BOY'S OWN TOY-MAKER. D. Appleton & Co., N.Y., 1860, 153pp., hb.

Lawson, Arthur H., HOMEMADE GAMES. J.B. Lippincott Co., Philadelphia, 1934, 266pp., hb.

Leeming, Joseph. FUN WITH PUZZLES. J.B. Lippincott Co., Philadelphia, 1946, 128pp., hb.

Leeming, Joseph. MORE FUN WITH PUZZLES. J.B. Lippincott Co., Philadelphia, 1947, 149pp., hb.

Loyd, Sam II (editor). CYCLOPEDIA OF PUZZLES. Lamb Publishing Co., N.Y., 1914, 384pp., hb.; (reprinted by Pinnacle Books, N.Y., 1976).

Loyd, Sam. THE EIGHTH BOOK OF TAN; SEVEN HUNDRED TANGRAMS BY SAM LOYD. Dover (Rev.Ed.), N.Y., (1903), 1968, 52pp., pb.

Loyd, Sam. (Edited by Martin Gardner). MATHEMATICAL PUZZLES OF SAM LOYD. Dover Pub., N.Y., 1959, 165pp., pb.

MAKE YOUR OWN PUZZLES. National Recreation Assoc., N.Y., 1952, 12pp., ph.

Meeus, J. and P.J. Torbijn. POLYCUBES. Cedic, Paris, 1977, 176pp., pb. (French).

METAMORFOSI DEL GIUOCO DETTO L'ENIMMA CHINESE. Landi Librajo Sul Canto Di Via Servi, Firenze, Italy, 1818, 28pp., pb., (Italian).

Minskin, E., PIONERSKAY A IGROTEKA. (Games for Pioneers). Young Guards, Moscow, 1966, 239pp., hb., (Russian).

Moscovich, Ivan. IVAN MOSCOVICH'S SUPER-GAMES. Hutchinson, London, 1984, 126pp., pb.

NEW BOOK OF PUZZLES - NO. 28. Royal Pub. Co.; S.S. Adams & Co., Asbury Park, N.J., 1914, 58pp., pb.

Pearson, A. Cyril (editor). THE TWENTIETH CENTURY STANDARD PUZZLE BOOK - Three parts in one volume. George Routledge & Sons, London, 1907, 571 pp., hb.

Proskauer, Julien J., PUZZLES FOR EVERYONE. Harper & Bros., N.Y., 1944, 176pp., hb.

PUZZLES. Mathematical, Scientific, and Dexterious. John Dicks Press Ltd., London, c1875, 62pp., ph.

Raabe, Juliette. CASSE-TETES. Pierre Horay Editeur, Paris, 1967, 238pp., hb., (French).

Read, Ronald C., TANGRAMS: 330 PUZZLES. Dover Pub., N.Y., 1965, 152pp., pb.

Rohrbough, Lynn. PUZZLECRAFT; Plans for Making and Solving 40 Puzzles in Wire, Wood, and String. (KIT-U) Cooperative Recreation Service, Delaware, Ohio, 1930, 24pp., ph.

Schnacke, Dick. AMERICAN FOLK TOYS - 85 American Folk Toys and How To Make Them. G.P. Putnam's Sons, N.Y., 1973, 219pp., hb.

Slocum, Jerry. MAKING AND SOLVING PUZZLES. Science and Mechanics Magazine, Vol. 26, No. 5, Oct. 1955 (pp. 121-126); also Magic Handbook, (pp. 107-112), Science and Mechanics Pub. Co., Chicago, Ill., 1961, 153pp., pb.

Stangberg, Robert. ROLIGA GATOR Och Andra Sallskapslekar. Natur Och Kultur, Stockholm, 1950, 194pp., hb. (Swedish).

St. John, Thomas M. FUN WITH PUZZLES, Thomas M. St. John, N.Y., 1898, 79pp., pb.

Stubbs, A. Duncan. MISCELLANEOUS PUZZLES. F. Warne & Co., London, 1931, 142pp., pb.

Takagi, Shigeo. PLAY PUZZLE (Encyclopedia of Puzzles), Heibon-Sha, Tokyo, 1981, 221pp., hb., (Japanese).

Takagi, Shigeo. PLAY PUZZLE - PART 2. Heibon-sha, Tokyo, 1982, 198pp., hb., (Japanese).

Tangerman, E.J., WHITTLING AND WOODCARVING, Whittlesey House, McGraw-Hill Book Co., Inc., N.Y., 1936, 293pp., hb.

Thiele, Rudiger. DIE GEFESSELTE ZEIT, Urania-Verlag, Leipzig, 1984, 215pp., hb., (German).

Thomas, R.M. (editor). PUZZLES AND HOW TO MAKE THEM. Handicrafts, Ltd., London, 1927, 68pp., pb.

Townsend, Charles. MERLIN'S PUZZLER. Hammond Inc., 1976, 122 pp., pb.

Townsend, Charles B., MERLIN'S PUZZLER, VOL. 2. Hammond Inc., 1977, 122 pp., pb.

Van Delft, Pieter, and Jack Botermans, CREATIVE PUZZLES OF THE WORLD. Harry N. Abrams, N.Y., 1978, 200pp., hb.

WEHMAN BROS' NEW BOOK OF 200 PUZZLES. Wehman Bros., N.Y., 1908, 58pp., pb.

Wells, Kenneth. WOODEN PUZZLES AND GAMES, INTRIGUING PROJECTS YOU CAN MAKE. Sterling Pub. Co., N.Y., 1983, 142pp., pb.

Wilson, Marguerite. SOMA PUZZLE SOLUTIONS. Creative Publications, Palo Alto, Ca., 1973, 44pp., ph.

Wyatt, Edwin M., PUZZLES IN WOOD. Bruce Pub. Co., Milwaukee, Wisc., 1928, 64pp., ph.; reprinted by Woodcraft Supply Corp., Woodburn, Mass., 1980.

Wyatt, Edwin M., WONDERS IN WOOD. Bruce Pub. Co., Milwaukee, Wisc., 1946, 76pp., ph.

Yoshigahara, Nobuyuki. PAZURU WOTUKURU (Puzzles to Make). Ohtsuki Shoten, Tokyo, Japan, 1984, 86pp., hb. (Japanese).

Yu, Chung-en. INGENIOUS RING PUZZLE BOOK. Shanghai Culture Pub. Co., Shanghai, China, 1958. English translation published by Jerry Slocum, Beverly Hills, Ca., 1981, 44pp., ph.

Zechlin, Katharina. GAMES YOU CAN BUILD YOURSELF. Sterling Pub., Co., Inc., N.Y., 1975, 80 pp., hb.

REFERENCE BOOKS AND ARTICLES

Afriat, S.N., THE RING OF LINKED RINGS. G. Duckworth & Co., London, 1982, 126pp., pb.

Andrews, W.S., MAGIC SQUARES AND CUBES. Open Court, Chicago, 1917, 419pp., hb.

Bain, George Grantham. THE PRINCE OF PUZZLE-MAKERS: AN INTERVIEW WITH SAM LOYD. Strand Magazine, Vol. 34, 1907, George Newness, Ltd., London, 800pp., (pp. 771-779), hb.

Ball, W. W. Rouse, Revised by H.S.M. Coxeter, MATHEMATICAL RECREATIONS AND ESSAYS. MacMillan & Co., London, 11th ed., 1939, 418pp., hb.

Bandelow, Christoph. INSIDE RUBIK'S CUBE AND BEYOND. Birkhauser, Boston, 1982, 120pp., pb.

Barnum, Phineas T., P.T. BARNUM'S ADVANCE COURIER. P.T. Barnum, N.Y., 1872, ph.

Berlekamp, Elwyn R., John Conway, & Richard Guy. WINNING WAYS FOR YOUR MATHEMATICAL PLAYS. Vol. 2, Games in Particular. Academic Press, N.Y., 1982, 850pp., pb.

Bestelmeier, Georg Hieronimus. BESTELMEIERR - KATALOG. Magazin Von Verschiedenen Kunst und Anderen Nutzlichenn Sachen Mit IIII Abbildungen. Edition Olms, Zurich (Nurnberg 1803), 1979, hb. (German).

Brears, Peter C.D., THE COLLECTOR'S BOOK OF ENGLISH COUNTRY POTTERY. David & Charles, London, 1974, 207pp., hb.

Burlington Fine Arts Club. EXHIBITION OF EARLY ENGLISH EARTHEN WARE. Burlington Fine Arts Club, London, 1914.

Crossman, Carl L., THE CHINA TRADE. The Pyne Press, Princeton, 1972, 275pp., hb.

Culin, Stewart. GAMES OF THE ORIENT. Chas. E. Tuttle Co., Rutland, Vermont, (1895), 1960, 177pp., pb.

Cutler, William H., THE SIX-PEACE BURR, Journal of Recreational Mathematics, Vol 10(4) 1977-1978. Baywood Pub.Co., Inc., Farmingdale, N.Y. pp. 241-250, pb.

Eaglestone, Arthur A., & T. A. Lockett. THE ROCKINGHAM POTTERY. Municipal Museum and Art Gallery, Rotherham, England, 1964, hb.

Fourrey, E., CURIOSITIES GEOMETRIQUES. Vuibert Et Nony Editeurs, Paris, 1907, 427pp., pb., (French).

Fults, John Lee. MAGIC SQUARES. Open Court Pub. Co., LaSalle, Ill., 1974, 103pp., pb.

Gardner, Martin. MARTIN GARDNER'S NEW MATHEMATICAL DIVERSIONS FROM SCIENTIFIC AMERICAN. Simon & Schuster, N.Y., 1966, 253pp., hb.

Gardner, Martin. MARTIN GARDNER'S SIXTH BOOK OF MATHEMATICAL GAMES FROM SCIENTIFIC AMERICAN. W. H. Freeman, San Francisco, 1971, 262pp., hb.

Gardner, Martin. MATHEMATICAL CARNIVAL. Alfred A. Knopf, N.Y., 1975, 274pp., hb.

Gardner, Martin. MATHEMATICAL CIRCUS. Alfred A. Knopf, N.Y., 1979, 272pp., hb.

Gardner, Martin, MATHEMATICAL MAGIC SHOW. Alfred A. Knopf, N.Y., 1977, 284pp., hb.

Gardner, Martin. MATHEMATICS, MAGIC AND MYSTERY. Dover Publications, N.Y., 1956, 176pp., pb.

Gardner, Martin. THE SECOND SCIENTIFIC AMERICAN BOOK OF MATHEMATICAL PUZZLES AND DIVERSIONS. Simon and Schuster, N.Y., 1961, 253pp., hb.

Gardner, Martin. THE SCIENTIFIC AMERICAN BOOK OF MATHEMATICAL PUZZLES AND DIVERSIONS. Simon and Schuster, N.Y., 1959, 178pp., hb.

Gardner, Martin. THE UNEXPECTED HANGING. Simon & Schuster, N.Y., 1969, 255pp., hb.

Gardner, Martin. WHEELS, LIFE, AND OTHER MATHEMATICAL AMUSEMENTS. W. H. Freeman & Co., N.Y., 1983, 261pp., hb.

Golomb, Solomon W., CHECKERBOARDS AND POLYOMINOES. AMERICAN Mathematical monthly, vol 61, December 1961, (pp675-682)

Hall, A. Neely. CARPENTRY AND MECHANICS FOR BOYS. Lothrop, Lee & Shepard Co., Boston, 1918, 385pp., hb.

Hannas, Linda. THE ENGLISH JIGSAW PUZZLE 1760 TO 1890. Wayland Publishers, London, 1972, 164pp., hb.

Hartswick, F. Gregory. THE TANGRAM BOOK: ADVENTURES OF THE BEAUTIFUL PRINCESS IN TRIANGLE LAND. Simon & Schuster, N.Y., 1925, 141pp., hb.

Hill, Donald R. (Trans). THE BOOK OF INGENIOUS DEVICES. D. Reidel Pub. Co., Dordrecht, Holland, 1979, 267pp., hb.

Honsberger, Ross. MATHEMATICAL GEMS II. The Mathematical Assoc. of America, 1976, 182pp., hb.

Hooper, W. RATIONAL RECREATIONS. B. Law and Son; and G.G. and J. Robinson, London, 1794, Vol. IV, 367 pp., hb.

Hopkins, Albert A. THE LURE OF THE LOCK. The General Society of Mechanics and Tradesmen, N.Y., 1928.

Hutton, Charles. RECREATIONS IN MATHEMATICS AND NATURAL PHILOSOPHY. Vol. I., G. Kearsley, London, 1803, 447 pp., hb.

Johnson Smith. OUR LATEST CATALOGUE OF SURPRISING NOVELTIES, PUZZLES, TRICKS, JOKE GOODS, USEFUL ARTICLES, ETC. Catalogue No. 147. Johnson Smith & Co., Detroit, Mich., 1937, 573pp., pb.

Joseph, Joan. FOLK TOYS AROUND THE WORLD AND HOW TO MAKE THEM. Parents Magazine Press, N.Y., 1972, 96pp., hb.

Kinnard, Clark (ed.). ENCYCLOPEDIA OF PUZZLES AND PASTIMES. Grosset & Dunlap, N.Y., (1928), 1946, 431pp., hb.

Kunz, George Frederick. RINGS FOR THE FINGER. Dover Pub., N.Y., (1917) 1973, 381pp., pb.

Lee, Jean Gordon. PHILADELPHIANS AND THE CHINA TRADE, 1784-1844. Philadelphia Museum of Art, Philadelphia, 1984, 232pp., pb.

Loyd, Sam II (editor). SAM LOYD AND HIS PUZZLES, an Autobiographical Review. Barse & Co., N.Y., 1928, 122pp., hb.

Lucas, Edouard. RECREATIONS MATHEMATIQUES - Vol. I-IV. Albert Blanchard, Paris, (1891) 1975, pgs. 254, 245, 200, 266, pb., (French).

Manasse, Mark and Victor K. Wei, some results on the panex puzzle AT+T Bell Labs, Murray Hills, N.J., 1985, 20pp. ph. (unpublished).

McClintock, Inez and Marshall, TOYS IN AMERICA. Public Affairs Press, Wash., D.C., 1961, 480pp., hb.

Meyers, J.L., HANDBOOK OF THE CESNOLA COLLECTION OF ANTIQUITIES FROM CYPRUS. New York, 1914.

Noble, Joseph Veach. SOME TRICK GREEK VASES. Proceedings of the American Philosophical Society, Vol. 112, No. 6, Dec. 1968, pp. 371-378.

O'Beirne, T.H., PUZZLES AND PARADOXES. Oxford University Press, N.Y., 1965, 238pp., hb.

Ozanam, Jacques. RECREATIONS MATHEMATIQUES ET PHYSIQUES. Chez Claude Jombert, Paris, 1735, Vol. IV, 446pp., hb. (French).

Pinto, Edward H. TREEN AND OTHER WOODEN BYGONES. Bell and Hyman, London (1969) 1979, hb.

Prime, William C. POTTERY AND PORCELAIN OF ALL TIMES AND NATIONS. Harper & Bros., N.Y., 1878, hb.

Remise, Jac. L'ARGUS DES JOUETS ANCIENS 1850-1918. Balland, Paris, 1978, 349pp., hb.

Singmaster, David. NOTES ON RUBIK'S MAGIC CUBE. Enslow Pub., Hillside, N.J., 1981, 73pp., pb.

Smith, David Eugene. HISTORY OF MATHEMATICS, Vol. II, Ginn & Co., Boston, 1925, 725pp., hb.

Steinhaus, Hugo. MATHEMATICAL SNAPSHOTS. Oxford University Press, N.Y., 1969, 3rd ed., 311pp., hb.

Tanavoli, Parviz & John T. Wertime. LOCKS FROM IRAN - Pre-Islamic to Twentieth Century., 151pp.

Tissandier, Gaston and Henry Frith, MARVELS OF INVENTION AND SCIENTIFIC PUZZLES. Ward, Lock & Co., London, nd., 113pp., hb.

Tissandier, Gaston. POPULAR SCIENTIFIC RECREATIONS. Ward, Lock, and Co., London, 1882, 781pp., hb.

TEAPOTS IN POTTERY AND PORCELAIN (Victoria & Albert Museum), Her Majesty's Stationery Office, London, 1948.

White, Alain. SAM LOYD AND HIS CHESS PROBLEMS. Whitehead & Miller, 1913, reprinted by Dover, N.Y., 1962, 471pp., hb.

White, Gwen. ANTIQUE TOYS AND THEIR BACKGROUND. B.T. Batsford, Ltd., London, 1971, 260pp., hb.

Woodcroft, Bennet. THE PNEUMATICS OF HERO OF ALEXANDRIA - From the Original Greek. Taylor Walton and Maberly, London, 1851, reprinted by MacDonald, London, with an introduction by Marie Boaz Hall.

Zwijnenberg, Peter A., DE GESCHIEDENIS VAN RICHTERS ANKERSTEEN BOUWDOZEN. Paz Mediakontakten, Alphen a/d Rijn, Holland, 1982, 115pp., pb. (Dutch).